Praise for

The Book of

Separation

A *New York Times Book Review* Editors' Choice

One of *O, The Oprah Magazine*'s
"Ten Books to Pick Up Right Now"

One of *Jewish Week*'s "Books to Read This Fall"

One of *Real Simple*'s "Best New Books to Read"

"Tova Mirvis has already established herself as a first-rate novelist with *The Ladies Auxiliary, The Outside World,* and *Visible City*. With *The Book of Separation,* Mirvis shifts genres, reveals some of the autobiographical germs of her fiction, and compellingly chronicles the process of separating from Orthodoxy . . . The respect for intra-Jewish difference that Mirvis models for her children — and for readers — is a precious gift to the Jewish literary world . . . Beautiful and poignant."　　　　*—Lilith Magazine*

"An intimate tale of departure . . . [Mirvis] movingly conveys the heartache that accompanies the abandonment of one way of life in search of another."　　　　*—New York Times Book Review*

"Poignant . . . [Mirvis] explores what it means to truly be yourself, even if it means giving up everything you've ever known."
　　　　—Real Simple

"We've all daydreamed about walking away from it all. Mirvis actually *did,* after years of soldiering through a good-enough life. This is the moving story of her life, post-divorce and post-Orthodox Judaism. She's an inspiring example of living — and loving — on your own terms." —*Glamour*

"Capable of both wry humor and darkly apt turns of phrase, Mirvis is a gifted writer reflecting on her identity: first through the prism of organized religion, then through a self-charted life." —*Chicago Tribune*

"Mirvis longs for freedom so much that you want it for her — and then look internally and want it for yourself, too . . . Inspiring." —*Jewish Book Council*

"This tender, touching book is filled with insights about intimacy, observance, and self-possession, as Mirvis comes of age, and learns to love and trust herself." —*Times of Israel*

"A beautifully written book . . . in which Mirvis applies her gifts as a novelist to reveal her own struggles. And it is a profound meditation on what it means to be true to oneself, and what costs doing so may exact." —*Jewish News of Northern California*

"The author's sensitive thematic treatment of belonging and individuality and her candor about the terror she experienced leaving the only community she had ever known makes for moving, inspiring reading. A thoughtful, courageous memoir of family, religion, and self-discovery." —*Kirkus Reviews*

"Mirvis's experience of Orthodox Judaism is vivid and particular, but her questions—about love and belonging, community and isolation, striking to new soul terrain without a map—are universal. Luminous, unsettling, and fiercely brave, Mirvis's memoir insists on a simple but earth-shattering truth: 'there are other ways to be.'" —*Shelf Awareness*, starred review

"A graceful and deeply affecting memoir . . . *The Book of Separation* is a brave and deeply personal memoir . . . Mirvis is such an engaging writer that it's a pleasure to spend time with her." —*Moment*

"Mirvis intimately chronicles her divorce and her separation from modern Orthodox Judaism in this bold memoir . . . Hers is a story of grief and rebirth. She is compassionate and judicious in her portrayal of Orthodox Judaism, even as she describes its repressive attitudes toward women; she discusses the diverse Jewish lifestyles, from Hasidic to secular. Her personal journey makes for an introspective and fascinating story." —*Publishers Weekly*

"Looking both backward and forward, Mirvis recounts with candor and close observation the social, psychological, and spiritual travail precipitated by leaving her narrow but well known world and entering a more secular, unfamiliar territory . . . Sharing the personal details and drama of her journey, Mirvis recounts the arduous path so many must take to emerge into their own, true identities." —*Booklist*

"[Mirvis] detail[s] her journey with grace and subtlety." —*Improper Bostonian*

"[Mirvis's] interior narrative voice draws readers in, asking if she can be loved for who she is, not who she was, especially in her withdrawal from her natal religion . . . A soothing picture of personal and religious divorce." —*Library Journal*

"A memoir from an accomplished novelist is always a gift, but this one stands out. When you tell me it's about growing up in and marrying within the Orthodox Jewish culture, I'm hooked —but when you tell me it's some of the best writing I've seen about growing up, evolving your beliefs, and finding your own way outside of the stories you've been told—and have told yourself—then I'm blown away, and I was." —KJ Dell'Antonia

"Tova Mirvis offers a warmly told and searchingly explored story of her divorce from both her first husband and her Orthodox Jewish faith. The intimate view of what it means to live an Orthodox life—the day to day reality of following its many guiding rules and principles—is fascinating to an outsider like me, and Tova's insights are both thought-provoking and generous. As she sorts through what pushed her away from the faith and traditions she grew up with, she also conveys what held her; her conflict over her 'separation' becomes our own."
—Jessica Shattuck, *New York Times* best-selling
author of *The Women in the Castle*

"*The Book of Separation* is an elegant, beautiful, carefully drawn story of love, tradition, inner conflict, and loss. This extraordinary memoir resonated with me more than I can say."
—Dani Shapiro, best-selling author of *Devotion* and
Hourglass: Time, Memory, Marriage

"To say that reading *The Book of Separation* made me feel less alone in the world would be a vast understatement. Tova Mirvis perfectly, beautifully, unsettlingly captures the particular horror — existential and otherwise — of dismantling a long marriage and starting one's life anew. This is a heartbreaking, breathtaking, life-altering book."

— Joanna Rakoff, author of *My Salinger Year*

"In *The Book of Separation,* Tova Mirvis brings us into her heart-wrenching decision to leave her marriage and the world of Orthodox Judaism behind. Her exploration of faith and self are truly miraculous. This book is a wonder!"

— Ann Hood, author of *The Book That Matters Most*

"With elegance, rare depth and unflinching honesty, Tova Mirvis offers up a chronicle of one woman's revolution against her own life. *The Book of Separation* is fiercely inspiring, and illuminates the too often dormant power within all of us to live in accordance with who we truly are."

— Heidi Pitlor, author of *The Daylight Marriage*

"Tova Mirvis's memoir, beautifully written and fiercely honest, is a moving reflection on what it means to take responsibility for one's own life. In the course of the book Mirvis takes leave of her husband, her religious community, and her inherited notions of how her life ought to go. By staring so unflinchingly into her confusions and fears, a portrait of quiet courage slowly assembles itself, radiating insights and inspiration for all."

— Rebecca Newberger Goldstein, author of
Plato at the Googleplex

The Book of Separation

The Book of
Separation

· A Memoir ·

Tova Mirvis

MARINER BOOKS
HOUGHTON MIFFLIN HARCOURT
BOSTON   NEW YORK

First Mariner Books edition 2018
Copyright © 2017 by Tova Mirvis
Reading Group Guide copyright © 2017 by Houghton Mifflin Harcourt
Publishing Company
Q&A with the author copyright © 2018 by Tova Mirvis

For information about permission to reproduce selections from this book,
write to trade.permissions@hmhco.com or to Permissions,
Houghton Mifflin Harcourt Publishing Company, 3 Park Avenue,
19th Floor, New York, New York 10016.

hmhco.com

Library of Congress Cataloging-in-Publication Data
Names: Mirvis, Tova author.
Title: The book of separation : a memoir / Tova Mirvis.
Description: Boston : Houghton Mifflin Harcourt, 2017.
Identifiers: LCCN 2017015328 (print) | LCCN 2017030254 (ebook) |
ISBN 9780544520547 (ebook) | ISBN 9780544520523 (hardcover) |
ISBN 9781328477873 (paperback)
Subjects: LCSH: Mirvis, Tova. | Authors, American — 20th century — Biography.
Classification: LCC PS3563.I7217 (ebook) | LCC PS3563.I7217 Z46 2017 (print) |
DDC 813/.54 [B] — dc23
LC record available at https://lccn.loc.gov/2017015328

Book design by Victoria Hartman

Printed in the United States of America
DOC 10 9 8 7 6 5 4 3 2 1

"The Journey" from *Dream Work,* copyright © 1986 by Mary Oliver. Used by permission of
Grove/Atlantic, Inc. Any third-party use of this material, outside of this publication, is
prohibited. Lines from "I Go Back to May 1937" from *The Gold Cell* by Sharon Olds,
copyright © 1987 by Sharon Olds. Used by permission of Alfred A. Knopf, an imprint of the
Knopf Doubleday Publishing Group, a division of Penguin Random House LLC. All rights
reserved.

For my family

Author's Note

The Book of Separation is based on my recollection and understanding of events that have shaped and changed me. I am aware that others may regard these same events in different ways. In writing this book, I have re-created dialogue from memory and, in a few instances, have simplified chronology for the sake of narrative flow. I have changed the names of everyone who appears in the book except for myself.

The Journey | BY MARY OLIVER

One day you finally knew
what you had to do, and began,
though the voices around you
kept shouting
their bad advice —
though the whole house
began to tremble
and you felt the old tug
at your ankles.
"Mend my life!"
each voice cried.
But you didn't stop.
You knew what you had to do,
though the wind pried
with its stiff fingers
at the very foundations —
though their melancholy
was terrible.
It was already late
enough, and a wild night,
and the road full of fallen
branches and stones.
But little by little,
as you left their voices behind,
the stars began to burn
through the sheets of clouds,
and there was a new voice,
which you slowly
recognized as your own,
that kept you company
as you strode deeper and deeper
into the world,
determined to do
the only thing you could do —
determined to save
the only life you could save.

I stood before a panel of rabbis. I was dressed in the outfit of the Orthodox Jewish woman I was supposed to be: a below-the-knee navy skirt and a cardigan buttoned over a short-sleeved shirt that without the sweater would have been considered immodest. But no matter how covered I was, I felt exposed. *What kind of shameful woman,* I imagined the rabbis thinking, *leaves her marriage; what kind of mother overturns her life?* Yet a month shy of my fortieth birthday, after almost seventeen years of marriage and three children, I had upended it all.

On one side of the conference room, the rabbis, in beards, black suits, and dark fedora hats, huddled together to examine the *get* — the divorce document I was waiting for them to confer upon me. It was black ink hand-scribed on beige parchment, written on behalf of my husband the prior week, when he had come before this same group of assembled men. It didn't matter that I was the one to end our marriage. Jewish law dictated that only a man had the power to issue a divorce.

It also didn't matter how I felt about being in this conference room before this religious tribunal whose job it was to enforce the very rules that I had long felt shackled by. My role was to remain silent as I followed the careful choreography of this ancient ceremony in which no deviations were allowed. A misspelled name, and the document could be nullified. Any tiny irregularity in the ceremony, and the validity of the divorce might one day be called into question.

To ensure that the court had the right woman, the rabbi from my synagogue had been deputized to verify my identity. On my cell phone the week before, I'd confirmed that I had no nicknames, no aliases or pseudonyms. My father, I answered, also had none. This kind of scrutiny wasn't new to me. I'd lived my life among the minute rules of Orthodox Judaism. Until now, I'd complied even when I questioned them — pretending when necessary, doing anything in order to stay inside. I might have fantasized about leaving, but it was never something I thought I'd actually do. If you left, you were in danger of losing everyone you loved. If you left, you were in danger of losing yourself.

When every letter of the document had been deemed correct, the rabbis stood. I tried to keep my face impassive, to pretend that nothing here could touch me.

One of the oldest of the rabbis read the document out loud, in Aramaic, dated the year 5772 from the creation of the world, in the city of Boston, by the Ocean Atlantic.

I, Tova Aliza, was released from the house of my husband.

I, Tova Aliza, was permitted to have authority over myself.

The words might have been ancient, but the freedom they promised seemed radical.

The piece of beige parchment was carefully folded into a

small triangle, and I was given further directions: One of the rabbis would drop the parchment into my hands and I was supposed to clasp it to my chest to show I was taking possession. Without saying a word, I was to turn and walk from the room. As soon as the door shut behind me, the divorce would go into effect.

The rabbi who had been appointed as my husband's emissary came over and stood directly in front of me. The other rabbis remained behind the table to witness and thus validate this act. I stood silently before him as instructed, but I knew that I had arrived not just at the end of my marriage but at the edge of the supposed-to-be world. Until now, this had been the only world that existed. Here was the way the world was made, and here was the way the world worked. Here was what I was to do and here was who I was supposed to be. Every decision I'd made up to this point had been stacked on top of these truths. But once the foundation had started to shake, everything else did as well. One by one, the pieces had begun to fall.

The rabbi dangled the folded piece of parchment from his fingers. I cupped my hands and waited.

Part 1

New Year, New You

It is September, the first Rosh Hashanah since the divorce, and I've set out on my own.

My three children are with their father, at his parents' house, where I'd spent the past decade of these holidays. My parents, sister, and grandparents are at home, in Memphis, where they will observe this celebration of the Jewish New Year in the Orthodox synagogue I attended every week of my childhood. My friends are in their homes, cooking for family gatherings. My brother, along with four of his eight children, has traveled with throngs of fellow Breslover Chasidim, an ultra-Orthodox sect, to Uman, a city in Ukraine, the site of their spiritual pilgrimage. And I am fleeing to Kripalu, a yoga and meditation retreat in Western Massachusetts.

Until this year, I celebrated every Rosh Hashanah the same way I had the one before. To spend this holiday anywhere but in the long solemn hours of synagogue would have been unfathomable. Now, without the rules wrapped tightly around me, I no longer know what to do. Dreading the arrival of this year's

High Holy Days, I'd considered pretending they didn't exist and decided to go to Kripalu only because yoga and meditation seemed to be the obligatory way of moving on. ("I assume you're doing yoga," an acquaintance said upon hearing the news of my divorce.) I've told few people where I'm going for the holiday because to do so would be to admit that I'm no longer Orthodox, something that I'm still unsure of myself.

Kripalu is three hours from my house in the Boston suburb of Newton, a highway drive that until recently would have been impossible for me unless I'd studied the maps in search of easy back roads and plotted a route that felt sufficiently safe. For almost a decade of living in the Boston area, I'd been gripped by a fear of driving, steadfastly avoiding rotaries, bridges, and tunnels, driving only when I had to, wishing I could still be in a driver's-ed car equipped with a passenger-side brake and someone who could stop me if I went too fast or too far. I was terrified of getting lost, most of all terrified of the highway. I couldn't bear the sight of those green signs announcing the Mass. Pike or I-95, couldn't merge into the stream of speeding cars. I had nightmares of making a wrong turn onto a wrong street that would lead me to an entry ramp that would take me onto a highway from which I'd never find my way back.

Yet I'm now on the Mass. Pike; the cars are passing me, too many and too fast, and, still shocked that I'm driving on the highway, I clutch the steering wheel, worried about getting into an accident. The biggest fear, though, is not of any injury I might sustain but of the fact that then people will know I'd planned to spend Rosh Hashanah at some suspect retreat center instead of praying in synagogue for a year of blessing, a year of goodness. At the start of all other years, I knew exactly what sort of goodness I was supposed to be praying for, but on this new year, there is no ready prayer, even if I could bring myself to utter one.

It's not just where I'm going for the holiday, but when — I'd left too late and now the sun is setting and the clock on my dashboard reminds me how close it is to the deadline of exactly 6:08 p.m. that, until recently, would have divided my day into unalterable domains of allowed and forbidden. It's forbidden to drive on this holiday, and it still feels impossible that I could break one of the religious rules prohibiting the use of electricity, against riding in a car. Every transgression feels like a first, each one new and destabilizing.

I speed up — better to break the laws of Massachusetts than the laws of religion that are still binding in my head. If I go faster, maybe I can make it to Kripalu before driving becomes forbidden. But the sun is sinking lower in the sky, and no matter how fast I go, I won't arrive before Rosh Hashanah officially begins. The only option now in accordance with Jewish law would be to pull over by the side of the road, knock on someone's door, and ask to stay for the next forty-eight hours, as though I were a hiker stranded in an unexpected blizzard. If this were a Jewish fairy tale of the sort I'd been raised on, I'd wander in the forest of Central Massachusetts until, in a clearing, with just minutes until the holiday began, I'd come upon a small cabin bathed in golden light and inside, lo and behold, a nice Jewish couple, probably childless, with the holiday candles ready to be lit, an extra place at their table waiting just for me.

I keep going, watching the dashboard clock as the numbers change to 6:08. Finally, I've traversed the line that divides me from my past. The drivers around me — shouldn't they have the same look of fear on their faces, distressed at finding themselves in their vehicles at this hour on this day? Even though I am in my getaway car, my every action is recorded, my every word, every thought, known and evaluated. The voices that have been speaking in a whisper this entire drive are now thundering. *If you veer this far, you will never be found. If you leave the path, you will be cut off and alone.* My iPhone, my trusty companion, might be ably guiding me toward my destination, but there are other ways to get lost. I've driven not just into Western Massachusetts but into the outermost region of who I was supposed to be.

The road transforms from the Mass. Pike of the city to the Mass. Pike of the country. Alongside the highway, a scattering of precocious trees are on the brink of change, eagerly dusted with yellow and red, as though they've arrived early to a party. I've passed the most congested areas of the drive, and now there are few cars ahead of me or behind. The offenses add up—I stop for gas, check my phone, turn up the radio; seemingly innocuous actions, yet forbidden too on this day, late entries to my ledger of wrongdoing. If God is in the details, sin lies there as well. By now it's entirely dark. The iPhone maps the way from the Mass. Pike onto winding roads that lead me through the Berkshire towns of Lee and Lenox. No matter how many miles I go, I still expect to look in my rearview mirror and see the people I once knew coming after me. In my mind, there is a stampede of feet, the incessant thrumming of voices: *She was driving on Rosh Hashanah,* they say. *We thought she was one of us.*

In this alternate universe, I can still turn the car around. I can find the map that marks the underground passages through which I will travel, not just down miles of highway but into the past, to the white Cape house in Newton where my husband and I and our three children once lived; the key would still turn in the lock, and there we are, gathered around a table set with our blue-and-white wedding china, observing Shabbat—the Jewish Sabbath. Then I will be standing at the sink washing dishes and looking out the window, fantasizing about escape while lamenting the fact that nothing, nothing, can change. I will be in synagogue, bedecked in my married woman's hat, imagining myself somewhere, anywhere, else.

A FEW YEARS BEFORE, in my in-laws' Orthodox synagogue, I stood in the back row of the small women's section, as I did every Rosh Hashanah. I was fenced in on one side by the *mechitzah* (which separates the men from the women in an Orthodox synagogue) and on the other side by two women who groaned and rolled their eyes anytime I or one of my sisters-in-law needed to pass by. Overhead, in a larger section, the majority of women sat in the balcony, looking down at the figures draped in prayer shawls, a congregation of men.

In what I'd now term a custody arrangement but for all my married years jokingly referred to as a prenup, my husband's parents, who lived in Brookline, a fifteen-minute drive from us, got Rosh Hashanah and Thanksgiving, while my parents, farther away, in Memphis, got the Passover seders. Rosh Hashanah inaugurates the autumn holidays, the start of the school year swiftly interrupted. For months before, there is talk, with an air of resigned hardship, about how the long string of holidays fall out this year—whether early or late, whether on weekends (which is preferable) or midweek (precluding any regular attendance at work). "How do you explain to your colleagues that you're out of the office again because it's Shemini Atzeret?" people exclaim about observing even the more minor holidays, all the while knowing they would never consider skipping any of them.

On this day it is decided, who shall live and who shall die, the congregation sang in Hebrew.

Remember us for life. Inscribe us in the book of life, we pleaded.

The rabbi — white-haired, white-bearded, and dressed in the thin white robe in which men are both married and buried — moved his hands in time to the prayers as though conducting; on his face was a look of beatific pleasure. I wanted to be moved but it was a performance I'd seen too many times. Here is the part of the service where you sit. Here you stand. Here you bow. Here you proclaim unwavering belief. I stared into my prayer book, hoping my face gave nothing away, but just in case, I pulled the brim of my black silk hat lower — as constricted as I felt by it, at least it provided a place to hide. I counted pages, averaged how many we were covering per minute, and calculated when we would be done — the same game I'd played as a child when time had passed unbearably slowly.

On the other side of the partition stood two of my brothers-in-law and my father-in-law, who'd become Orthodox as a young man. Each of them had a black-and-white tallis — the prayer shawl worn by married men — draped over his shoulders. My husband, Aaron, stood next to them in his navy-blue suit and tallis. From behind the *mechitzah,* I watched how he swayed to the words, knowing how moved he felt by the High Holy Day tunes.

Layla, my almost three-year-old daughter, was upstairs in the play group with the other nursery-age children, who weren't expected to sit through the nearly five-hour service. I went to check on her, incurring the annoyance of the women seated next to me as I apologetically squeezed past. In the upstairs classrooms, local college girls looked after the kids, who were dressed in miniature suits and flowered dresses, all wearing name tags made before the holiday began because writing was among the many forbidden tasks on this day. As I watched my daughter play, I removed my hat for a few minutes, to give myself a break from the pressure of it wrapped around my head. When I returned to the sanctuary, I put the hat back on and watched my two sons, Noam and Josh — who, at eleven and seven, were not interested in the play group — standing beside Aaron. They were dressed in khakis and blue button-down shirts, Red Sox—logo yarmulkes clipped to their light brown hair — yarmulkes were required of boys and men as a sign that God was always above. I'd packed books and snacks to keep them occupied during the service, as though it were a long car ride we had ahead of us, but that wasn't enough to stem the boredom that made them squirm and whisper. They hadn't yet mastered that most necessary skill: how not to be where you are.

Instead of reciting the prayers, I surveyed the dresses of those around me and the hats of the married women, especially the outlandish one worn by a woman across the aisle, festooned with a webbed black veil and scarlet-speckled feathers. Most women had on more staid wool hats, and a few of them tucked all their hair underneath in accordance with the strictest of Orthodox injunctions that a married woman's hair must always be covered, that it was little different than her breasts or thighs. Some of the younger married women had started opting for less obtrusive scarves or twenties-era cloches or even wide headbands, which seemed more like decorative afterthoughts than anything seriously intended to cover, a means of probing the edges while remaining inside. Each of these hats conveyed a world and a worldview. Like birds, we could be spotted and identified by the feathers and crowns on our heads.

I tried to pray, but my mind kept wandering. Under all these brims and bows, what were people really thinking? There were few clues, only the fantasies I spun out. Did any of these women ever worry, as I did, that too much thinking might unravel their lives? You were supposed to believe that this way of life was the only true one. You were supposed to tell yourself that the rituals and restrictions were binding and beautiful. And if you felt any rumblings of dissatisfaction, you were supposed to believe that the problem lay with you. My own discontent, I hoped, remained well hidden. It wasn't the sort of thing I would have shared with my mother-in-law or sisters-in-law, who sat beside me wearing hats of their own. Along with the actual rules, there was another set of laws, equally stringent yet more unforgiving, enforced not by a belief in God but by communal eyes that were just as all-seeing and all-knowing. Inside my head, a voice constantly whispered: *What will they think?*

I'd learned to squelch the questions. I knew how to ease doubt with the routine of ritual: Invite guests for festive meals on Shabbat. Prepare the hot-water urn before sundown every Friday so I didn't have to perform the forbidden act of boiling liquid on Shabbat. Unscrew the light in the refrigerator and set the timers in our house so I didn't have to perform the forbidden act of switching on a light on Shabbat. Check every package of food I bought for the proper kosher certification. Check my underwear for signs of bleeding that would make me sexually off-limits to my husband. Immerse myself in the mikvah, the ritual bath, a week after my period ended so that I would once again be permitted to him. Change the dish racks in the sink according to the kind of meal I'd prepared, wash the dishes with sponges designated for meat or for dairy so that the two never mixed. Sit on the women's side of the synagogue and tell myself that this didn't bother me. Believe in modern interpretations to make the rules sound more palatable. Advocate for liberal positions within Orthodoxy so that women could be more included. Tell myself that I could live with the remaining contradictions. Console myself with the thought of being part of a chain of tradition. Listen to the men recite the prayers, deliver the sermons, make the rules. Light the candles for Shabbat on Fridays, light the menorah for Chanukah for eight nights, prepare baskets of food for friends on Purim, vacuum the car for any drop of forbidden leavened food before Passover. Doubt quietly, but don't talk about it, don't act on it.

Now it was time for the shofar—the blowing of the ram's horn that was the highlight of the Rosh Hashanah service—and the children, released from the play group, came rushing into the sanctuary like prisoners on furlough. Eager to hear the shofar, which they'd been learning about in school for weeks, they crowded to the front of the men's section, where the view was better. The man blowing the shofar wore his black-and-white-striped tallis over his head, and the speckled ram's horn emerged from underneath this zebralike covering, turning him into some sort of hybrid animal at whom we all gazed expectantly. Layla was still young enough to be allowed in the men's section, and her white-blond curls and hot-pink dress stood out in the sea of black and white as Aaron held her, his head draped with his tallis as well. Seen from this vantage point, he looked like every other man.

Instead of the usual soft murmur of conversation, there was silence in the sanctuary. We were required to hear every single note of the shofar — all one hundred blasts — in order to satisfy our obligation. *Does it really matter if we don't actually hear each one,* I quietly wondered as Aaron leaned forward in concentration, as intent on fulfilling this command as he was with the others that governed our shared lives, sometimes pulling manuals from our bookshelf to remind himself of the specific rules for a holiday. When he did that, I felt uneasy at how readily he followed even the smallest details of the law, but how could I argue with his devotion, which should have been mine as well? Now, too, I bristled as I watched him, feeling like I was spying on a stranger. What he took refuge in was the same thing that I wished to flee. If I ever tried to share how deadened I felt whenever I stood supposedly in prayer, he professed understanding but smiled nervously, hoping my discontent would disappear before it became something to be reckoned with. If I said too much, I saw in his eyes a look of fear, the same kind I felt myself.

It was safer not to talk about it. And I saw little reason to, because I was convinced that nothing could change. These words I'd held on to for years now: *nothing can change.* It was far too late to question my marriage or the Orthodox life in which we were steeped. Change might be something I longed for but never something I dared to bring about. I had long ago passed the exit ramp; with three kids, a husband, and a home in the Orthodox community, I couldn't have thoughts of leaving. People who left Orthodoxy did so earlier in their lives, during college or in the years soon after, when they could still choose who they wanted to be.

That year, we'd gone with the kids to New York City, where we'd watched street performers who folded themselves, arms over legs over necks, into smaller and smaller glass boxes. I smiled and clapped along with the crowd at what seemed to be an impossible feat of enclosure, but even after we wandered on to the next spectacle, I couldn't stop thinking about these performers, feeling like I was one of them.

"Sometimes it's hard for me to be Orthodox," I'd once said tentatively to my best friend, Ariel, as I continued to feel my own sense of enclosure. Like me, she was a writer and Jewish. But because she wasn't Orthodox, it was easier to broach this subject with her.

"I've wondered why the rules don't bother you more," she admitted carefully.

"I try not to let myself think about it. I work so hard just to hold it all together," I told her, but afraid of my words, I didn't say anything else about it, and she, out of respect, didn't ask.

More than anything, I wanted these feelings to go away, but they only grew stronger. One Shabbat, I had been at the synagogue we attended every week, waiting to enter the social hall after the service ended. It was like any Shabbat morning, like every Shabbat morning. People talked, laughed, milled around, and so did I, though my arms were folded across my chest, my fingers tightly digging into my arms as though I needed to hold myself intact. A debilitating headache came over me, the pain concentrated along the line where my hat met my head. Around me, people continued their conversations, but, startled by the pain, I rushed from the crowd. It was a brain tumor, an aneurysm. Afraid of what was erupting inside me, I pushed through the glass doors of the building. On the steps of the synagogue, I ripped the hat off my head, and the pain disappeared.

"*Tekiah,*" a man called out now, bringing everyone in my in-laws' synagogue to expectant attention, and a long unbroken sound emerged from the shofar—a siren, a wail.

Shevarim—three broken blasts, like hiccups.

Then *teruah*—nine small blasts, plaintive sobs.

A new year, a new possibility. No matter how many times I'd heard it, the sound of the shofar was piercing. I tried to force back this burst of doubt, to locate the spot where I was getting lost. Did I believe there was a God? Did I believe there was a God who was involved in the world? Did I believe there was a God who revealed His word to Moses on Mount Sinai? Did I believe there was a God who made known His teachings in the oral law? Did I believe that the oral law was passed down from Moses to his disciples, to the judges of the rabbinical courts, to the rabbis, to me? Did I believe these laws were binding upon me? Did I believe in a God who cared about the smallest details of what I ate and wore—God the Scorekeeper, God the Pun-isher, God the King?

We all believe, claimed the prayer that was sung by the men in front of me and the women beside me and in the balcony above. *Do we really?* asked the voice growing more brazen in-side me. There was no fighting it now. It was a late doubt, slow in asserting itself, but now it broke through me, pushed me, dared me. What if someone, me, for instance, were to take on the role of heckler, yell out that, in fact, I wasn't so sure? The stalwarts all around would shush me, all disturbances quashed, all dissent hidden away. But surely inside some of these minds burned this same strange fire, these same doubt-riddled thoughts.

⁓

THE DAY AT KRIPALU begins early, with morning yoga at six thirty. I put on my regulation black yoga pants quietly, so as not to wake my roommate, and I slip out of the room.

Either randomly or by the design of the Kripalu registration office, I'm sharing a small dormlike room with a secular Jewish poet who was born in the Warsaw Ghetto and survived the Holocaust in hiding. Where the registration form asked for my occupation, I'd put down *novelist*, so perhaps the administrators at Kripalu enjoyed making matches; perhaps, says the Orthodox voice in my head, it's *bashert*, "meant to be." The night before, I'd arrived too late for dinner, so my Rosh Hashanah meal was a granola bar from the lobby kiosk that I ate in the room with the poet as we lay like college roommates in our narrow side-by-side beds. Exhausted from caring for an elderly mother and a partner suffering from congestive heart failure, she had yet to make it out of the room for yoga or any of the activities offered. All she had the strength to do was sleep.

"What about you? Why are you here?" she asked me as she stretched out, her eyes closing as we spoke.

"It's Rosh Hashanah, but I'm not sure I'm celebrating it," I told her, thinking of my overnight bag where I'd stashed a round raisin challah and a small jar of honey that I should have been eating as part of my holiday meal, dipping first the challah and then an apple slice into the honey. At the last minute, I'd also grabbed the shofar given to my older son as a bar mitzvah gift

—not that I knew how to blow it, and not that I could envision myself, even at a place like Kripalu, standing in a field, raising a ram's horn to my lips, and letting forth a blast. I'd intended to bring a Rosh Hashanah prayer book with me too but hadn't been able to find mine. Maybe after the divorce division of books, I no longer owned one.

There had been no time to search the shelves for a lost prayer book. Aaron had come to pick up the kids for the holiday and once they left, I threw my last things in a bag and went to see William, the man with whom I've become involved. I was supposedly just stopping by his apartment to say a quick goodbye, but once I was there, it was hard to leave.

We sat together on the soft gray couch in his apartment in the Avalon, where he's lived for a little over a year, since his own divorce. The Avalon, a large complex, has an air of industrial neutrality. With its modern fixtures and clean white walls, it's a mecca for the divorced—an in-between place for those who no longer know what home is supposed to look like.

William is tall, with green eyes and dark brown hair. He is a physician, ten years older than me; like me, he has three kids, though his are older and away at school. It was Sunday afternoon, but he was in scrubs and sleepy, having been on call and awake in the hospital all night. When I got there, he went into the kitchen and emerged a few minutes later carrying a plate with slices of tomato and fresh mozzarella cheese, which he'd artistically arranged, and presented it to me with a dramatic flourish.

I ate everything, wanting to curl up inside this apartment, inside his arms, and wait out the days until Rosh Hashanah ended. I was still in a state of disbelief that I wasn't packing up the kids' clothing in order to spend the holiday with Aaron's parents. But here in this hideaway, there would be no new year taking place, no repentance prayers playing in a constant loop. I checked my watch, already nervous about the drive to Kripalu.

"I really should go," I said. "It's Rosh Hashanah and I'm not sure if I'm observing it in my own way or just waiting for it to be over."

William, too, is Jewish, though it occupies little of him. He grew up with no sense of religious obligation. When he talks about his Jewishness, it is about his many relatives who were killed in the Holocaust and about his grandparents, who were immigrants to the old Boston Jewish neighborhoods of Mattapan and Roxbury.

"Before you, I rarely thought about any of this. I could go for months without thinking about religion," he said.

This I know about him: He is not someone who would be willing to live under so many rules. He prides himself on his independence. He is a "free-range William," we joke. His strength is what has attracted me from the start.

"I still can't go an hour without thinking about it," I said.

"I couldn't live that way," he said, and his voice changed, becoming a little quizzical, a little pitying. He was still sitting next to me, but something about him became harder to access.

"I don't know how to stop being something I always was," I said.

AN AURA OF DEVOTION permeates the corridors at Kripalu, a hushed hurried feeling as people move toward the main yoga hall. There, they solemnly remove their shoes, then, in the darkened space, they curl on their mats. Except for the fact that there's a gold Buddha statue up front, the room looks like the sanctuaries I'm accustomed to—there's even a balcony overhead, though if all the women were relegated to it, the main hall would be nearly empty.

Once the class begins, however, there's no mistaking this for a synagogue. Yoga pose, with its erect dignity, bears little in common with how we sit in synagogue, where we rustle, whisper, and sway. The teacher starts by quoting Swami Kripalu: The greatest form of spiritual practice is self-observation without judgment. I can no more imagine self-observation without judgment than I can imagine walking without moving my feet. Everywhere, there's the assault of voices, a firing squad of eyes. *You are bad,* I hear in my head. *Bad, bad, bad,* the Buddha at the front of the room sneers. I am the opposite of yoga.

My body attempts downward dog, but instead of letting go of these coursing thoughts, I'm deeper inside them. I am supposed to be with my children. I am supposed to still have a husband. I am not supposed to be doing yoga on this day. I am not supposed to feel so lost and alone. Instead of focusing on my breath, my mind races in endless laps and retrieves a Chasidic story a formerly Orthodox friend once shared with me: There was a wayward yeshiva student who went to his rabbi and confessed that he no longer believed. Newly free, he would eat nonkosher food, sleep with women, bask in all that was once forbidden. His rabbi looked at him and said, "You can partake of the pleasures, but you will never enjoy them." I imagine that rabbi issuing a warning to me as well: *You can go to your nice Kripalu, you can listen to talk of letting go, you can breathe, bend, and pose, but your mind will always belong to us.*

"Namaste," the teacher says at the end of class, which means "the divine in me pays homage to the divine in you." All around me, heads bow in devotion, hands clasped to hearts, but I resist taking part. Surely I'm the only one here hoping not to find God but to lose Him.

I try a hula-hooping class and learn — self-discovery, at last! — that when I close my eyes and stop thinking about what I'm doing, I can hula-hoop indefinitely. I splurge on craniosacral therapy at the advice of a friend, and as the therapist lightly touches my head, I tell her my story, as though with these simple adjustments, she can alleviate the knot of guilt and fear.

On the second day, when Kripalu is starting to feel like a mental institution in which all inmates wear black yoga pants, the woman who leads yoga dance advises us to let go of the stale, hardened spaces within ourselves.

"What would your body feel like if it were free?" she asks.

Standing in the back of the room in case my self-consciousness requires me to make a quick escape, I have no answer. I'm wary of trading one false devotion for another. Any talk of meaning and purpose, any reference to a beatific divine light, falls under the tarp of suspicion. As the people around me start to dance, prancing and floating and light and free, my legs feel wooden, my body heavy and lumbering. All I can think of are the bugs my elementary-school classmates and I used to collect at recess, tiny black crawlers that, when threatened by the pokes and prods of our fingers, curled into tight balls.

"As you dance," the instructor says, "make eye contact with people you don't know. Release your fear. Break the barriers that prevent you from connecting." There's a languid soulful song playing, and I dance a little, hands above my head in a sheepish ballerina spin. My longing for the kids comes over me. They will be back from synagogue by now, sitting around my former in-laws' dining-room table, their aunts and uncles and cousins assembled, traditional holiday fare like brisket, breaded chicken, and an assortment of kugels before them. I make tentative eye contact with a few people dancing near me. Except for my roommate, I've barely spoken to anyone, but if I start to talk I might become one of those people you meet on airplanes or in coffee shops who pour out their tales of woe.

I take a magenta scarf from the shimmery pile, feeling ridiculous. I'm not sure if being here is less or more absurd than standing in a different sanctuary in a different costume counting out the blasts of a ram's horn. What if the people in the sanctuary in which I've spent the Rosh Hashanahs of years past were to break out in such movements? *Dance your prayers, your sins, your wishes.* The women would lift their hats so they could see unimpeded. The men would hold their prayer shawls like billowing scarves. Arms outstretched, they would open their hands, their hearts, to the world: *We are in child pose, in submission to God above us. We are in mountain pose, in worship of the creation we celebrate today.*

In this room, I feel my clenched resistance begin to give way. It's a little easier to face my fears, a list lying in wait—nightmares of my hands slipping from the roof of a building, of falling off the edge of a cliff, falling from an airplane, falling from a thin wire, falling for no reason at all, just falling. The fear most of all that I would come unmoored from all that was supposed to hold me.

What I have most feared is now what I have chosen.

It's a good thing there are no mirrors in here. For one rare moment, I stop thinking. My arms come free from my body and I twirl and circle the room. It doesn't matter who else is here, who might see me, or what they, or I, might think. My arms are waving branches. I am part of the grass, under the sky.

In this moment, it feels both exceedingly simple and impossibly out of reach: there are other ways to be.

Day of Judgment

With a few hours until Yom Kippur begins, Aaron comes to pick up the kids — according to our new schedule, this year, this holiday belongs to him as well. Yom Kippur, which comes ten days after the beginning of Rosh Hashanah, is the Day of Atonement, the most solemn day in the Jewish calendar. Aaron is in a hurry to get the kids to his house so they have enough time to eat before the fast, which begins at sundown. A sense of urgency surrounds us, exacerbating the anxious solemnity already present in the hours leading up to this holiday, during which we won't eat, drink, or shower, during which we ignore most of the physical needs of our bodies.

Trying not to look at me, Aaron stands in the entryway of the house I'm renting from a friend of a friend for a year or possibly two, until she's ready to sell it. It looks strikingly like the old house we all lived in together, as though I've intentionally re-created an approximation of what was before. This house, though, has half the furniture that used to be ours and is now mine—a few weeks before we each moved, Aaron and I had divided the contents of the house "like a sports draft," Noam, our oldest child, quipped as Aaron and I sat in the backyard on the wooden chairs and table that would soon belong to me alone, a late-round pick. With each selection—*You take the gray sectional couch we bought when we first moved to Boston; I'll take the breakfront in which we'd stored our wedding china*—we were disassembling our lives. The mirror we bought while on vacation in Cape May, New Jersey. The Ikea desk we'd put together in the first weeks of our marriage. The desk had been in possession of more parts than we'd anticipated, none of which fit together smoothly due to the incomprehensible directions—our first lesson in married life. We'd assumed the desk would last only a few years, but it had far exceeded our expectations—the seventy-five-dollar desk from Ikea had outlasted even us.

Awkwardly, I hand Aaron the bag I assemble each time he comes to pick up the kids—today it's the kids' dress clothes for synagogue and books to entertain them while they're there. Intent on avoiding any conversation that might lead to a fight, we discuss only practicalities. In front of the kids, we are restrained, trying to foster the illusion that divorce happens quietly, politely.

Even so, despite my attempt at sounding natural, my voice is false, my body rigid and on guard. Aware, as I always am, of his anger toward me, I can leave no vulnerable spots unprotected. In his mind, this is all my fault. Every conversation risks reverting to a drumbeat of blame: I have changed. I have broken the rules. I am bad, I am bad, I am bad. "You have no right to your own version of this story," he said on the doorstep of my house a few weeks earlier, when I tried to explain again why I had chosen this. Even as every part of me rose in revolt at his statement, his words played in an endless loop in my head, no longer just in his voice but in my own as well.

"We need to go now," Noam says, aware of how close it is to sundown.

"Do we have to?" asks Josh, more interested in finishing the video game he's in the middle of than in fulfilling the obligation to pray and repent.

Noam is now thirteen, perceptive, thoughtful, and responsible. Josh, who is nine, has an impish smile and is both exuberant and reflective. Layla, almost five, has a shock of curly blond hair and a free spirit. Inside me, there live spaces carved out in their images, as though my body still carries the shell of each of them.

"This is the plan," I say carefully, worried that everything I say could be used against me. I have been the mother who picks the kids up at school every day, makes dinner, packs school lunches, reads bedtime stories, and tucks them into bed each night, but now, because of the divorce, I feel like I am constantly on trial. I need to prove that I am still capable, responsible, and, of course, good.

The need to uphold the agreement has been drilled into me by our burgeoning staff of lawyers and therapists. In our temporary agreement, the weekdays are divided, as are the weekends. The holidays too have been divvied up so meticulously that even the lawyers who weren't Jewish became versed in the details of every Jewish holiday. We had originally tried mediation, but that turned out to be an expensive way to argue while the mediator helplessly murmured, "I know this must be so hard for you." There was too much anger, too much pain — an entire marriage's worth compressed and then released. Now we each have lawyers, which feels like a surreal fact, as though we can still wake from this nightmare that I've purposely chosen. There have been months of negotiating — angry e-mails, bitter texts — about the parenting plan, about the division of whatever money we have left, about anything over which two people can fight.

While the religious divorce was finalized in the *get* ceremony in May, the civil agreement is slated to be completed in December, a few months from now. We had arrived at a temporary agreement in August, a few hours before a pretrial hearing. Early one morning, I'd waited in line to have my bag x-rayed by security before I entered the courthouse, but that seemed pointless; the whole building could have been brought down by all the explosive anger inside. Here in this building lay the collective underbelly of love. The marriage license bureau should be housed here, all brides made to pass through. They should show films of this place to engaged couples, like those of deadly car wrecks screened in driver's ed.

Inside the courthouse, I saw Aaron on the other side of the mezzanine. At the sight of him, I veered between guilt and anger. I couldn't stop staring at him in the way I sometimes mined the kids' faces for remnants of the babies they once were. He was two people simultaneously, still the man I was married to, still the man I was divorcing, yet it felt impossible that he was either — impossible that we were ever married, impossible that we were getting divorced. I felt his anger every time he looked at me, but in that tense, coiled anger, there was safety. When it lifted, there would be room for the sorrow, his and mine, which was what I feared most of all.

As we waited for our time with the judge, our lawyers completed last-minute negotiations. Aaron and I sat for hours on wood benches on opposite sides of the mezzanine—like children in trouble at school while the adults determined the punishment. When finally an agreement was reached, we signed a document headed with both our names—names I was so used to seeing together, though hardly in this oppositional formulation, lined up as though preparing for war.

On the wall of the courtroom that looked like a DMV, a sign announced that a failure to dress appropriately would result in a penalty, although the nature of the penalty wasn't specified, nor did the sign indicate what exactly was considered inappropriate. I'd opted for synagogue-wear—a knee-length black skirt, a purple blouse with a ruffle around the collar, and low heels— trying to look proper, respectful, good. But apparently no one dresses up to get divorced. The people around me wore tank tops, shorts, and flip-flops as they waited for the judge to dispense rulings on their lives. Not realizing these were public proceedings, I'd imagined that the judge would sit privately with us, a wise, all-knowing marriage counselor whose opinion was binding. Each detail of the parenting plan—should the kids be picked up by Aaron at 6:00 p.m. as he wanted or at 6:30 p.m. as I preferred—would be given careful judicial review; perhaps he'd split the disputed time in half and arrive at a Solomonic 6:15. Instead, parenting plans, financial arrangements, all forms of bitter grievances were dealt with in minutes in front of an audience of lawyers and other petitioners who halfheartedly listened, tired of waiting but relieved to hear of separations more fraught than their own.

Before our names were called, a tiny wispy-haired man in a brown suit did battle with an obese ex-wife, who stood with the aid of a cane, over missed alimony payments and alleged attempts to hide income.

"But Judge," the man said in a thin, whiny voice, "she has a history of claiming she's on the verge of being evicted."

Who was right, who was wrong? Here everyone was both and neither, wrong and wronged. We awaited our ten minutes with the judge, then were quickly given a seal of approval for the temporary agreement—the provisional map until December, when the borders between our now-divided country would be permanently negotiated.

WITH THE START OF YOM KIPPUR rapidly approaching, I walk the kids out to Aaron's car, a dark blue Honda Pilot, the companion to my light brown one. I hug the kids goodbye but what I really want to do is apologize to them profusely then grab hold of them and keep them here with me—tuck them somehow inside my body if need be and revert to an earlier stage of motherhood, when they were always part of me. I had once been a mother who aspired to smooth away all imperfections, present my children with a world that was safe and whole. I glued photographs into albums to create the definitive stories of their early years. I changed the words of songs as I rocked them to sleep; *down will come baby,* not *cradle and all,* but *safely in my arms.* When an old lady swallowed a fly, there was no *perhaps she'll die* but *perhaps she'll cry*—the outer limit of the bad that could exist. Of course I knew, even back then, that no absolute protection could, or even should, be ensured. I knew that events beyond our control might shake us loose from the story of how things were supposed to be. But I would never have believed that I would be the one to bring it about.

When Aaron and the children leave, I want to chase after the kids and tell them I didn't mean it, didn't mean any of this. I don't want to go back inside the house, which will feel eerily quiet—an empty stage set. Everything that appeared three-dimensional—the furnishings, the view out the window—will turn out to have been painted on cardboard. I hadn't been able to imagine, until I'd arrived here, how it would feel to watch the kids drive off to what seems like an alternate life that exists half a mile away; how it would feel to scroll through the calendar in dread of which days with them I would miss. I didn't know that alongside the pain of separation, I would hear, screaming inside my head, a constant, accusing voice: *You wanted this. You chose this.*

It's getting dark and I haven't yet decided how I will observe this holiday that once filled me with trepidation. As much as I want to hide from the press of rules, I can gather no distance; for someone who is trying to leave, I haven't made it very far. I'm considering blocking from my mind the image of Jews the world over fasting and praying for forgiveness, yet to skip this day feels far graver than sitting out Rosh Hashanah. The punishment for not observing Yom Kippur is *karet*—your soul shall be cut off from your people, this supposedly the ultimate penalty. But it occurs to me, as I stand outside, that this is exactly how I feel, like an astronaut whose connection to the spaceship is severed; outside the law of gravity, you endlessly float.

A few days before, a friend had told me about the nontraditional spiritual service she and her family were going to in Weston, a few towns over, in a barn in someone's backyard. "You should come with us," she'd said.

"I'll think about it," I told her, not sure whether I wanted to embrace a more freewheeling religious practice or do away with religion altogether.

When I go back inside the quiet house now and check my e-mail, I see that my friend has forwarded me a message from the leader of the barn service. It contains an exercise to help prepare for the purpose of the day.

In the e-mail, he noted that the central command of Yom Kippur — *va'aneetem et nafshoteichem* — was typically interpreted as a need to "afflict our souls." But there were other possible meanings, he wrote. The word that we usually translated as "afflicted" could also mean "answer, respond to, be occupied with, busy ourselves with, or sing." The word that was usually translated as "soul" could also mean "body, life, self, desire, or passion." Yom Kippur, he told us, was a call to examine how the phrase applied in our own lives.

We are given an assignment: Decide which meanings of the phrase *va'aneetem et nafshoteichem* are most moving to us. Do we want to think of this as a day of afflicting our souls, or of answering our passions, or of occupying ourselves with our lives? We are to consider the combinations of sentences that these varying definitions can make and choose the ones that express our deepest longings. Then we are to ask ourselves how we put this into practice. For example, how would we finish the sentence *I afflict my body when I . . . ?* Or *I answer my soul when I . . . ?* Or *I am responding to my passion when I . . . ?*

We are to write our answers on index cards and hand them in at the service, where they will be shared with the group. When I was newly married — a young Orthodox woman with my hair covered, as was required of me — I was enrolled in a creative writing graduate program. In one class, a teacher instructed all the students to write down our deepest secrets. We didn't have to read them aloud or show them to anyone; just writing the words was a feat of bravery. All around me, my classmates started to write. I'd stared anxiously at the blank sheet, aware that there were sentences that could hardly be thought, let alone written down. I had no great secret in mind; all I could have written was that I harbored a fear that also felt like a fantasy that one day my orderly life would erupt. Afraid to let this sentence linger in my head for too long, I folded the blank paper into a small square and threw it away when I left the classroom.

Now, though, when I've learned that those bare-all sentences never stay buried for long, I quickly write something on an index card and put it in my bag.

Going to the barn service, I text William. All day we text back and forth, so much that just the sight of my phone makes me think of him. At night, when the kids are asleep, we talk on the phone. I whisper so as not to wake Layla, who sleeps in my bed these days and shifts at the sound of my laughter.

Enjoy, William writes.

Want to come with me? I ask.

No religion for me, he answers, as I knew he would. He is skeptical, rational, scientific. He decries false piety, organized religion, public demonstrations of righteousness. For him, religion is designed to divide people; it's not a search for truth but an exclusive club. In being with him, I know that I've chosen the opposite of what came before.

Please? I persist.

You don't believe in it, so why are you holding on? he writes back.

I have no simple answer for this.

A few minutes later, I'm rifling through my closet looking for a pair of nonleather shoes, which are required by Jewish law as a sign of deprivation on Yom Kippur, when my phone beeps again. My heart leaps, as it always does, when I see William's name.

I can drive there with you if you want and wait for you outside, he texts, an offer I appreciate, but I tell him I can go by myself. My religious journey is one I need to make on my own.

IT'S ALMOST DARK by the time I head out to Weston; my car is my chief vehicle of transgression. Not wanting anyone I know to see me driving on this day, I carefully plot my route — the map inside my head is still marked with streets that are impassable on Shabbat and on holidays, roads allowed and forbidden. On the streets I take, no one I know will be walking to synagogue, noticing me in my car. By driving to this service, I'm supposedly doing something wrong, yet all along the street where the service is being held, cars are lined up, people emerging, doing something they believe to be good. The feeling of wrongdoing appears to be mine alone.

Really, this is a barn in name only — it's actually a beautifully refurbished structure out behind a sprawling house. There is a small basket filled with index cards by the front door, and I add my own card to the heaping pile.

I walk in tentatively, wishing the kids were with me. In one of the rows of this barn turned synagogue, I see my friend, her husband, and their children. They saved me a seat in case I decided to attend, and this act of friendship fills my eyes with tears — as does any small kindness these days.

We sit in a semicircle of rows. The leader is an earnest, soft-spoken rheumatologist with a soulful voice. The mood is warm and gentle as he plays the guitar and a congregant beats a drum, both technically forbidden today according to Orthodox rules. Until this year, I might have been intrigued by this barn service, but I would never have considered attending it. It was too different from the Orthodox services I was used to, and there were too many barriers—not just that driving to the service was forbidden but that it didn't comply with the rules of Orthodoxy requiring men and women to sit separately, requiring the traditional liturgy to remain unchanged. It wouldn't matter if I found the experience moving, not if it meant trespassing upon any of the laws. I was so used to feeling compelled, I had long ago ceased to consider what I wanted this to mean. Even now, when the singing is rousing and heartfelt—a room of people passionately engaged—I sit stiffly, unmoved. I can't help but see it all through my Orthodox eyes. *Too crunchy,* I think, *too spiritual;* I tabulate all the ways this service doesn't adhere to the letter of the law.

"Is this your first time here?" a woman on the other side of me asks. She's in her fifties, with straight brown hair and maroon lipstick, wearing a sleeveless black sheath dress and black leather pumps.

"It is," I say, and she asks me where I've gone to Yom Kippur services in prior years.

"I used to be Orthodox," I say, as though this can explain everything.

"I'm a convert," she says, "but my husband"—she gestures to the man sitting next to her—"also grew up Orthodox."

His eyes meet mine in understanding, and I wonder: Are the synagogues he used to attend ghosted over this one? Does he feel the unrelenting internal voice that won't stop asking what is true, what is real?

"We wanted to celebrate Yom Kippur," she explained, "but we needed somewhere we would feel comfortable."

"How long since you've been Orthodox?" I ask him.

He thinks it over. "Thirty years. I left right after college. It's been a lifetime."

The service continues with the same prayers, in the same tunes, as the ones I grew up with. Sitting in this place, I'm simultaneously here and back inside the Yom Kippurs of my childhood, when, in the lead-up to this holiest of days, my brother, sister, and I gleefully asked one another for forgiveness for anything we might have done wrong. It was thrilling to have sins for which we needed to be forgiven — a visit to the adult side of the world. To be difficult, we sometimes refused to bestow forgiveness, but this was a precarious proposition. If you turned someone down for forgiveness three times, the sin was no longer on the original offender but on you.

All year, we complied with the rules, the world divided by stark lines. We were to be a separate nation, pure and holy. We were to follow the commandments as set down in the Torah. We learned to classify and judge. Every person, every action, could be plotted on a grid, good or bad. This is what God wants, we were told at every turn, only He wasn't referred to as God but as Hashem, a nickname reserved for those who were closest to Him. He didn't exist on high, removed from the daily dealings, but lived in the here and now, inside the most private and seemingly insignificant moments. Every bite of food came either allowed or forbidden. On Saturday night, three stars had to appear in the sky, the sign that the sun had fully set, before Shabbat was declared officially over. On every doorway of every house, we hung a mezuzah, a small decorative case holding a parchment bearing the Shema prayer. If anything went wrong—a car accident, a diagnosis of cancer—we were advised to check the parchments for a smudged letter that had left us unguarded, as though we'd forgotten to lock our front doors. Every night, I said the same Shema prayer, which proclaimed my belief in God, then I recited the list of *God bless*es, as my mother had taught me. I named all my relatives, then my friends, leaving off only those I happened to be in a fight with on a particular day. I knew that being good could protect you from harm. Only obedience could keep you safe. God, I knew, was like a parent who dispensed soothing comforts with one hand, terrible punishments with the other. My mind constantly fired off a series of what-ifs: What if someone I loved was in a car accident? What if the Holocaust happened again? I had a recurring nightmare that I was driving with my mother and then she disappeared and I had to drive but didn't know how. The nightmare unfolded again and again, even though I loved the antique-car ride at Libertyland, the local amusement park, thrilled to think I was actually piloting the car—only years later did I realize the car was running on a track, my steering an illusion. When I was too racked with fear to fall back to sleep, I tiptoed into my parents' bedroom and woke my mother, who walked me to bed and sat beside me as she smoothed my hair. Together we recited a psalm —*The Lord is my light and my salvation; whom shall I fear?*— words I wanted to hold like a torch that would illuminate the way until morning. I fell asleep trusting that my parents were watching over the house and that God, awake late into the night, was standing guard as well.

At the Memphis Hebrew Academy, which I attended starting in nursery school, the boys wore a uniform of blue pants and white button-down shirts, and the girls wore red-and-black-plaid jumpers, like the Christian girls in the St. Louis Academy down the street. It shocked me, as we drove past their school on the way to ours, that these kids were taught a religion as steadfastly as we were. Had I been born into their faith, would I, too, have believed this to be truth? But the thought was too unsettling. Obviously, they had to be wrong. How lucky I was; of the billions of people on earth, I was among those born to the sole truth. I knew that I was supposed to be proud of who I was, yet when I went out with my brother and father in their yarmulkes, it was hard not to think about the time that a few boys from our neighborhood had yelled "Heil Hitler!" at us. I hoped that any non-Jews we passed might think of the yarmulkes as just some sort of miniature hats.

We might have been a small Orthodox community in the midst of a larger city, but at school, ours was the only one that existed. The seeming anomaly of Orthodox Jews living in Memphis didn't matter. The Jerusalem of the South, our leaders proudly dubbed the community. A Jewish oasis in a vast Southern desert. Every morning, we stood by our desks and recited the same daily prayers said in every corner of the Orthodox world. Every month, a magazine whose Hebrew name translated as "Our World" arrived from Brooklyn. It contained cartoons depicting the adventures of a yarmulke-wearing mouse named Mendel and invited us to join the army of God. We learned about the *yetzer hara* — the evil inclination — a serpentine impulse that lived inside us and was in danger of slithering out if we didn't vigilantly guard against its escape. In first grade, we learned to read Hebrew. In second grade, we earned gold stars if we could recite verses of the Torah by heart, if we knew the blessings for different foods. Having memorized more verses than anyone in my class and having mastered which blessing was said for even the trickiest of foods, I was eager to be quizzed by the teacher. After each right answer I delivered, I took the star — the same kind that God was surely placing by my name in His divine ledger — and stuck it to the front of my notebook, forming constellations. Each star was confirmation not just of my knowledge but of my goodness. There was nothing more important that I could be. Even my own name reminded me of this fact. I was named after my great-grandmother Gertrude, whose Yiddish name was Gittel, which means "good." The Hebrew word for "good" is *tova*.

On Yom Kippur, I sat in the women's section next to my mother and sister, across the *mechitzah* that divided us from my father and brother and the other men. The walls were purple, the chairs were a speckled red fabric, the ceiling silver-paneled. Visitors from out of town sometimes commented that the décor made them think of Elvis Presley, whose famous Graceland was just a few miles away, but to me, this sanctuary was simply a second home. On Kol Nidrei, the prayer highlight of the year, all the Torah scrolls were taken from the ark. The sanctuary was packed with the regulars, who, because driving was forbidden on Shabbat, lived within walking distance of the synagogue, as we did. Like ours, these families were solid entities, made of husbands, wives, and children. The rare divorced women lay at the outskirts, occasional Shabbat guests who were to be pitied, outsiders who were the near equivalent of the non-Orthodox who drove to synagogue but parked a few blocks down so no one would catch a glimpse of them in their cars. As though they'd appeared magically in the neighborhood, they walked the remainder of the way. These infrequent attendees were marked by the uncertain manner in which they held their prayer books; by the black doilies the women wore instead of hats; by the prayer shawls the men wore, which were provided by the synagogue and were silken and small, like scarves, not the flowing wool capes of the regulars. The papery black visitors' yarmulkes perched on top of these men's heads might as well have borne the label *I Do Not Belong*.

I was curious about these congregants—didn't they care that they were breaking Shabbat? *Breaking* was the word we used to describe their infractions, and I had imagined them clumsily shattering something precious and fragile. Or (this idea seemed dangerous even to entertain) was it possible that they didn't believe that by driving to synagogue—just one sin out of what I knew must be legion—they were violating the word of God? "Nonreligious Jews are like babies stolen at birth, not responsible for their trespasses," our more tolerant teachers and rabbis explained. Our job was to beckon them deeper inside.

I sat by my mother, determined to fast all twenty-five hours of Yom Kippur, staying next to her as we recited the prayer reminding us that on this day, the judgment for each of us for the coming year was sealed: who would live, who would die, who by fire and who by sword. Aware that my very life hung in the balance, I stayed even as the day dragged on, to the sermon and then to the long descriptions of the ancient Temple service. Using the English translation that was printed alongside the Hebrew in the prayer book, I studied the preparations the high priest had made as he readied himself to enter the Holy of Ho-

lies, the part of the Temple forbidden on all other days. He cer-
emonially washed himself and donned his priestly vestments,
preparing to offer sacrifices and pray for forgiveness on behalf of
the people. He displayed a cord of wool dyed red. If the sins of
the people were forgiven, the wool would turn white.

One year at the start of the Yom Kippur service, I discovered
that I had a hangnail, which was forbidden to tear off on Shabbat and even more so on Yom Kippur. I tried to ignore its presence, but once I was aware of it, there was no way to make my
fingers leave it alone. Unable to concentrate on the prayers, I
fiddled with the nail behind my back. If my mother saw me, I
knew she would encircle my hand with hers, as both an affec-
tionate gesture and a means of preventing this forbidden act. I
tried to imagine what God would say. With all He had to worry
about on this day, was He really concerned with my hangnail?
The debate raged in my head. If I pulled off the hangnail, I
could once again pray undistracted, but if I pulled it off, I would
be breaking one of the laws of the day. In this small sliver of nail
lay a daunting theological quandary. Finally, guilt-ridden but
hoping that God was as slow to anger as our prayers proclaimed,
I ripped it off.

"All vows, swears, oaths, promises that I may make from this
Yom Kippur to the next are now nullified, voided, ended," sang
the cantor in the synagogue I'd grown up in, as does the leader
now in the barn that has filled to capacity.

The words, a second time, louder now for the stragglers, the
latecomers.

"All vows, swears, oaths, promises."

And a third time. "Nullified, voided, ended."

What we had promised we could undo. What we had committed ourselves to, we could still change.

In my parents' synagogue, the Torah scrolls, all seven of them, would have been removed from the ark. The parchment scrolls were rolled around wood spindles, cloaked in white velvet robes, and topped with silver crowns. They would be solemnly carried around the sanctuary by a parade of honored men who held them gingerly over their shoulders, as though they were carrying elaborately dressed sleeping children.

In this barn service, there is only one Torah scroll that is taken from the small ark. A poem is read, a song is sung, and it's time now for the basket of index cards to be passed around and read aloud.

"'I answer my soul when I reach out to those in need,'" someone behind me reads.

"'I occupy myself with my passion when I paint, sing, and dance.'"

My voice shakes when it's my turn to read the card I've selected. Even though the words aren't my own, I feel as though I'm baring my most private secret.

"'I respond to my soul when I remember that I'm not the only one who is imperfect. I am not the only one who falls short.'"

A woman in front of me turns around to smile in agreement —I don't know if she's the one whose words I've read or if they just speak to her, as they do to me.

"'I answer my self when I'm allowed to think what I think, feel what I feel,'" reads a woman across the room, and my face flushes at the sound of words that are mine.

A harmless wish, when read in someone else's voice.

People are invited outside into the dark yard to recite the silent portion of the evening prayers or offer their own improvised prayers. As much as I too want to stand under a star-filled canopy — to trade the tightness of one world for the seeming openness of another — I can't go outside. I'm unable to open myself to what's being offered. So many years of observing without believing has left my soul, if such a thing exists, callused.

I think about my kids, who are with Aaron at a Yom Kippur service like the one I'd always attended. I think of William — maybe he has worked late, maybe he went out to dinner or a movie with friends. For him, this was an ordinary night. Still in my seat, in a room mostly emptied out, I return, from habit, to saying the confessional prayers that I've always said. Though I feel the urge to shield myself from every ritual and rule, there is no hiding from this prayer.

Ashamnu, bagadnu, gazalnu.

We have sinned, we have transgressed, we have stolen.

The sins for which we atone are recited collectively. Not even on the Day of Judgment did we have to face God alone. Guilt is communal, but so is penance; no lonely *I* but an ever-present *we*.

For the sin we have sinned before You with our illicit thoughts.

For the sin we have sinned before You knowingly and unknowingly, with an outstretched hand, with a hardened heart.

Guilt swoops in, a large-winged bird that can find me anywhere. A flock of impossible questions. Did happiness matter? Did loneliness? Were you allowed to change your life? Were you allowed to change if it caused other people pain? Could you make yourself believe something? Could you make yourself love someone? Could you make yourself not love someone?

The crowing voice: *You are bad*.

For these words there is no cleansing; no high priest's red cord shall magically turn white.

Bad; the word is clawed and it grabs me.

Bad; the word beats in my chest.

To atone, we are to cast our sins into flowing water. We are to swing a live chicken over our heads and request that God transfer our sins to this animal. I too want relief from my sins but have no stream of water, no squawking fowl, just my own words, which replace the ones written on the pages of the prayer book.

For the sin we have sinned by harboring doubt.

For the sin we have sinned by trying to make it through with tepid belief.

For the sin we have sinned by trying to hold everything together; for the sin of no longer being able, or willing, to do so.

For the sin we have sinned by wanting to live a life in which we believed; for the sin of acting when we knew this might destroy everything.

Along with each of these words, I should be curling my hand into a fist, as the tradition requires, my shoulders rounded forward in contrition as I pound away at my chest. I make the obligatory fist, but my hand recoils just as it's about to touch down on my body.

For the sin of fantasy, for the sin of despair, for the sin of hope, for the sin of desire, for the sin of possibility.

For the sin of opening our hearts to someone new.

For the sin of causing pain; for the sin of dishonesty; for the sin of falling, falling, falling; for the sin of leaving in the hope of love.

For the sin of pursuing that which made us feel alive.

Instead of striking my chest, I uncurl my fist and place my hand over my heart, as though pledging allegiance to some other truth.

Home

My father holds out a spoon heaped with sautéed mushrooms —cremini, portobello, and shiitake—which will serve as the filling for the phyllo-dough turnovers he is making.

"More seasoning?" he asks as I take a bite.

"Delicious," I pronounce. I assemble my own less gourmet dish of stuffed zucchini, mixing unmeasured amounts of bread crumbs, mushrooms, spices, and the zucchini innards that I've scooped out.

In my parents' kitchen in Memphis, where the kids and I have come for Sukkot—the next, after Yom Kippur, in the long list of autumn holidays—cast-iron sauté pans sizzle on the stovetop. The room bursts with color. The walls of the kitchen are buttery yellow. Blue frosted-glass light fixtures dangle from the burnt-sienna ceiling. Bottles of balsamic vinegar and olive oil, sprigs of rosemary clipped from the garden, cloves of garlic and shallots with their papery husks scattered around, are arrayed on the countertops. The table holds bags from the latest outing to the grocery store—we've made several trips to collect all the necessary ingredients.

As I stir and sample, my father chops and seasons to make tuna tartare. For my father, cooking is not obligation but art. He is a cardiologist by day, a chef by night. Everywhere else, my father is quiet, but bent over a cutting board, stirring at the stove, he comes to life, talking eagerly of whisks and garlic presses, of new recipes and combinations of flavor.

My mother bustles around as sous-chef, cleaning up rinds, cores, and peels. She's grown her thick, wavy hair long in recent years and it has slowly turned from streaked to mostly gray. She wears bright colors and loose flowing skirts, beaded jewelry and comfortable shoes. She takes tai chi classes; she is a storyteller; she adheres to various self-help philosophies, none of which conflict with her strict religious observance. For her, cooking is utilitarian. Her art forms are the Jewish folktales she tells and her paintings, which hang on the walls around us, portraits of my grandmother, my kids, my siblings, and me. My sister's bedroom has been turned into my mother's studio; small tubes of paint cover the desk. She's in love, she says, with color.

"Are the kids excited for Sukkot?" my mother asks.

"I think so," I say. It's an innocent question, but I hear what lurks below.

"How does it work with the kids?" she wants to know, and we are off, into the perilous double helix of divorce and religion. It's hard to remember what we used to talk about. Now the questions abound—not only how the kids' time will be divided but who shall retain possession of their beliefs.

"You know I'm not really Orthodox anymore," I remind her,

as I have several times already, although without detailing what exactly this means. Each time, I detect a flicker of disbelief on her face, as though I'm describing an impossibility. But I can hardly blame her — I'm still surprised myself.

"I respect your own choices, but with the kids, don't you think . . ." My mother trails off.

"You can leave as long as you're willing to leave alone? You can quietly stray as long as the kids remain?" I finish the sentence for her.

"I just think —" she starts to say.

"Am I supposed to pretend?" I interrupt, lowering my voice so that the kids playing in the next room don't hear. Even as I argue with her, I worry she's right — how many changes can the kids face in one year? How can they comfortably navigate their different worlds — their father's and mine? I'm cagey with the kids about no longer being Orthodox. They have seen me break some of the prohibitions, but I have yet to say, *The rules with which we have raised you, I no longer observe; the truths I have instilled in you, I no longer believe.* I'm not sure which is the greater betrayal: to change course at this late date, or to continue to raise them in a system in which I don't believe.

My mother doesn't answer. There will be no stark rejection, no hard-sell coercion — though Orthodox, my parents are too open and accepting for the outright shunning that often happens in more stringently Orthodox families when the parts of a family cease to match one another. Parents stop speaking to children, children stop speaking to parents, all in the name of God. With every sentence I say, though, I am afraid of becoming unrecognizable, no longer the good daughter I am supposed to be.

I worry that I will lose the sense that I belong here in this house, the only place that still feels like home.

ONCE THE DISHES are put in the oven—my zucchini lined up in the pan like a fleet of green canoes—I leave the kitchen to go check on the kids, who are playing happily. I study them as though searching for symptoms of a dreaded fever, worried that the divorce fills their minds as persistently as it does mine, that they too cannot stop noting that this is the first Sukkot of the divorce, that during this year, everything is a first. When I was their age, divorce existed only in books or the occasional after-school TV special, part of the swath of problems that affected other people. *A broken home,* it was always called, and I'd imagined a house cut in half, suffering the kind of wreckage we saw on the news after a tornado had touched down nearby.

In the den, the boys are plugged into a variety of screens, and Layla is playing with the bins of toys saved from my childhood—the wood blocks and the oversize red metal fire truck, the small Fisher-Price people I had once named Bayla and Faygie, and the milk crate of naked Barbies who, in earlier days, were dressed in sparkling gowns and bore names like Tiffany and Chrissy. "Those are good names for nice Jewish dolls," my mother once quipped and I was taken aback. I hadn't realized that the Barbies were automatically Jewish because they were mine.

There are few aspects of my family not imbued with Jewishness; it is braided through every memory, part of nearly every conversation and every relationship. On every wall of this house, there is contemporary Israeli art. Books overflow onto every free surface—this is a house made not only of bricks but of books.

On my parents' shelves, novels and volumes of poetry mingle with Jewish texts and books of Jewish folktales, books about Israel and Jewish spirituality and philosophical works by Modern Orthodox rabbis who advocate integrating secular ideas with religious ones. At least on these shelves, there is an easy commingling of disparate ideas.

In large frames displayed around the house, there are family photos of my siblings and me. My younger sister, Dahlia, who has long dark blond curls and striking green eyes, is unmarried at the age of thirty-seven. She is a therapist and lives on the Upper West Side of Manhattan, one among the many Orthodox singles who live close to one another, awaiting marriage. In a picture of my older brother, Akiva, at his wedding—which took place the same summer as mine—he is clean-shaven, the white-knit yarmulke of the Modern Orthodox on his head. His wife, in sequins and tulle, leans against him playfully. In a more recent photo, Akiva has a full beard and long ringlet side-curls and wears a black ceremonial coat and a round fur-trimmed hat like those once worn by Russian and Polish nobility. His wife's hair is entirely covered with a gold turban, and their children are dressed in black and white, their hair cut short except for the side-curls that frame the boys' faces. Now adherents to ultra-Orthodox Chasidism—a mystical movement started in the eighteenth century advocating for a greater emphasis on forging a spiritual connection to God—they live in the Israeli city of Tzfat; they are not allowed secular studies, not allowed exposure to art, to literature, to the outside world.

All these photos are not just family memories but photographic evidence of the presumed threats to Modern Orthodoxy, which views itself as being under siege from the right, from the left, and from inside. There is the problem of kids rejecting the so-called pick-and-choose laxness of Modern Orthodoxy and becoming right-wing Orthodox. There is the problem of kids falling through the holes created by the relative openness and becoming nonobservant. And if that's not bad enough, there's the problem of singles who don't get married at the conventional time and who linger for years, feeling that the community has no place for them.

Now my siblings and I represent all of these. My parents, I imagine, must sometimes feel like they have whiplash from the varying paths we have taken. But even so, they have maintained this middle ground. They believe that you can remain strictly Orthodox without being a separatist. You can grapple with modern ideas, engage in art and science, believe in a limited feminism if you must, although not so much that it pulls you away. Teach your children to span two worlds and trust that they can navigate between them. But here lay the dilemma. If you allowed yourself to be a critical thinker, was religion exempt from this examination? If you raised children to think for themselves, what did you do if they thought in ways that were foreign to you? If you believed in free choice, what did you do if your children chose something else?

"Do you know what it feels like to live something you don't believe?" I ask my parents when I come back into the kitchen. Each time I say this outright, I leave a little more. To leave a marriage, to leave a religion, you never go just once. You have to leave again and again.

It's quiet in here and in the den, too, where the kids have probably made use of their special sonar that can detect when something of interest is being discussed by the adults. I look from my mother to my father. She is passionate, creative, and free-spirited, deeply engaged with religious ritual and spirituality. He makes fewer outward displays of religiosity but is in possession of an intellectual curiosity, an abiding commitment, and a quiet integrity. For both of them, there have been times when they have not fit neatly inside the Orthodox community, yet it remains the place where they belong.

"What would you do if you felt this way?" I persist. The few moments in which they are silent tick painfully past.

"You're in a tough position," my father says.

"It's confusing for the kids," my mother says.

I seek refuge in my childhood bedroom, the past intact on shelves and in the walk-in closet, where I once liked to curl up on Shabbat in a nest of pillows and read. On Shabbat, when traveling by car was forbidden, books were a permissible mode of escape. They released me from the trapped feeling I had each Friday at sundown, when the rules went into effect and it felt like we were being stranded on a desert island.

In the books I read, siblings lived parentless in boxcars; children embarked on forest adventures; a girl encountered a family who would live forever. I read of witches and ghosts, of teenage twins—one good, one bad—who went to football games and proms. No one I met in books lived as we did, but in real life, almost everyone I knew was Orthodox.

My maternal grandmother grew up in Memphis in a secular Zionist household; her father was a native Memphian and her mother an immigrant from Grodno, a city on the Poland-Russia border. My grandmother became Orthodox on her own, as a teenager. Before that, she sometimes went to the wealthier Reform temple in downtown Memphis, where she felt like an outsider. One day, searching for something more, she decided to attend the less affluent Orthodox synagogue, made up mostly of Eastern European immigrants. She was the first one to arrive at the youth service. The second to arrive was my grandfather, then a blond-haired, blue-eyed young Orthodox man, the American-born son of Polish immigrants.

My grandmother's transformation to Orthodoxy was conveyed in storied tones, the religious equivalent of a fairy tale about a princess returned to her rightful home. If a rift was created between her and her parents, if she was regarded as rejecting their secular beliefs, I never knew about it, though I was aware that sometimes her father drove to our house on Shabbat but parked a few blocks away so that we wouldn't actually see him desecrate the day. The gesture was appreciated, but still, family members quietly discussed whether we were allowed to have him over in the first place. By inviting him to a place that he had to drive to, we were causing him to sin — the equivalent, our rabbis explained, of placing a stumbling block before a blind man. All Jews, we were told, were responsible for one another. Our concern about the sins of non-Orthodox Jews was often held up as an example of our kindness and compassion, but even so, I used to wonder how my great-grandfather would have felt had he known he was our equivalent of a blind man.

My grandmother sent her children to the Memphis Hebrew Academy, which she helped found, the centerpiece of a now burgeoning Orthodox community; she dressed her daughters for the Children's Ball, when mixed dancing was still allowed, and organized the school's float in the Cotton Carnival Parade. Eventually, she sent a son to a right-wing Orthodox yeshiva in Lakewood, New Jersey, and a daughter to a women's seminary in New York. Only my mother went to college, to the women's branch of the Modern Orthodox Yeshiva University, which prided itself on integrating secular and religious studies.

Though fully Orthodox, we were considered the least religious branch of my mother's family. Modern Orthodoxy was often regarded with suspicion, seen as an intellectual way of rationalizing a laxness about the laws. To my mother's brother's wedding, my father wore one of right-wing Orthodoxy's trademark black fedoras (a concession and an act of falseness that he sometimes marvels at now and says he wouldn't repeat), and my mother covered her hair with a short curly wig that later joined our collection of dress-up clothes. My siblings and I studied the pictures of our parents dressed to fit into this alternate world. Though I was aware, from a young age, of the differences between Modern Orthodoxy and right-wing Orthodoxy, the stricter proscriptions cast an ever-present shadow. "Pants aren't modest," one of my cousins informed me about my jeans, and I'd been annoyed at what she said but at the same time felt I had reason to be ashamed.

There were always reasons to feel this coil of anger and shame. In fourth grade, we learned that Eve had caused Adam to sin with her unwillingness to follow God's directions. As a punishment, God told her that her desire will be for her husband, and *va timshol ba* — "he will rule over her" — the text said. For homework, I needed to translate this verse, among others, and at the small white desk in my bedroom, I felt a low rumbling of anger, the same slow burn I felt in school when the boys screamed out the morning blessing designated for them, thanking God for not making them women. Without being told, we, the girls in the class, knew to use small sweet voices when we recited our counterpart version thanking God for making us "according to Thy will." *You don't have to feel that way,* we were told if we complained to our teachers about this blessing or any other perceived slight to us as girls and women. *You're too sensitive. You've been corrupted by the outside. You're looking at it the wrong way. You don't realize that these supposed denigrations are actually the opposite, because you, girls and women, don't need all the rituals that men require. Because you are special, more spiritual, naturally close to God.*

My mother came into my room and I pointed to the offending words about Eve being ruled over by Adam.

"How can the Torah say that?" I asked.

The book that I had been taught to revere, seemingly turned against me.

Her eyes filled with sympathy but also conviction. "You can't take it that way. It doesn't mean it like that," she explained, but I could see that she understood the problem. She considered herself an Orthodox feminist even before that term became widespread and vilified. Anywhere but in the religious arena, she would have argued against the notion of male domination. But the Torah was protected land — the words were sacred. It might have sounded confusing but she believed that, however imperfectly, feminism could coexist with Orthodoxy. A contradiction like this didn't have the power to undo her belief. The text couldn't be wrong; the rabbis couldn't be wrong. If sexism was wrong, the text couldn't be sexist. You were either reading it wrong or feeling it wrong. The laws couldn't change, the words couldn't change — nothing, in fact, could change — yet you could turn the words, reframe them, and reshape them, do anything so that you could still fit inside.

I continued to feel that burn of anger but tried to allow my mother's words to spread over me, like a calm hand cooling a feverish forehead. I didn't want to fall outside her comfort, didn't want to walk across a dividing line as familial as it was religious. There was one truth I knew without having to be told, not just in my family but in my community, among everyone that I knew: to observe was to be good, and to be good was to be loved.

Searching for a way out of the problem the text presented, my mother and I read a biblical commentary that explained that this supposedly offending phrase referred to the fact that the man shall rule over the woman in the sexual act. It wasn't exactly clear to me how this explanation made the words any better, but I was too embarrassed to ask my mother and find out. I may not have understood what the commentator meant by *the sexual act,* but I did know that it had to do with a part of the world that needed to remain hidden.

When I was in ninth grade, my friends and I went to the Mall of Memphis, where we tried on prom dresses that we'd never be allowed to wear, for a prom we'd never be allowed to have. From the outside, no one could tell we were Orthodox — unlike the boys, we didn't to have to wear yarmulkes everywhere we went — which was a relief. But even so, there was no forgetting. Usually when I browsed through racks of clothing, I automatically separated out what was allowed, what was not. At home, my parents let me wear pants — this was one of the so-called laxities of Modern Orthodoxy — but I did so with the awareness that it wasn't really permitted. It seemed like maybe the rabbis were right — I did feel different in jeans, strangely powerful and strong. But at school, the rules were stricter. Could you see my collarbone? Could you see my knees? Was this skirt too short, this shirt too sheer, too tight, too sexy? My friends and I folded dresses over our arms and hurried into the changing rooms. In the three-sided mirrors, I surveyed myself in a strapless satin gown, marveling at the bare shoulders and arms, the beginning of cleavage. This was an impossible version of myself; it was as though these were fun-house mirrors distorting who I really was. I was used to all the ways my body needed to be covered but less accustomed to what could be revealed. My friends and I laughed at our reflections and quickly took off the gowns, worried that the salespeople surveying us could tell that we didn't belong inside these dresses, that they'd suspect us not of shoplifting, but of impersonating teens we would never become.

"If you're going to be a role model, you need to wear skirts," one of my youth-group leaders told me when I was in tenth grade. This was just before we went on a weekend retreat. Every few months we would go on one of these conventions for teenagers from observant and nonobservant homes. We traveled to cities with large Jewish populations, like St. Louis, and small ones, like Omaha and Wichita, to instill in Jewish teens a love of Orthodox Judaism. *Influence them. Convince them. Sway them,* we were urged regarding those who weren't Orthodox — runaway bunnies or little lost lambs who could be gently coaxed home. I listened to my adviser's admonition against wearing pants because, more than my freedom, I cared about his approval.

After a long overnight bus ride to our intended destination, we would arrive a few hours before Shabbat.

"You are the next link in the chain," we were told as we sang and danced in separate circles, boys and girls.

"You are the bright light in the darkness."

"How do we know it's true?" my friends and I asked a rabbi on Shabbat afternoon at one of these conventions. In class we usually raised questions about the existence of God only to waste time, but here I really wanted to know. I still lay awake at night tormented by the what-ifs, but now many of them were of the religious sort. All around me, I heard the drumbeat of supposed truth. *Without God, there is no meaning. Without the Torah, there is no goodness.* But what if there emerged some irrefutable proof that the Torah wasn't true? I wasn't sure if I was dreading this or hoping for it; I didn't know how it would feel to watch everything that I had been taught was true crumble, just as I didn't know exactly what form such a revelation might take—I doubted that a refutation of the Torah would be announced from heaven. But the practical questions notwithstanding, what if it was proven, beyond any doubt, that the Torah was not the word of God? Would I want to know, I interrogated myself, or would I prefer to cover my eyes and carry on unchanged? On the one hand, the forbidden world would spring free—all of a sudden we would be able to watch TV on Shabbat and eat at the restaurants whose commercials we watched and that tempted us to compile lists of which we'd try first if we could. (Taco Bell, then KFC, but not Red Lobster, which seemed disgusting.) But after the excitement faded, surely the earth would sway dangerously. It would be the same as discovering you weren't part of your own family, like learning that your parents didn't actually love you.

At a prior convention, this rabbi had come upon me huddling close to a cute boy in the basement of the synagogue, and he had pointedly put a pillow between us. According to the To-

rah, it was forbidden to touch boys; wrong to kiss, wrong even
to hold hands. Because I was one of the good girls, the rabbi
had looked at me with surprise. He was right to react in this
way. I had never kissed a boy; barely touched one, for that matter. Though I cringed at the thought of disappointing anyone, I studied the so-called bad girls in my class, the ones who
wore short skirts and, it was rumored, at one of these conventions, had snuck out of their houses at night to hang out with,
and possibly kiss, boys. Didn't they feel that their every action
was watched, judged? Didn't they feel communal eyes burning marks of shame onto their skin? It was something I had always known: you existed only as you were created in the eyes of
others.

This boy and I sat close, our arms brushing against each other's. We'd pretended not to notice, though with the lights off and
no one else around, the tickle of his skin against mine was the
only sensation that existed—the rest of my body came to a
standstill in the face of this discovery. I'd been taught about how
sinful and soul-damaging it was to have any physical contact
with boys, but no one had talked about the feeling that more of
your body could come to life.

Here at this convention, though, as my friends and I asked
questions about God, the rabbi wasn't police officer but teacher.
He didn't have to offer me a disappointed shake of the head and
a reminder that I was someone from whom he expected more.
He described his own crisis of faith, when he decided he couldn't
live on the fence. Though it was clear what he'd chosen—one
look at his beard and black hat dispelled any questions—I still
wanted to hear him speak of the existence of these doubts. It was
easy to fall for the illusion that there was only contentment, only

righteousness, but I was hungry for someone to expose the underworld of dissenting feelings—even to admit it existed at all. We all believe, I heard again and again, but was it possible that there were outliers who didn't always believe exactly as they were required to? Was there some hidden place where people admitted what they really thought—maybe inside a small box that locked with a mini-key like the one that closed my diary or in some subterranean room where, in the dark of night, they laid bare their confessions? Only in fleeting moments was there ever a hint that this alternate world existed—scandals that ripped a jagged fissure in the way the community was supposed to look, discussed by the adults at the Shabbat table, the topic abruptly changed when the children wandered back in for dessert. Each overheard story offered a small piece of understanding that I was only starting to assemble. People weren't necessarily who they appeared to be. Good and bad weren't always so neatly divided.

With my friends and I sitting around him, the rabbi told us that according to the Torah, animals needed to have split hoofs and chew their cuds in order to be considered kosher. However, a certain number of animals had one of these traits but not the other.

"The proof that the Torah was written by God," he said, "was that the text states the exact number of animals in this ambiguous category."

If a human being wrote the Torah, how would he know how many animals had one trait and not the other? Why would he risk specifying the number of animals, a fact that could easily be disproven when new lands were discovered and our knowledge of the earth expanded?

"To this day"—he paused dramatically—"that number holds."

The hair on the back of my neck bristled. Here was proof. The Torah, the laws, the rabbis were true after all.

"Remember the certainty you feel in this moment," he said. "You won't be able to hold on to it, but you can remember that right here, right now, you did feel it."

When Shabbat was over, we sat on the floor of the synagogue social hall. With the lights dimmed and the band playing softly, we swayed back and forth. *A pure heart God created in me,* we sang in Hebrew as a candle was passed from person to person. This was the high point of the weekend, why we had traveled all these miles. We would name how we had grown. We would inspire our peers to grow as well.

"I came feeling like I had no friends, but now I belong," said a girl who cried as she held the candle, her face flickering in and out of view.

"I'm going to tell my parents I want to go to yeshiva instead of public school," said a lanky teenage boy with spiked hair.

The candle came to me. "I hope I never lose the certainty I felt over this Shabbat," I said. But already that bristling sensation at the back of my neck—the feeling that I was being shown indisputable facts—was fading.

But don't give in to doubt. Don't be influenced by the pull of the outside. Keep the flame of tradition burning. Bear the torch, be a light unto the nations. So many Jews had died, we were told, without the freedom we possessed. With the lights still dimmed, one of the rabbis told a story about a man who died and went to heaven. With God watching, the angels piled the man's good deeds on one side of a scale and his bad deeds on the other. The scale teetered back and forth and then, lo and behold, it came out exactly even.

"Go back to earth," the angels advised this soul. "Bring three good deeds to sway the Holy One, blessed be He, so that you may be admitted to heaven."

The soul flew to earth and found a Jew performing one of God's commandments. He scooped up the good deed and carried it to the waiting angels. But it wasn't enough — "We need two more," said the angels — so the soul flew back to earth and found a second good deed, which he brought to heaven.

But it wasn't enough. One more. So the soul flew across the ocean, across the years. To Russia. To a small village. The czar and a band of Cossacks were riding horses through the street. Atrocities and suffering the likes of which you've never seen, the rabbi told us, his voice rising and falling dramatically. A Jewish girl, thirteen years old, tied to a horse by her long hair. Dragged through the streets. A crowd of jeering onlookers.

"A last request," the girl begged.

The czar was intrigued, amused. Who was this girl who dared to ask such a thing?

"Quiet," he commanded. "Let us hear her wish."

"Two straight pins," she pleaded.

The crowd scoffed as she was handed the pins. But this didn't deter her.

She took the pins and stuck one through each side of her skirt, plunging them into her flesh so that her skirt wouldn't ride up, so that her modesty would be preserved.

I was still with anticipation as I imagined this girl who would do anything to remain covered. The only thing stopping me from being covered was the impediment of my own flawed self.

To heaven the soul flew, clasping a bloody pin. Upon presenting it to the jury of angels, to God Himself, he was admitted to heaven.

AT THE YESHIVA of the South, where I was one of eighteen girls in the entire high school, safety pins were kept in the office to fasten shut a low-cut blouse or a skirt with an offending slit. Mothers had to be called if a new skirt needed to be procured; a spare skirt was kept in the office for those times when a mother wasn't reachable. Modesty mattered above all. Singing was immodest (though not being allowed to sing didn't bother me as much as the other laws—I had a terrible voice and steadfastly refused to sing in front of anyone). Our bodies too were immodest—to see a woman's thigh was to see her nakedness. Pants showed the forbidden form of legs. Knees were equally problematic. So was any writing on our shirts that would draw men's eyes to our chests. We might have been distractions, temptations, but modesty cleansed us of any potential sin. Modesty prevented us from tempting the weak men, who were less spiritual than we were. Modesty was for our own benefit, so that we remembered we were holy. After all, *the glory of the king's daughter is within* —so said the psalm that was produced to snuff out any disgruntlement. We might have been the king's daughters, but God, the rabbis, and all the men were the kings.

We were taught, we were told, we were watched. The rabbis existed not just in the classroom but inside my head, small disapproving figures monitoring both what I did and what I thought. They spoke not as individuals but in a collective voice. In the face of this, my own voice seemed weak and uncertain. The only available subversions were small. I mastered the art of adjusting my skirts, rolling them up or pulling them down on my hips depending on who was around. Shame and defiance wound themselves together. The male teachers reported any immodesty to the female teachers, which made us quietly ask one another, "Well, why were they looking?" But everyone was looking; this was a given. Our knees, elbows, and hair were discussed in black-scripted rabbinic texts, featured prominently in the school rules, in notes sent home reporting infractions. We were always subject to inspection, our bodies divided and measured and mapped.

The days, too, were divided, secular subjects in the morning, Judaic studies in the afternoon. We were taught to believe in reward and punishment and the world to come. We were supposed to believe the laws were eternal and unchanging. We talked of God as though we could understand His every move. "Think of life as a board game," a teacher told us. "Would the inventors of Monopoly have created the game and neglected to give you the rules?" The Torah was a rule book as authoritative as the instruction pamphlet in a fresh set of Monopoly, the money rainbow-arrayed and all the properties organized by color. Everything happened for a reason, we were told, yet when a teenager from our community was killed in an accident, when a young woman died unexpectedly, there was no denying that events didn't always make sense. Only then were we grudgingly forced to encounter a God whose ways we couldn't understand.

In between prepping vocabulary words for the SATs and practicing lines for a Shakespeare play, we learned that we were not to talk to any of the three forlorn boys who made up the entirety of a separate and equally restless boys' high school that was housed in a different wing of the building—here, at least, there was room for mystery. These three lone boys wore basketball jackets (though there weren't enough of them for an actual team) donated by a crusading member of the community in exchange for their agreement to wear dress jackets for morning prayers, a sign of religious devotion. We weren't supposed to talk to them—since we started high school, they had become off-limits, creatures we glimpsed out the window of our classrooms as they played two-on-one basketball on the playground or when we happened to walk past them in the school hallway as they went in one door and we went out another.

As forbidden as these boys were to us now, the same boys, or their equivalents, would become permissible when it was time to get married, which we would all do, preferably within a few years of our high-school graduations. On a school trip to North Carolina—for which we brought coolers full of kosher food— our teachers created a game in which we identified the qualities we valued most in a potential husband. An illusory feeling of love was hardly reason enough to get married. Instead, you needed shared religious values, an agreed-upon path to walk together. We rolled our eyes at the activity—we were far more interested in locating some real-life boys—but played along nonetheless. There were slips of paper and we were to select the ones naming the traits we desired: Someone who studied Torah all day. Someone who would make a good father. Someone who was handsome. Someone who was lenient enough to watch TV. I selected the qualities I thought I wanted—yes to TV, no to learning Torah all day—but since I had yet to have a boyfriend, it was hard to be sure of exactly what I was looking for in a husband.

In a class on the books of Prophets, we learned about King

David, who spied the beautiful Bathsheba bathing upon a roof-top and desired her and took her for his wife. I was sitting at my small wooden desk, sticking the sharp tip of my pencil into the hem of my almost-to-the-knee-if-you-looked-at-it-from-just-the-right-angle faded denim skirt—my most ardent goal was to fringe my way around the entire skirt before the end of the school year. I stared at the clock, whose faint ticking was audible if you listened closely, willing not just the hours to pass but the years.

"'King David gave word that her husband, Uriah, was to be sent to the front lines of the battle so that he would be killed,'" we translated from the Hebrew.

When we were in elementary school, our teachers had skipped over the juicy portions of the Torah. Only when there was no other choice would they reluctantly acknowledge that the Patriarchs and Matriarchs weren't always perfect. At the story of Bathsheba and David, I stirred to attention. This was starting to sound a little like *Days of Our Lives,* which I watched during summer vacations and was allowed to tape once a week. Every Friday afternoon, I rushed home to Bo and Hope, even though my mother pointed out that we didn't share their values.

It bore some resemblance too to the novels that existed on the other side of the line drawn between the secular and religious. In English class that year, I'd fallen in love with *The Scarlet Letter.* Here, in the pages of Nathaniel Hawthorne, was blustery New England; here were other people's rules, so strict that they made my own seem almost lax in comparison. And here, in no uncertain terms, was the punishment for sin. When Hester wears the embroidered *A* on her chest, "every gesture, every word, and even the silence of those with whom she came in contact . . . expressed, that she was banished, and as much alone as if she inhabited another sphere." And yet, that letter allows her to see people more fully. "She shuddered to believe, yet could not help believing, that it gave her a sympathetic knowledge of the hidden sin in other hearts . . . the outward guise of purity was but a lie, and that, if truth were everywhere to be shown, a scarlet letter would blaze forth on many a bosom besides Hester Prynne's." Seeing my love of books, my English teacher—a non-Jewish poet who smoked a pipe and had a renegade spirit that was gloriously out of place in the school—encouraged me to talk to him about what I was reading. "You're going to love college. You can explore anything you're interested in," he told me.

"King David didn't sin," my Jewish studies teacher insisted, trying to tamp down our curious looks.

She showed us a rabbinic commentator's explanation for why King David's act of sleeping with another man's wife wasn't wrong: Every man issued a *get* to his wife before he went to war so that, in the event that he didn't return, the wife wouldn't be rendered an *agunah,* a chained woman whose husband was unable or unwilling to issue a divorce and who thus could not remarry. As soon as Uriah was killed, the divorce retroactively went into effect, so when King David slept with Bathsheva, she retroactively was not married and was thus permissible to him.

I stared back in confusion—this explanation for why King David hadn't sinned sounded a little contorted, the sort of excuse I wouldn't dare offer for breaking a rule. Questions of desire and power seemed so apparent in the actual text but not in the version we were given. I said nothing, because to outwardly challenge a teacher would have been worse than not doing your homework or talking out of turn. I sunk lower in my seat and focused on the hem of my skirt. *Be good,* said this teacher. *Be good,* the community said. *Be good,* my name reminded me. But could the inside of your mind be made to conform as readily as your body could — your thoughts covered with the equivalent of a long skirt? I knew without needing to be told that an indispensable part of being good was a willingness to hide what you really thought. There was one way to be good and there were infinite ways to be bad.

The teacher drew a diagram on the chalkboard, as though a little clarification was all that was needed.

"It's hard to understand," she conceded. "But he didn't sin."

There was always an underlayer, I was realizing. Even the rules contained secret passageways, trapdoors, and hiding spots that could be accessed when necessary. But this I didn't say. I parroted the teacher's explanation on the test and received an A.

As much as I admired my English teacher, I imagined myself becoming like my religious teachers. I would get married young; I would be a good Jewish wife, sheltered inside the promise of contentment as far as the eye could see. Only sometimes did I allow myself to spin out other possible stories, imagining a version of myself in college — sophisticated and worldly and no longer religious — but that was as far as the story could go. I didn't know what other kinds of lives might look like.

It was my senior year of high school and I was trying to decide what to do next. I was applying to college and also to gap-year Orthodox schools in Israel, which was the customary path for Modern Orthodox teenagers like myself — spend one year immersed in religious study, a last-chance inoculation against the dangers of secular college. At the same time, there was also the danger of kids being so inspired by their years in Israel that they became too religious and refused to come back home. Above all, the parents' central wish: *Be as religious as we are, no more and no less.* I'd grown up hearing the nervous talk about a distant cousin who had gone to secular college and not returned. *She's not religious anymore* — words so shocking they needed to be mouthed rather than said aloud. Though I barely knew her, this cousin was the bellwether of what could happen if you ventured too close to the edge — she Icarus, Barnard the sun. How would I answer the challenge of someone schooled in evolutionary science? What if a nonreligious roommate invited me to a party where there would be the temptations of sex and drinking? The college campus was formed not of the green lawns and brick walkways pictured on the glossy brochures but of slippery slopes down which we Orthodox students would slide, dark forests that could consume us if we dared to stray from the path. To survive these perils, we needed not courage but obedience.

Sufficiently warned, I decided to go to Israel for the year. I was interested in attending a women's yeshiva that was on the liberal side of Orthodoxy, regarded as groundbreaking for teaching women how to engage in serious Talmud study. This school was where my parents wanted me to go — my father in particular had reservations about a youth-group adviser's efforts to steer me rightward, toward a seminary that would offer heaping doses of inspiration and moral instruction. Girls would study only those texts that applied directly to women. The students who returned for a second year were set up on dates and married off. Among its detractors, the school had a reputation for brainwashing, but apparently this wasn't a problem; "If our brains are being washed," the students reportedly (probably apocryphally)

said, "it's only because they need washing." Two of my classmates were intent on going there, and they had recently started
wearing long flared skirts and prim sweaters, pantyhose and
flats. They hadn't yet been accepted to this seminary, but already
they looked like they belonged.

Though I hadn't completed an application, I decided at the
last minute to have an interview with the head of the seminary
when he came to visit our school. Not having planned to meet
with him in advance, I was wearing an oversize gray Princeton
sweatshirt, my jean skirt, and a pair of leggings, a yeshiva-girl
version of teenage grunge.

He was a round, pleasant-faced man with a black yarmulke
large enough to cover his nearly bald head. When he asked me
why I wanted to go to his school, I knew I was supposed to say
that I wanted to strengthen my belief and grow spiritually. But
my teeth clenched and my stomach seized with that slow burn of
anger that I was starting to recognize as resistance.

"Do girls learn Talmud?" I asked, but already knew the answer.

He raised his eyebrows as though I'd asked if I'd be allowed
to use the boys' bathroom. He gave the answer that I'd known
he would—that Talmud study was for men, whereas women,
who were already more spiritual, needed to study only the practical areas of Jewish law that would enable them to be good
wives and mothers.

"She has a bad attitude. We would have to spend the first
half of the year just breaking that down," he later told my youth-
group adviser, and I had been half ashamed, half proud.

I decided to attend the more liberal school in Israel and study
Talmud. A few weeks later I was accepted to Columbia. My ad-

viser sat stonily when I informed him of my plans. "It would almost be better for you not to go to Israel at all," he said and I felt as though I'd failed him, or he'd failed me.

That summer, as a counselor at an Orthodox sleep-away camp outside of Memphis, I had my first boyfriend. He too was Orthodox but he wore tank tops and lifted weights, like someone who'd stepped out of one of the teen novels I devoured. I'd been shocked when I realized he liked me.

By day, I shepherded my campers to morning prayers, then to swimming and kickball. At night, my boyfriend and I walked out to the fields, flashlights in hand. We were supposed to be on patrol for wayward campers, but instead we sat next to each other in the grass. The heat was viscous during the day, the air thick and muggy, but at night, it was cooler. Thrilled and scared, I let him put his arm around me. He smelled of Drakkar and Deep Woods Off. He leaned toward me and put his lips to mine. My heart beating fast, more from fear than desire, I kissed him back, afraid my inexperience was apparent. I looked around, even more afraid that the camp director or the other counselors would stumble upon us, flashlights beaming on our faces. Desire, I knew, was just another word for bad. I imagined my teachers watching, scolding. *We thought she was a good girl,* they'd say from the guard post inside my head — eventually those voices start coming from not just around you but inside you. There was no need for security cameras installed on walls or in the shrubbery because they were embedded in my skin, expertly camouflaged inside the lens of my eye, like some new technology decades away from invention.

With his arms around me, I leaned back into the grass, which was unexpectedly cool against my legs. I pulled him toward me, surprised that my body knew how to do this. Having been warned about all the ways this was wrong, I hadn't realized that desire would feel like a different kind of curiosity, a rising urge to know.

We were still kissing when I thought I heard voices coming toward us. I pushed him off me and sat up quickly. I didn't see anyone, but still, I scooted away from him, trying to clear my face of any hint of what I'd discovered. Here was shame and danger, yet in a small spot that remained protected, here also was the entry to a forbidden realm that felt lush and pink and blooming.

Soon I would be leaving for Israel for the year. After spending months immersed in Jewish books, I would surely repent for this sin and for the other sins I hoped to amass in the next few weeks. My goodness would be retroactively restored. But until then, I was free to kiss him again. This was my final chance. Sin, because repentance was near.

⁓

"Let's go outside," I say to my kids, who have spread out around my parents' house. They follow me out into the backyard, where my parents' *sukkah* is. We're commanded to sit in these huts for seven days, temporary homes like the ones the Jews built when they left Egypt and traveled in the desert. This is also the holiday of the harvest. In elementary school, we occasionally colored in mimeographed pages containing a few stalks of wheat in honor of the holiday, but other than that, there had been little talk of nature. We studied primarily the rules for how tall each wall of the *sukkah* needed to be, who was required to sit inside it and who was not.

My parents' *sukkah* is made from wooden doors hung from a wood frame that my father built. My mother is in charge of the art, and on each of the doors she has painted a biblical figure: King David with red curly hair, playing a harp; Moses's sister, Miriam, holding a tambourine that she used to lead the women in dancing and singing after the Israelites crossed the Red Sea.

If my children's participation in the holiday is lackluster, it will be attributed to my bad influence, so I try to rouse my kids' interest in making *sukkah* decorations. My leaving still feels so tenuous, so fragile, that any nice memory seems like a potential threat—each ritual, however nice it may be, bears the looming shadow of the larger system. Still, I can't help but think about how much I have always loved this holiday, so much so that in the divorce negotiations, I offered Aaron every Rosh Hashanah with the kids so that I could always have this holiday with them. It's not the rules of required dimensions and allowable building materials that I love but the story, the themes, and, most of all, the opportunity for art projects. I tell the kids how, when I was a child, my siblings and I strung frozen cranberries onto thread, making long strands that we hung across the length of the *sukkah*. I tell them how my father woke us early on the Sunday preceding the holiday and my siblings and I climbed a ladder, which my father held steady, and stepped onto the gently sloped roof of our ranch house, where we assisted in laying out the bamboo poles that went across the top of the *sukkah*.

"Can we go on the roof?" Noam asks.

"We can make paper chains," I offer lamely after I tell the kids that they can't go on the roof, and not just because the bamboo mats, purchased online at Sukkah.com, no longer require three little helpers. I can't imagine that I could hold the ladder as steady as my father did. It's too easy to envision them falling.

I expect protests, but any disappointment is short-lived. Just beyond the *sukkah* is my parents' hammock—my favorite spot at home, and maybe anywhere—and I make a run for it.

The kids pile on me with giddy energy, and though there isn't really room for all four of us, we squeeze together. Holding them close rouses my longing for their baby selves, yet every memory feels painful. Are those early days more lost to me now than they would have been? Divorce fractures the story; it draws an ever-present divide between then and now. Every memory is either preamble or postscript—every memory feels like it took place not just long ago but across enemy lines, and there is no way to sneak safely back across. I was endangering myself if I flipped through the photo albums that I made for each of the kids, filled with their baby pictures and birthday parties and trips to Cape Cod.

"We should live here," Josh decides.

"I call Mommy's old bedroom!" Layla says.

Out here, there are few signs of autumn, though it's early October and the scorching Memphis summer has finally abated. A few trees will tentatively change color but nothing like the reds and yellows that already adorn my neighborhood in Newton.

"I can't imagine living anywhere else," my grandmother once said to me in her Southern drawl as she sat in the house she'd lived in for more than forty years. Memphis wasn't just the place we happened to live but where we had been rooted for five generations. To be from a place—for a Southerner, this was the crucial thing. It was not just your address but some core element of who you were. In Memphis, the years could unravel, all experiences peel from me, and, even more so now, this is the place that would still explain me to myself. In Newton, where we now live, any sense of belonging has been shattered. Newton, a small city that is really more like an idyllic town, has a beautiful library and playgrounds busy with kids in their Little League gear, but for Aaron and me, what had mattered most was the Orthodox community—the synagogues and the kosher bagel store and the kosher ice cream store and the scores of people who lived as we did.

As I am no longer part of this community, the idea of home feels tenuous, irreparably broken. I stumble over the word *home* every time I say it, not sure that I can still lay claim to its comforts. I wish, impossibly, that the kids and I could stay in Memphis—that I could give in to a leftover childhood urge to be folded up, taken in. Time will turn back, and I will become once again the teenager who lived here, the kids present by some magical doing not my own. They will feel rooted here, the next generation in this long-standing lineage.

"The new house feels like a hotel," Josh says now, as though he can read my mind, and Layla, who is lying on top of me, her hair fluffing in my face, nods in agreement.

"I miss the old house," she says.

Noam, who is being trampled by his younger siblings, shuffles for a better spot on the hammock. His silence worries me, though I'm not sure of the way inside. It's not just the old house they're all missing—it's easier to speak of the loss of the house, harder to say that it was where we all lived together.

"It won't always feel like this," I answer, and I tell them how when my parents moved to this ranch house when I was six, it seemed like a mansion, the large living room a movie theater, the sunken bathtub a swimming pool. All these years later, this house feels far too permanent to ever be taken apart. I try to say more, about the idea of home and change and loss, but the exact lesson I'm attempting to impart is lost even on me.

"I feel the same way," I admit but don't say that it's not just the new house but life itself that feels like a temporary locale. Nor do I speak of how I go out of my way to avoid passing our old street, dreading the sight of the Cape house where I used to have nightmares of growing frightfully large, my head protruding from the chimney, my arms from the windows, wearing the house like a too-short dress.

The need to sell the house was one of the few things Aaron and I could agree on in our divorce negotiations. We wouldn't have been able to come to a decision about who would keep it, and neither of us could have afforded it in any case. Until a permanent plan was put in place, we had taken turns being in the house—*nesting,* as this was known in the divorce lexicon. To potential buyers, no mention was made of the fact that the house was being sold due to divorce; it was as though a grisly murder had taken place there. I cleared away anything that could reveal what was transpiring—no lawyers' papers left lying around—but, then, what did unhappiness look like? Could it be recognized in a bowl slightly out of place, a mirror hung askew? In preparation for showing the house, we had a few small repairs done, but there was nothing we could do about the larger issues—the roof needing to be reshingled, the exterior needing to be painted—that we had allowed to go untended.

The day after our first open house, there were three offers, one of them made by a young Jewish couple who, having seen the telltale signs of religious observance in our house—the Shabbat candelabra on the breakfront, the calligraphed Jewish marriage contract still on our wall—thought they knew how to sway us to choose them.

We imagine that we will be as happy in this house as you were. We will raise our family here and fill our Shabbat table with as much love and joy as you did, said the note that the real estate agent read to Aaron and me as we sat stonily in her office.

We sold the house to a Chinese couple who offered no letter, nothing but a bid higher than all others and a no-mortgage clause.

BACK INSIDE MY PARENTS' HOUSE, with the holiday preparations almost done, I'm again staring at the display of photos, my wedding photo in particular. In my own house now, all such pictures are stashed in the basement, in a still-unpacked box. But faced with this picture, I can't look away. The photo feels like an impossibility, someone else dressed to appear as me. My eyes might be shining, my cheek pressed close to Aaron's, but I believe, in my raw state, that any happiness must be discredited. If I could perform some sort of emotional forensics exam on this photo, surely my smile would reveal my uncertainty. Doubt would flicker in my eyes.

My mother comes up behind me and puts her arm around me, and we pull back from the argument that looms.

"Don't you think it's time to take this picture down?" I whisper.

"Maybe it's good for the kids to see it?" she murmurs.

"I'm not sure what's good for them anymore," I say.

"I'm not trying to judge," my mother says. "I just want to understand what you want for the kids and for yourself."

"I don't know yet," I say, a paltry answer when people all around me seem to have answers in abundance.

"I realize it's hard," my mother says.

"It's hard for you too."

"It takes away," she admits.

"I'm allowed to believe something different," I say, but it's late, so late, to be having this conversation. I feel like I've arrived at a delayed-onset adolescence, like I'm becoming the rebellious teenager I never was. Back in this house, it comes over me; a part of me had ceased to grow up. I was still in need of permission. By staying inside even when I chafed, I learned to hide what I thought. By getting married so young, I didn't arrive earlier at adulthood but later.

As we stand here, I think about my mother's struggle to separate from her own mother. Growing up, I heard stories of how my grandmother used to scrub clean my mother's knees, how she had her lie down on the counter and washed her hair over the sink, then cracked eggs over her hair to make it shine. My grandmother wanted desperately for my mother to be regarded as sweet and pretty and kind. "It's going to end with me," my mother had once valiantly proclaimed when she was seventeen during a fight with her mother about this insistence on maintaining appearances, caring so much about what others thought. It's a story I've always loved for its rebellious sentiment, even though it turned out not to be true and here we are, debating one of its variants. Did you have to match the person your mother intended you to be? Could you be who you really were and still be loved?

It seems like such a simple proposition—that you can love someone yet see the world so differently from that person. As nice as this sounds, I know that when you change, you risk losing the people closest to you. After a divorce, every relationship has to be remade, and it's as true of the religious sort of divorce as it is of the marital sort. Religion is not just one facet of my family but its central core—part of every story told, every promise offered. Orthodoxy was more than what we believed—it was the enclosing walls of this house, its sheltering roof, its steadfast foundation.

And this, I understand anew, is why it's so hard to leave. Leaving isn't just about engaging in a set of once-forbidden actions. It's about changing the family story. Orthodoxy has always been my home, and to leave it is to leave home as well.

At sundown, when the Sukkot holiday officially begins, it's drizzling, but we do as required and go outside, where my father holds a silver cup filled with wine and recites the Kiddush blessing over it. As we are about to move inside for the rest of the meal, the rain stops, and we can eat in the *sukkah* after all.

We sit together, as my family has for decades. When I was little, we used to hear singing coming from other families' *sukkahs* down the street. All over this neighborhood, all over neighborhoods like ours, people were sitting in the same small huts, under the same bamboo and branch roofs through which we could see the stars. We weren't alone out here, not alone in our lives. As a little girl, staring up at the sky, I used to imagine that from outer space, all our *sukkahs* were visible—small dots of light in an otherwise dark night.

It's cool out, and the kids are bundled up next to me. The

navy-blue fleece I've borrowed from my father is large enough that Layla pulls it over herself too. At night, she's still sleeping in my bed, and I lie awake watching her. Sensing my wakefulness, she will shift, rotate, and murmur, "Hug me," and I will, the two of us cocooned inside our blankets. When she was a baby, I lamented each passing week, wanting to remain indefinitely inside the hazy early days when I never had to be apart from her. When she was older, she, like her brothers, cried when I dropped her off at nursery school. In the throes of separation anxiety, she wrapped her arms around my leg in protest, unable to fathom that I could go and still return.

Now, a separation comes earlier than it otherwise would. There is the need, according to our team of therapists and the stack of divorce books I've checked out from the library, to remind the kids that even though their parents don't love each other as they once did, their love for their children remains permanent and unchanged. But despite every reassurance that I can offer, I cannot shelter them or any of us from the pain. There are areas of their lives to which I have little access, as though when they're not with me, they cease to be mine. Suffering now from my own form of separation anxiety, I have the urge to cling to them as they sometimes do to me.

In the *sukkah*, this temporary hut that is half sheltered, half exposed, we are supposed to feel the impermanence of our lives. We leave our secure houses and go outside, where we dwell more vulnerably in God's hands. The God part, I'm no longer sure about, but this year I need no reenactment of impermanence, no reminder that everything seemingly fixed can topple.

Not Ours

After the onslaught of Jewish holidays, the last thing I want is another celebration, but Halloween is a week away.

"Why can't we trick-or-treat?" Josh asks.

"It's not a Jewish holiday," I answer automatically—the standard Orthodox explanation, as though this year were no different than any other and my kids would still do as I'd once done, wait with bated breath for the doorbell to ring, then hand out candy to the costumed kids. This was as close as my siblings and I could get to a holiday that—my mother explained— wasn't ours.

"Neither is Thanksgiving, and we celebrate that," Josh shoots back.

"It wasn't something we did as kids," I say.

"But didn't you want to?" he asks.

"It never seemed like an option," I say, and I tell him how each October, my elementary school principal sent home a letter detailing the pagan origins of Halloween and stating unequivocally that Jews shouldn't participate. Despite the letter, a few of my not-exactly-Orthodox classmates did go trick-or-treating, and though it was never acknowledged outright, there were murmurings the next day in school about costumes and candy. Having taken to heart the admonitions of the letter, I found it hard to imagine some of my friends, usually dressed in their regulation school uniforms, costumed like ghosts or witches and let loose in the night. Halloween was nearly as foreign as Christmas, when our neighbors' houses twinkled with lights, and we sometimes drove around to see the most elaborate displays. There was always a sense of loneliness to these outings and to the season. We were surrounded by something that had nothing to do with us.

"Ask Daddy," I say when the Halloween disputations continue unabated, afraid to allow them to go trick-or-treating—one more change for which I will be responsible.

Though I sometimes write Aaron long e-mails in my head, I don't know how to broach the complicated subject of our religious differences. There can be no calm conversation between us. Among our failures as a couple was that we couldn't agree on a worldview or navigate the hardest of issues as a team, and now we need to do what is even harder: navigate them when we are increasingly estranged. There are no provisions in the separation agreement currently being negotiated for who retains the rights over the kids' observances and beliefs, but even so, I worry about the Orthodox expectation that I will cede all decisions of observance to him, that though I am noncompliant, I will teach my children that Orthodoxy is still where the truth resides.

Confusing for the kids. I hear my mother's voice in my head, but a larger threat looms.

"Are you worried a judge could hold not being Orthodox

against you?" she asked me a few weeks earlier when we talked, as we always did, about the final divorce hearing, which is in December.

My mother is right to be worried. We both read an article about a woman in an ultra-Orthodox enclave in New York who ceased to be Orthodox and then lost custody of her kids. I hear about children purposely alienated from a parent who is no longer religious, community members hiring lawyers on behalf of the still-Orthodox spouse, claiming that they are merely acting in the best interest of the kids. On blogs, I read about parents terrified of seeking divorce for fear that they will lose their children to a more religious spouse. And it's not only among the ultra-Orthodox. I hear about a Modern Orthodox husband suing his ex-wife for full custody because she wasn't sufficiently observant. You are allowed to leave as long as you surrender your children at the border. To your kids' questions, you should offer answers you don't believe. Agree to a daily, sometimes hourly, enforcement of rules that feel like iron bars.

"I live in the United States of America," I proclaimed in response.

"I don't want you to be so angry," my mother murmured. You weren't supposed to be angry — this was a flaw that would invalidate any complaint. But then and now, I am angry — at this presumption that religious rules trumped even a parent's love and presence. A parent or child could be bound and sacrificed, if necessary, on its altar. *You are harming your children if you say what you really believe. You are taking them off the one true path.* No matter how often I tell myself I have left, these Orthodox edicts continue to live in my head, unwelcome guests who will never shut up. In all my years of fantasizing about leaving, I hadn't understood that you could go yet remain stuck inside. *You can partake of the pleasures, but you will never enjoy them.* Now when I think about that Chasidic tale my friend told me, I hear not merely a warning but gleeful satisfaction. It wasn't the actions that held you tightest but the imprint they made in your mind. I'm realizing that this was an intentional part of the design, like one of those invisible dog fences installed at the edge of a yard. Others might have the illusion that you could run free, but born to this, you always knew where the electrified boundary lay.

Josh asks his father about trick-or-treating, as I suggest, and later reports back that Aaron said that if they were with him on that night, they wouldn't be allowed to go, but because Halloween falls on my night, the decision is mine, a response that makes me feel surprised but grateful. We are like rulers of neighboring kingdoms—we have no jurisdiction beyond our own borders. Our children are dual citizens. I have the urge to check the calendars to see how the next decade of Halloweens will fall. Is this how all decisions will be made? Though there can be no open discussion between us, his response makes me wonder if he is as uncertain as I am about how to parent with someone who has different beliefs.

At the pluralist Jewish day school that Noam and Josh attend —itself a departure from what was expected of us—the teachers talk of how different families do different things. We had nervously visited the school when, years before, Noam was unhappy at the local Modern Orthodox elementary school. It never occurred to us that our children would go anywhere else, but every afternoon when I picked Noam up, I saw how unhappy he was. On that first visit to what would eventually become Noam's new school, I'd stood in the back of the room used as a synagogue. The boys and girls sat together as a female rabbi played the guitar and another teacher beat a bongo drum. I wasn't supposed to be so moved by what I saw—this, after all, was wrong—yet I felt disappointed that this pluralist, progressive community couldn't be ours. If we sent our son here, how would we ensure that he remained Orthodox? How would we navigate the complications of people who didn't practice as we did? Though we worried what our community would think, we decided to make the change because Noam was so unhappy. And it worked—he looked forward to going to school each morning and came home excited about what he had learned. It was his first experience of being with people who didn't observe as we did, but he proudly wore his yarmulke and understood that others believed differently. For me, as well, the school became a place where I felt at home. There was no single way to be. Engage and wrestle with the differences, the school taught. Be willing to have conversations with other families about what they do. But for us now, that message needs to be taken further. Inside our family, we do different things. Inside our family, we are different families.

"There's not one good thing about being Jewish," Josh declares angrily as I tuck him into bed at night. His resistance to religion has been steadily mounting. For a number of years before the divorce, he hadn't wanted to go to synagogue. For the past year, he has complained about having to study Jewish subjects in school and has refused to wear a yarmulke.

"Not one good thing?" I ask.

"Chanukah," he concedes. He means, of course, the presents, as opposed to any theological affinity with the holiday that celebrates a small band of Jews who fought for religious freedom from the Hellenizing Greeks. But that doesn't forestall his critique of Judaism, which begins with the problem of believing in the existence of God due to the reporting of miracles, in particular the notion that God spoke to the Jews on Mount Sinai.

"If I had a megaphone, I could lie and say, 'I'm God, listen to me,'" he says. The Egyptians, he reasons, drowned in the Red Sea because they were in chariots.

Before I can offer him one of the proofs that the rabbis present to insurgent questioners, he tears up.

"Do you know how many things I can't do that I care about, all because of something I don't care about?" he says.

He can't play on basketball teams that practice on Shabbat. He can't eat nonkosher pizza like his non-Orthodox friends from school. Once, a year before, he went out for nonkosher pizza with those friends, but he had done so knowing it wasn't allowed.

"Do you really believe God cares about pizza?" he presses me.

"I don't," I admit.

"Then why do I have to?" he asks.

Curled up next to Josh in his bed, I hear in my head the script I once would have followed, lines that would indoctrinate Josh with the belief that we are special and separate so he would accept that he has all he needs right where he is. If that fails, I'm supposed to select words that will wield guilt and instill fear.

"I'm forced, all the time," he says. "Do you even know how that feels?"

"I do know," I say.

He sits up in bed, trying to see me better. He looks as though he is contemplating the farthest reaches of existence.

"I've been Orthodox my whole life and now I've decided I don't want to be," I tell him.

"Have *you* ever . . ." he starts, but then he pauses, apparently deciding whether he dares to venture further. I await the rest of his question nervously.

"Have you ever had nonkosher pizza?" he asks. He lies back down. As I put together my response, his eyes are trained on me, his hand on my arm as though he needs to hold me here in case I float away.

"I have," I admit.

He doesn't ask for details—for now, it's enough to simply absorb this new fact about me.

"Will you take me for pizza?" he asks a few minute later, his voice softer and heavier with impending sleep.

I murmur that I will one day but I worry what Aaron would think if he heard this conversation. I'm unsure of what else to say. I hug Josh as he drifts off to sleep, not sure anymore how much of myself I can share with my own children, equally unsure where the separation is between the kids' stories and mine. In motherhood, all of you is demanded, but sometimes that means giving your children the parts of you that are uncertain and unresolved.

Instead of hurrying to finish the bedtime routine, I linger, aware that the era of cuddling is waning. Josh is half little boy, half preteen; each time I look at him, a different version greets me. One day, surely, I will wake up and, seemingly overnight, new boundaries will have been set in place; snuggling with his mother will belong to the distant past.

When I think he's fallen asleep, I try to extricate myself, but as I disentangle my arm, he surprises me, still awake.

"God," he announces softly but vehemently, "is a poop-head."

I TAKE JOSH AND LAYLA trick-or-treating; Noam has other plans and doesn't want to join us. We go with non-Orthodox Jewish friends who don't believe that by asking for chocolate, they are becoming pagans or idolaters — they regard this as an American tradition that doesn't need to mean more. Their neighborhood is a short distance from the center of the Ortho-dox community, those few blocks assuaging my fear that we'll knock on a door and a former fellow Orthodox congregant will answer. It crosses my mind as the kids assemble their costumes that the best way for me to hide would be to wear one as well.

My mother had called as we were heading out, and I didn't mention our plans for the evening. "Can you call me later?" I asked. Surely at the age of forty, I'm too old to be hiding Halloween from my mother, but I wanted to get off the phone before I gave anything away.

By early evening, families are out in groups, the mood friendly and neighborly. I hadn't realized how communal this night would feel, like an evening block party. As the kids and I walk from street to street, I self-consciously scan for any config-uration in which adults don't come two by two. I steal glimpses into people's homes. From this vantage point, everyone else's life seems neatly ordered, pleasant, and intact. I should know better, yet I fall for the illusion every time.

"Happy Halloween," we call to witches and princesses, Red Sox players and vampires.

"Happy Halloween," I say as a man hands a chocolate bar to Layla, who is dressed like the Tooth Fairy.

So this is how you do it in America, I text William as we walk. William, of course, went trick-or-treating every year with his kids and finds it funny that this ordinary event is so foreign to me.

My mind searches for a familiar correlative in order to ease the disorientation that makes me feel like an immigrant in my own town. Though the holiday of Purim, with its costumes and baskets of candy, is the obvious comparison, I think longingly of a ritual the night before Passover, when we made our way through a dark house, candles in hand, on a scavenger hunt of sorts, searching for any remnant of bread, which was forbidden once the holiday began. Each time we came upon one of the cubes of bread my mother had placed on bookshelves and dressers beforehand, we shook our heads in mock surprise. *Bread the night before Passover!* Using the light of the candle, my father swept the piece of bread with a feather—carefully, carefully, so as not to leave behind any crumbs—into a wooden spoon and then deposited it in a plastic bag. The next morning, the pieces of bread were burned in a small foil pan in the driveway as we recited a blessing declaring that any forbidden food still in our possession—knowingly or unknowingly—should be like the dust of the earth. Anything we had was no longer ours.

When the three of us arrive home from trick-or-treating,

Josh and Layla dump the candy on the living-room floor and the initial gorge ensues.

"I can't believe I've missed out on this my whole life," Josh declares.

"We went trick-or-treating," Layla gleefully informs my mother, who calls back as the candy binge reaches its sugary height.

I get on the phone with her for only a few minutes and say little. When I hang up, I pilfer some chocolate, wondering if my kids and I have newly laid claim to a holiday, and a world, that is slowly becoming ours.

Between This Day and All Others

Is it a Mommy Shabbat?" Layla asks as I drive her home from nursery school on a November Friday afternoon.

Though she's not entirely sure of the days of the week, the schedule is fixed in her mind, the days divided into Mommy and Daddy. Next to me in the car is the picture of the two of us that she made that day in school, a figure with wild brown curls holding the hand of a smaller figure with equally wild yellow curls, crowns on both our heads. In life, too, her blond curls make a halo. Her imaginary world is thick and fully formed, the real effortlessly intertwined with the pretend. She dwells in a kingdom of fairies and princesses and she sings of a Disney version of true love — but has the idea of happily-ever-after already been upended?

"It's a Mommy Shabbat," I tell her, relieved that I don't have to be apart from the kids for two days. Even so, fear about Shabbat looms — I worry the kids will feel both the divorce and the religious divide more acutely on this day. For me, Shabbat now comes every other week, on the weekends I'm with the kids, as though God too is subject to a custody agreement. Shabbat, we are taught, is the most beautiful day of the week, yet for me it's not the day of rest but the day of discomfort. I'm burned through by it, soured and used up by all the years of feeling trapped. Just the word *Shabbat* makes my body tense and my throat tighten —a late-onset allergy.

And yet, even so, half an hour before sundown—in November, this is a little after five o'clock—I'm in my kitchen cooking Shabbat dinner. The kitchen in my house is still strictly kosher; the rules are so ingrained in me that I follow them without having to think about it. In this regard, my guiding mantra is to do as I have always done, with the same level of meticulousness, in order to ensure that my family will still eat in my house.

I pull out ingredients, and the countertop grows crowded with the food I'm preparing—a large Shabbat dinner, though not the same dishes I once made. When I unpacked in this house, I'd stored my most frequently used cookbooks on the highest shelf, next to the recipe binder I'd compiled when I was newly married. It contained recipes I'd copied from my aunt, whose beautiful Shabbat meals I aspired to make, apricot-glazed chicken and carrot kugel and sweet pecan-crusted noodle ring.

A few minutes before Shabbat officially starts, the air becomes thick with prohibition. I'm not yet finished cooking, something that once would have caused me to anxiously race to finish in time. I would have a list in my head of all that I needed to do before the exact moment Shabbat descended. Had I remembered to preheat the oven, since it was forbidden to turn it on? Had I remembered to turn off the bedroom lights, since I wouldn't be able to do so later?

"Shabbat's in five minutes," Noam calls to me from his room, the one pocket of this house where Shabbat exists as it always has.

"Are you all set?" I call back to him.

"Phone's off," he says, then he turns off his bedroom light and puts away his computer.

Noam has remained strict in his religious observance. He wears his yarmulke wherever he goes. His eighth-grade classmates are all connected now by their texting and instant messaging, but he won't use his phone on Shabbat. He eats only food that is certified kosher. "Is it hard?" I asked him a few years ago about wearing his yarmulke not just to school but to a non-Jewish day camp he attended. I knew that, had it been me, I would have been far less resolute. "It's a good way to start a conversation," he'd said, and I understood. The yarmulke wasn't simply something he wore but a central part of who he was.

"I'm still cooking," I admit sheepishly now when he comes into the kitchen, feeling like I'm confessing to a crime. "I cook on Shabbat. I'm not really Orthodox anymore."

"Um, Mom? Don't you think I know that by now?" he says.

It's a relief to hear him say this—to not be hiding what apparently exists in plain sight.

"What does that feel like for you?" I ask but am afraid of the answer. What scares me even more, though, is the possibility of religion drawing a dividing line between us. All those stories I have heard over the years haunt me: a son who became Orthodox and now won't eat in his parents' home; a daughter who became so religious that she will no longer speak to her family.

"I don't know," he says. "Everything feels different."

"I know. For me too."

The day passes into Shabbat but I turn on the stove, hearing in my head the biblical prohibition *Thou shalt kindle no flame.* I've never been so aware of the laws of Shabbat as I am when I'm transgressing them. *Watch as she lowers the flame,* that third-party narrator intones in my head, as though this were some kind of reality show about criminals that I'm starring in. Each action is broken into a hundred actions, all of which are forbidden. It feels impossible that there might come a day when it's simply a Friday night and I am just cooking a meal.

On the counter next to us, my phone beeps and after glancing at the text, I try to decipher the look that flashes across Noam's face. He's newly entered the age of separation; more of his life is becoming sealed off from me. I'm allowed unobstructed views only in rare moments—a lifting of the gate and you're ushered, briefly, inside.

"Is it hard not to use your phone?" I ask him.

"Sometimes, but I also like having it off. It's a good break," he says.

"It still feels funny for me to cook on Shabbat," I admit. "Sometimes I forget for a minute that I'm not keeping Shabbat like I used to and I feel surprised at what I've just done."

To this, I get a shrug and a teenager's *eh*. Instead of getting me to back off, as it's surely intended to, it makes me encourage him to say more. Even when I'm afraid of what I might hear, I no longer have the luxury, if I ever did, of hiding from what is painful and complicated. Before the divorce, my children and I could indulge in the fantasy that I had no needs separate from theirs, that any feelings I possessed could not possibly extend beyond the permitted range. I was their mother; it seemed, at the time, all they needed to know of me.

After divorce, though, there is no such illusion. The façade is stripped away. My children now know that I'm just another person trying to find her way.

"Does it feel hard that we don't all do Shabbat like we used to?" I persist at the risk of receiving another *eh* from Noam.

"I don't know. It's easier when everyone does it," he says.

Although he's probably already too much of a teenager to appreciate the gesture, I put my arms around him and he leans into the hug.

"I will still help you do it. Even if I'm not doing it myself," I tell him.

EVEN THOUGH IT'S NOW past sundown and so, technically, lighting candles is forbidden, I set up the thick white Shabbat candles, burn down the bottoms until they're securely inside the brass candelabra my mother once used. Out of habit, I still set up all five candles—one for each member of a family, if not this family.

With the kindling of the Shabbat candles, peace is meant to spread over the house, a soft golden glow. But as the spirit of Shabbat descends, so too does the image of how it's supposed to be. The way it is now is compared against an idyllic then that existed only in my mind. The mother who happily prepares the food; the children who are bathed and dressed in their finest clothing; the father who recites the blessing over the wine, holding a polished silver goblet. Not just one imagined family but a row of Shabbat-observing houses, a storybook planet in which candles flicker in every window. Shabbat was not a day of private observance; it was one of communal belonging. We lived in the plural, our lives rocked to the same gentle rhythm. An *eruv* surrounded Orthodox neighborhoods—a piece of twine attached to telephone wires so that, as part of a complicated rabbinic loophole, a public space was transformed into a private one, which enabled us to carry on Shabbat, an act that otherwise would have been prohibited. Even more than the symbolic enclosure encircling the neighborhood, a hundred lines of connection wrapped around us.

Though we are still within walking distance of it, the Orthodox neighborhood where we used to live feels like an inaccessible strip of land. "Be prepared to lose some friends," advised the rabbi of our synagogue when I first shared with him the news that Aaron and I were separating. I was surprised because I hadn't yet learned that in a divorce, anything not pinned down can fall away. I didn't yet understand how divorce stirs up an anxious nest of feelings — someone else's decision is regarded as a referendum on your own life.

Soon after the news of our divorce went public, I stopped going to synagogue. In that building, I was aware of the divorce at every moment, as though it were a neon sign across my forehead. I felt vulnerable to the curious looks, to comments I didn't know whether to interpret as biting or well-meaning. "People want to know what happened," said one of my closest friends from synagogue, one who, like many others, was soon to become a former friend. I was starting to understand what the rabbi had told me about losing friends — there were friendships you could take with you and friendships that had to stay in the spot where they began. Many of my friendships, I realized, existed only as long as I remained the person I was expected to be.

If I had wanted to stay inside the world, this would have been the time to launch a public relations campaign and make a play for whatever friends and allies I could capture. But it didn't seem worth fighting for a place in a community I couldn't remain in if I really left Orthodoxy. It was easier to retreat and cede the territory to Aaron; it had become clear that in a divorce, community and friendships were among the spoils to be divided. Little, it seemed to me then, could belong to us both.

In the weeks that followed, I began to hear what was being said about me. According to rumors, apparently I had come home one day and out of the blue announced that I wanted a divorce. I had gone crazy, some said. I was bad, others declared. I was hardly thrilled about the accusation of crazy, but bad was the one that hit the hardest.

As months passed, I started to become aware that people I'd once seen in synagogue every week now looked at me suspiciously. For the most part, it is my friends from outside the Orthodox community—mostly the parents of my kids' friends from school—who have let me know that they are still here; these were friendships I could take with me. My best friend, Ariel, remains someone in whom I can confide. When I run into people from my old community, it's a welcome relief when my greeting is returned, and a true gift on the occasions when it's returned warmly. A former neighbor who remains as close and connected as ever. A woman from the community who gives me a hug in the fruit market. A man from synagogue e-mails to say that he is wishing me well. A mother my age makes the simple yet generous gesture of chatting with me in line as we wait to buy coffee, as though no time has passed since she last saw me. Each of these kind moments looms large, a small bolstering reminder that leaving doesn't have to cut you off entirely.

But all too often it's surprise or discomfort that flickers in people's eyes, as though I ought to have moved away or ceased to exist. When I round the corner of an aisle in the grocery store and recognize an old acquaintance, my eyes surely give off a flash of fear. I can never predict who will say hello and who will shun me. From some, there is an awkward, pursed-lipped hello, as though the word is a precious object that they have been forced to surrender. Others pretend not to see me, checking their watches or busying themselves with their phones or looking slightly away. And from still others, there is the purposefully withheld greeting. Resolute and guarded — they stand as if in possession of backup they can call in if necessary — they look directly at me but don't say hello, as though in the space I occupy, there's nothing but air.

In the grocery store recently, I said hello to a woman I'd known for years, but she just looked at me — or, rather, slightly past me. Her eyes narrowed, her lips pursed, and she turned her full attention to the tomatoes in front of her.

It came over me: I was being shunned, right there in the produce section.

I knew I should let this non-hello slip quietly by, as I did with all the others, telling myself that these slights were the punishment to be exacted for leaving, consoling myself with the thought that the angriest people were probably the ones locked inside their own misery. But there had been too many of these moments of being shunned — a word that should no longer exist in my emotional lexicon, that should have been relegated to stories of stocks and medieval towns and Puritan New England.

"Hello," I said again to the woman, my heart pounding as I waited to see if she was still going to ignore me. *Why does it matter if she says hello?* I asked myself. She's not someone I've ever liked, yet I understood the meaning; I needed to know that in her eyes, I no longer existed. It was not a proper shunning if the person being shunned was unaware that she was being shunned.

Her shoulders stiffened; her mouth tightened into a small circle. To respond to my hello seemed a physical impossibility for her — she looked outraged that such a feat was being asked of her. Her eyes still downcast, she finally produced a begrudging sound, like a greeting issued from miles underwater, then returned to her careful tomato selection, checking for any too-ripe spots.

As the weeks, then months, passed, it surprised me how badly I wanted an invitation for a Shabbat meal — a gesture to let me know I was still welcome inside. It made me catalog all the people I'd failed to e-mail over the years or say hello to when I walked past, all the people who existed outside my own circle of vision — not because I intended to be mean but because I had no idea how in need of a kind word they might have been or because I was afraid of wading into something potentially uncomfortable. I knew how someone else's upheaval could threaten your own tenuous security, but I didn't yet understand how much a small gesture meant when you were the one to feel so loosely moored. *We are a special community,* those on the inside like to say to others equally on the inside, but it's easy to welcome those who are safely within. If you no longer matched, you no longer mattered. If you didn't show up in synagogue, you no longer counted — yet those moments when it was hardest to be part of a community were often when you most needed to be, when an outstretched arm, a kind word, could help hold you aloft.

I miss some of these people, fellow congregants, community members, but mostly, I miss the feeling of being situated inside a particular world. If the Earth's spinning were halted for a minute, I could have placed my finger on this one small spot and said: *I belong here*.

I CALL THE KIDS to the table, which I've set for four. I don't invite William over when the kids are home. Though they know I have a boyfriend—a term that feels impossible still, even to my own ears—I'm waiting to have him over so that my children won't regard him as one more change when there have been too many already. For now, William exists in a separate part of my life that takes place only when the kids aren't home. And knowing how little interest William has in any form of religion, it's hard to imagine how these disparate parts might ever become intertwined.

Maybe in a first love you can let yourself believe that any complicated issue will stay buried, but in a later love, there's no fooling yourself—everything submerged rises in the end. If William wasn't before, he is now all too aware of how often religion will be part of our lives. Maybe if I had left earlier, it would have been easier to carve a clear-cut separation, but too much of my life has been lived inside. My children have been raised, until now, in this world. The questions have started to multiply. If I remain tied to Orthodoxy, will William have to be connected to it as well? If I celebrate Shabbat with the kids, will he eventually have to take part? If my months are always punctuated by the Jewish holidays, will his have to be too?

"I don't know if I can let go of everything," I've said to him when the subject comes up, as it does increasingly these days— if discussing religion counts for anything, then we are among its greatest adherents. There are so many other things I want to talk to him about. He has a list of activities he is eager to try: hiking in national parks, teaching me to play tennis, taking up ballroom dancing. When he talks of the new hobbies he wants to throw himself into, I feel a world of possibilities opening. Yet even so, I remain preoccupied with the thing I am trying to leave. An unease settles over us now every time we wind our way back to this subject.

"You can be part of it, but I don't want to have to be involved in something I don't believe in," he said, and I wanted to both agree wholeheartedly and argue. I appreciate the way he tells me exactly what he is thinking, yet his opinions leave me tangled and spent. I don't want to fold myself into his certainty. He rouses me to push back against his every word.

"I don't want to have to do everything alone," I said.

"I'm afraid you won't be happy until I agree to be Orthodox."

"You know I'm not Orthodox anymore," I protested.

"A part of you still is," he said. Can you be happy, I wonder, with someone who doesn't come from the same place as you, even when it's a place you're trying to leave? Once again, religious differences are a source of conflict — the same kind of issue, just on the other side.

When the kids come to the table, we sing "Shalom Aleichem" — the song that has started every Shabbat dinner I've ever attended, my whole family gathered round — but with only our four voices, the prayer feels slight and vulnerable.

Here is the freedom and, alongside it, the price to be paid: loneliness.

All I can think about is the legend I heard multiple times growing up, about the two Shabbat angels, one good and one bad, who visit each Jewish home on Friday night. They accompany the husband home from synagogue, and as he enters the house, they peer in the windows. Are the wife and children dressed in their Shabbat best? Is the table set; is the family gathered round?

If so, the good angel is delighted to see God's word obeyed and he blesses the house: "May every Shabbat be as this one." And the bad angel has no choice but to hold back his sinfulness and answer "Amen, may it be so."

And if no dinner is prepared and no candles are lit, and the family is not gathered round, the bad angel is gleeful at the sight of so many sins and he laughs scornfully and blesses the house: "May every Shabbat be as this one." And the good angel, anguished as he is, has no choice but to utter "Amen."

Placing my hands on top of each kid's head in turn, as my father did each week, I bless them one by one with the traditional words: May God bless you and keep you, may God spread His light over you.

"Should I say Kiddush or do you want to?" I ask Noam when it's time for the blessing over the wine, which is supposed to be made by the man of the house.

Already past the age of bar mitzvah, Noam is now able to make the blessings on my behalf—he is required, some would say, to perform this commandment, and he cannot have his obligation fulfilled by me, a female who has no obligation of her own. My son belongs to the official community now in a way I, a woman, never will.

"I'll do it," Noam says, and he recites the blessing sanctifying this day, reading from a small prayer booklet; he doesn't yet know this by heart, though he surely will soon. In just the past few months, his voice has turned from a child's to an adult's. He sounds a little like Aaron, and as he gets older, I notice how much he is starting to look like him as well.

We dig into the challah and eat the meal I've prepared. Josh tells us about a game that his class played in school that week, called Rose, Bud, Thorn, in which the teacher asked each student to name one good thing that happened that week, one thing he or she is looking forward to, and one bad thing that happened. We play it now among ourselves, each of the kids sifting through their experiences to name their roses, their buds, their thorns.

As they talk, the idyllic image of how it is supposed to look begins to fall away. I see instead just their individual faces, hear their particular voices. These months, with just the four of us, I feel closer to them than I ever have, everything outside us stripped away. We are in that in-between state, when the past is still a looming presence and the future is made of lines so faint we can't fully see them yet, but slowly, a new possibility is coming into being.

When we have finished eating, the kids and I clear the table. We don't sing the traditional Shabbat songs. We don't say the blessings recited at the end of a meal. The white candles have burned down almost entirely but still make bright flickering ovals when I turn off the dining-room lights. I'm not going to think about how those Shabbat angels would classify our night.

IN THE MORNING, we don't go to synagogue. I don't miss it —getting dressed up, putting on a hat, purposely arriving late so I can sit through the bare minimum of the service. It's probably one of the last weeks before the weather grows cold, the start of the long Boston winter, and I try to get the kids to walk to the nearby playground, walk anywhere that is allowed. I persuade them to play board games, mostly Ticket to Ride, which we love, lining up small plastic trains along tracks between cities, and I want to grab them and have all of us hop a train for one of these far-off places. The four of us will flee Shabbat as though it exists in space, not time; travel across so many time zones that this day will have ended.

"Is it still Shabbat?" Layla asks.

"Just a little longer," I say, wishing the sun would set early and we would be free.

"But are we even keeping Shabbat?" she asks.

"There are lots of ways to celebrate Shabbat. We're doing it our own way," I say, trying to sound like I mean it.

As the day drags on, Josh turns on the TV, another act technically forbidden on Shabbat but that I have decided to allow. In the year before the divorce, Josh used to sneak down to the basement playroom of our old house on Shabbat afternoons and watch TV. It was against the rules, but he hadn't felt as daunted by that as I would have when I was his age. Aaron and I always used to joke that our kids were far more assertive than either of us ever were, and taken aback by the force of his resistance, we'd made only halfhearted efforts to stop him. Now watching TV on Shabbat is no longer something that needs to be hidden. During the week, I'm bothered by the incessant sound of electronics, but on this day I welcome the noise.

Noam will watch if it's on—this is not technically a violation of the laws of the day—but he won't press the button himself. In the space between the laws, there exist these loopholes. You could not turn a light switch on but you could set a timer beforehand to do it for you. You could not directly ask a non-Jew to perform a forbidden act for you, but you could do so indirectly. My mother used to knock on our non-Jewish neighbor's door on Shabbat and say leadingly, "The light in the refrigerator is on . . . ," hoping in this roundabout way to elicit an offer to come turn it off. Eventually, upon seeing my mother at her front door, our neighbor automatically came over to correct whatever predicament had befallen us.

"If you let us watch TV, why can't we drive?" Josh asks, a good question, and there are a hundred more good questions that can easily follow: If you don't believe in this, why do any of it? And if you do believe in this, why do less than all of it? In the past, when one of the kids asked why we observed a particular rule or why a certain act was forbidden, I knew what I was supposed to say. Even if I could never bring myself to say with absolute conviction that we did it because God said we should, I did talk about how the Torah was what we followed in all areas of our lives. I invoked tradition and community and said that this was who we were.

"Add it to the pile of religious confusion," I tell the kids now.

They laugh at the image, and so do I. We are all lulled by the TV, finding vegetative consolation in the shows' nontraditional families: adopted children being raised by a Texas nanny and a cranky butler; a family of restaurateur-wizards; a songwriter girl in Miami living with her father while her mother, divorced, is in Africa tending to apes. Around us, in real life, divorce is a rarity. When the school directory arrived in the mail at the start of the school year, I scanned the names and counted how few families were configured like ours.

An episode of *Shake It Up* comes on, a Disney sitcom about

teenage dance stars and a divorced mother who is on the verge of remarriage to a police officer who is so anxious that he can't stop sweating profusely. The mood in the living room tightens at the mention of divorce and remarriage, and I study the kids for any sign of what they are thinking.

"How does it make you feel when you see this?" I ask, trying for casual interest.

There is little but a murmured acknowledgment of my question. On the show, the day of the wedding arrives at last. With a burst of exuberance, the family dances down the aisle. Relaxing, I bask in the scene and want to say to my kids, *See, we're not the only ones. Families come lots of different ways. Happiness is still possible.*

But then, a plot twist: The parents have been spotted in a kiss. The parents still have feelings for each other. The news breaks moments before the marriage ceremony is over. The wedding is called off. The children's hope of reunion is realized. Even better, there are no hard feelings—the sweating police officer is the most relieved of all.

It's almost enough to make me want to reinstate the no-TV-on-Shabbat rule. I'm afraid to look at my children. When the show ends, I shut off the TV for the remainder of the day.

THE SKY DARKENS. Shabbat ends close to six o'clock. We can drive somewhere—anywhere. Go bowling! Ice skating! To a movie! And even if we go nowhere, I no longer feel trapped.

To mark the end of the Shabbat I'm supposed to recite the Havdalah prayer, smelling the sweet cloves to console us over Shabbat's departure, holding up a braided candle like a torch to light the way into the coming week. I'm supposed to make the blessing—one more that I'd heard every week but never recited myself—praising He who separates between holy and profane, between light and dark, between Israel and the nations, between the seventh day and all other days. But these words extolling such clear-cut divisions aren't ones I want to say, not when I'm trying to navigate painful but necessary rifts in so many parts of my life. Not everything, I am realizing anew, can be so easily separated. This week, as every week now, I leave the candle and spice box in the drawer.

Israel

A few days after Thanksgiving, my brother's daughter — the lone girl among seven sons — is becoming a bat mitzvah, and I'm going to Israel for four days for the celebration.

Even when my parents generously offered to buy me a plane ticket, I wasn't sure I'd go, afraid of seeing my brother and his family, afraid of my relatives in Israel, all of whom are strictly religious. They know, of course, about the divorce; in my extended family, as far back as I can trace, I count only one other divorce. But my religious leave-taking makes me even more suspect — it feels like an almost impossible proposition, to be different yet still belong. It's easier to become the marginal relative seen rarely at family gatherings, whispered and wondered about. As tempting as that feels right now, it's all the more reason why I need to go. I don't want to preemptively cede my place in my family out of fear of how I will be viewed.

Packing requires pulling out old clothes, searching for skirts that approximate knee-length, cardigans that provide the necessary sleeve length. It's an undercover mission back into a former land. Every skirt of mine seems too short, every ordinary shirt plunges too low. Assembling what I will bring makes me aware, more than any other time, of my body. Collarbones, knees, and elbows become landmarks that demarcate your position in contested territory. It still hasn't sunk in that I can now wear whatever I want. This past summer, when I first wore something sleeveless (the most forbidden dress-code infraction of them all), I loved the feeling of my arms bare and unencumbered, but even so, I made sure to have a cardigan handy, not in case I got cold but in case I ran into someone Orthodox.

As I wait to board the flight to Tel Aviv, a group of Orthodox men sitting at the gate gathers to recite the afternoon prayers. There are nine of them but they need one more for the required quorum of ten men that constitutes communal prayer. They scan the crowd looking for another man — their eyes pass over the women without seeing them. They rouse a bearded, yarmulked man from his preoccupation with charging his iPhone to ask if he will join them. It doesn't matter that they don't know one another — in this extended community, there are no strangers.

The man admits that he hasn't yet fulfilled his obligation to pray but nonetheless he declines to participate. Is he too trying to shed the person he outwardly appears to be? I am overexcited at the prospect that he might be pretending as well. When informed that he is the much-needed tenth man, he grimaces but joins. He stands back from the other men, but they all face the same way — eastward, the required direction for prayer — as the designated leader softly mumbles the words they all know by heart.

Watching them too are the other passengers waiting for the

flight to Tel Aviv. Many of them can't be unfamiliar with this sight, yet they still seem mildly annoyed. One passenger who notices me watching gives me a knowing smile. In jeans, which I'll wear until I change into a skirt in the Israeli airport bathroom (there should be kiosks there for those like me — leave your forbidden clothing at the airport, reclaim them upon your departure), I'm taken for someone who is not Orthodox. I still feel like a spy, though I'm not sure for which side.

WHEN I ARRIVE in Jerusalem, my family is on a day trip to the city of Hebron, visiting the tombs of the Patriarchs and Matriarchs, and I set off in search of falafel. Walking around Ben Yehuda Street, I spot the American girls on their post-high-school year in Israel. Some of the girls wear ankle-length denim skirts and have an angelic air; others are dressed in knee-high boots and tight skirts, albeit regulation length, and look styled and hardened, able to pass the modesty requirements but only technically.

A few decades earlier, I was one of the girls in a long baggy jean skirt with an earnest, serious expression. During the year I spent in Israel, between high school and college, I studied Talmud all morning, then Bible and Jewish law in the afternoon. Unlike high school, where feminism was a bad word and women's places were limited and defined, this school encouraged us to wrestle with the texts in accordance with the belief that women's roles within Orthodoxy could slowly evolve.

On our first Shabbat at school, we ate dinner at long tables in the book-lined study hall, and one of the female teachers made the Kiddush blessings over the wine, though there were men present. As she recited the words I'd heard every week, I stared

at her. My curiosity was aroused as some of the girls around me
—many of whom would be attending Barnard or Penn or Columbia—traded glances warily: Just how feminist was this
place? I shared their uncertainty. "She's trampling upon the very
laws she claims to be observing," my former teachers and rabbis
would have said, reminding us that though society around us
might change, the laws of God and the rabbis did not.

After the blessings over the braided challahs, also recited by
a woman, the teacher took out photocopied pages of Jewish texts
and taught us why, according to a more liberal interpretation of
the law, it was permissible for a woman to recite these blessings,
even on behalf of men. Women couldn't lead prayers or read
from the Torah scrolls in front of men, but the laws for making
Kiddush could be reinterpreted so as to allow women to do it.

In my high school, girls weren't permitted to study Talmud,
so I lacked the necessary skills to understand these pages of Aramaic words, to wrestle sentences to uncover their hidden meanings, to hold each interpretation of what a word meant and then
the various interpretations of each of those interpretations. Much
of my life was based on these texts but they were incomprehensible to me. I stared blankly at my study partner, who was only
slightly more knowledgeable than I was. The oversize folio
pages of the Talmud—the cryptic unpunctuated lines of Aramaic, the tiny Hebrew letters of the rabbinic commentaries—
were like unintelligible maps, leaving me to wander, lost, inside
the tangle of streets.

It surprised me how badly I wanted to find my way. When I
didn't have to shape myself into a form that felt too tight, I liked
what I was learning—essentially a legal tract detailing the rules
of returning property, the financial obligations of ownership,

like a book of torts that bore the invisible hand of God. It wasn't spiritual or theological concepts being debated, just the minute details of the law. One word necessitated an explanatory sentence. A paragraph required an extended commentary. Each interpretation inspired two subsequent interpretations. I pushed my mind as hard as I ever had, teasing out which rabbi agreed with which position and for which reasons. How could their disparate opinions be brought into agreement? How could a countertext refute an opposing viewpoint?

I put in long hours in the study hall, consumed with the desire to hand myself over entirely to these religious texts. During Yom Kippur, I prayed fervently for forgiveness for my fringed too-short high-school denim skirt, for having wanted to ask too many questions of my teachers, and most of all for having kissed my camp boyfriend. This was the worst sin I could come up with, or at least the most tangible one — something concrete on which to pin the feeling that I used to be a little bit bad but now I was becoming entirely good.

During the holiday of Sukkot, I spent time with my brother, Akiva, who was a year older than me and was studying in an Israeli yeshiva. That I was so serious and focused during this year of religious study came as a surprise to me, but there had never been any doubt that Akiva would love his time in Israel. "That one is going to be a rabbi," predicted a friend of my mother once when, years before, she'd come over and heard Akiva belting out the prayers. When he was little, he used to keep a suitcase packed under his bed so that he'd be prepared if the Messiah arrived — as centuries of Jews had prayed for — and we were quickly gathered in from our long exile. It sounded nice enough as a theoretical prayer, but as a teenager, I wouldn't have minded if the Messiah tarried a little longer. I worried that if God finally made good on that age-old promise, I would have to stop caring about clothes and boys and soap operas and move to Israel, where we would have to live in the throes of religious devotion; Temple sacrifices in lieu of *Days of Our Lives*.

Akiva and I went, on Sukkot, to one of the ultra-Orthodox neighborhoods in Jerusalem where, every night, the various sects of Chasidim held celebrations. On the main floor, Akiva joined the bearded, hatted, frock-coated men who danced in ecstatic circles while I went upstairs to sit with the women who peered down from the balcony, faces pressed to the metal grating for a glimpse. Did being relegated up here bother them? Did they ever wonder what lay beyond this barrier, or had they gleaned some secret to contentment that my Modern Orthodox friends and I had failed to understand? I searched their expressions for clues. Did any of them, maybe once in a while, ever want something else? Akiva could blend into the dancing circles of men, but the differences between me and these women seemed so vast as to make us barely part of the same religion. I preferred to watch the men, who displayed spiritual passion of the sort I'd never experienced. For me, religious devotion lived far more quietly: a dedicated spouse who made no grand displays of love, offered no flashy gifts, but day after day dutifully packed a lunch, prepared a dinner, rubbed a sore back.

WEEKS PASSED, then a few months. I sat in front of my Talmudic tracts and pushed my way in. Slowly, slowly, I reached the beginning of comprehension, so that the letters organized themselves into recognizable locales, their black lines now like roads onto which I could venture. A word sharpened into meaning. I knew that one. And then another, and another. A word became a question, which led to another question. One word turned a sentence back on itself, offering a refutation.

For the first time, I understood how the laws progressed from a biblical phrase to a Talmudic explication to a rabbinic dictate. I was part of this chain—not just a subject of the laws but part of their transmission. The texts belonged to me as well. I adopted a theology of obedience to God's will in which it was good to question but necessary to obey. The loftiest of inquiries about belief weren't what mattered—instead, it was each small moment, every specific act. I could debate the exact nature of a divine being as long as I prayed to Him three times a day at the proper moments, reciting each word not necessarily with passion but with precision. I could question various understandings of commandments as long as I accepted my obligation to say the right blessings before and after I ate. I would not pick and choose which laws I would observe. Each rule was a load-bearing wall in the overarching structure. I would study Jewish texts every day. I would not touch boys, not even a casual hug, because this was forbidden. I would stop wearing jeans. I didn't necessarily believe they were immodest but I wanted to align myself with the group to which I now fully belonged.

Here—at last—was the promise of goodness. All I had to do was be steadfast in my observance. Here—at last—was the pleasure of belief: to feel certainty about who I already was.

There wasn't enough time left—the months were passing too quickly, and there was so much I didn't know. As my time there came to an end, I toyed with the idea of returning for a second year but was swayed by the Columbia sweatshirt I'd worn for months and the college-course catalog with its seemingly endless choices. Before I left Israel, I went to a Jewish bookstore — not to one in an ultra-Orthodox neighborhood, where banners admonished women to dress modestly and where booksellers refused to sell many religious texts to girls, but to a Modern Orthodox one in the Old City of Jerusalem, where every book was permitted to me. I browsed the floor-to-ceiling shelves: commentaries on the Bible, explications of various aspects of Jewish law, philosophical treatises on God and the commandments. Each of them seemed crucial — it was impossible not to know their entire contents. I lingered for hours, wishing I could pour each of these books inside me. I carried home my heavy bags filled with the volumes I'd selected, solid reminders of the path I was now on.

In the last week of school, I sat on the bed in my dorm and took out my notebook, which I'd used to write letters to family and friends, and this time I wrote myself a letter: *Do not change back. Do not go to college and be swayed. Do not return to believing tepidly, to observing nominally.* I described the new person I was trying to be, a young woman firm in her convictions, learned and strong, who didn't waver or bend. She was still engaged in the outside world, but the truth lay fortressed inside her. I could see her so clearly — all I needed to do was press the edges of my old self against this new image so that we formed a single figure.

When I came back from my year in Israel, Akiva was home as well, though in a few weeks he would be going back again to Israel, where he'd decided to attend college. A few days after we both returned, we were in his room talking. There was a pause in the conversation, and Akiva looked at me awkwardly, like he wanted to tell me something but wasn't sure how.

"According to the *Shulchan Aruch,* it's impermissible for a brother to hug his sister," he said.

At first the words were theoretical — a theoretical brother, an imaginary sister, a hypothetical touch. I knew he wasn't trying to make me feel bad. It was nothing personal, we were just discussing the rules in which we both believed and that we agreed could never be compromised. But I also knew that when we were both in Israel that year, I had hugged him every time I saw him. Now I felt as though I'd done something wrong. I didn't know what to say, because how could you argue with the truth? The book he was quoting was one I'd studied as well, but now it was turning against me.

Shame touched down on my face, my arms, my legs. It didn't matter that I'd changed. My body itself was the problem, as though it had stood too close, hugged too long, as though the rabbis warning him back were the same rabbis in high school who had noticed my too-short skirt.

Akiva returned to Israel and I started college, where I requested an all-female floor in the first-year dorm and an Orthodox roommate so that we would be each other's buttresses against the outside. I was one of "the skirts," the strictly Orthodox girls in the large and active Columbia Jewish community. Our wearing only skirts was the means by which we were judged and categorized — not a private religious decision but a public manifesto. I ate with the other Orthodox Jews in the kosher area of the dining hall, and in between our classes, we studied Jewish texts in the small study hall lined with books. I woke at seven, a few hours before my first class, and I hurried to morning prayers across the nearly empty campus — only the athletes and the Orthodox Jews were awake at this hour. There were a few months during my first year when I briefly returned to wearing pants, but then I stopped, not only because I was worried about how God would regard such a slippage, but, more practically, because I cared immensely about what the Orthodox boys at Columbia would think. "He probably wouldn't date someone who wears pants," my roommate said of a boy I was interested in. At her words, I folded up my jeans and placed them once again out of reach. This time, I promised myself, I was putting them away for good.

There was a clear expectation that if you went into the outside world, you would limit what you took in. I'd heard too many warnings: the yeshiva boy who studied philosophy and left the path; the English major who enrolled in a biblical criticism class and never recovered. I studied in Butler Library, where Plato and Aristotle and Voltaire were memorialized on the grand marble façade, but the cautionary stories of the students who left Orthodoxy were the ones carved into my psyche. Other people might have viewed college as a chance to figure out who they were; I wasn't here to discover who I wanted to be but to remain who I already was.

It was easier if I closed myself off. I made few friends who weren't Orthodox. It was too hard to have to explain myself all the time, as my Orthodox roommate and I had done with our first-year suitemates (one Korean, one Mormon), asking them to please leave the bathroom light on from Friday night to Saturday night because we couldn't touch the switch. There were far too many rules to explain all of them, but the one about the light switch in the bathroom seemed important for them to know.

"So are these rules just for this weekend or every weekend?" someone on our floor asked when she heard about our request, then she tried to act like our explanation about the light switch falling into one of the thirty-nine categories of work that were forbidden on Shabbat made perfect sense to her. Until we started putting a piece of tape across the switch as a reminder, we grew accustomed to going to the bathroom in the dark.

In a poetry seminar, where the lights in the classroom were kept off to enhance the mood, I sat among those with hair dyed and noses pierced. The college they attended was complete with raucous parties and smoky bars and lots of sex—it might as well have been miles away from the one my Orthodox circle of friends and I attended, intent on remaining safe at all costs. Every day before class, I had to remind myself of what one of my favorite writers, Eudora Welty, had written: "A sheltered life can be a daring life as well. For all serious daring starts from within." Only when the professor read aloud the poems we had written did I feel that I belonged in the room.

In a required literature course, we studied the Bible alongside *The Iliad* and *The Odyssey*—this was as close as I would come to biblical criticism. The reading load was lighter for me during the week we studied Genesis—those stories were as familiar to me as those from my own childhood. When I wrote papers or participated in the class discussion, I had to remind myself to use the English names—Rivka was called Rebecca, Yosef was known as Joseph, as though they too were adopting disguises to live more comfortably in the outside world.

In a class discussion of the week's reading, a fellow student raised her hand.

"I can't believe people base their whole lives on the Bible. It's like living your life according to *The Iliad*!" she exclaimed.

My entire life dismissed so cavalierly, yet I didn't know what to say in its defense. I didn't want to raise my hand and put forth the belief that a blind poet had written *The Iliad* but an all-seeing God had written the Bible. If challenged, I'd have had no idea how to respond.

While I was in college, Akiva and I talked less, ostensibly because we were both busy and far away from each other. When I called him, I hoped to be reminded of the person I'd decided to be. More than anything, I was afraid of losing the certainty I'd gained during my year in Israel. In Israel, he became a rabbi, but in his late twenties, he switched from the Modern Orthodox knit yarmulke that my father wore to a black velvet one, from a small cropped beard to a longer one, from khakis and button-down shirts to the ultra-Orthodox uniform of black and white. He joined one of the more mystical Chasidic sects that emphasized the need to cultivate a joyous connection to God and reject the outside world. He said that he had decided to grow his beard and side-curls when he looked in the mirror and the clean-shaven face wasn't who he expected to see. Each of these changes, Akiva told me at the time, felt small, his whole life leading him, step by step, down this path. My parents were concerned about his transformation, worried that he was discarding the moderation with which we'd been raised. But despite any misgivings, my parents accepted who he wanted to be. They understood that he wanted to live in accordance with his beliefs. *Roots to grow and wings to soar,* my parents had written on birthday and graduation cards so frequently that the saying had become something of a family joke. I don't think any of us realized yet how often our family would wrestle with what happened when these roots and wings pulled in opposing directions.

⌒

ON SHABBAT MORNING, we walk in a procession to the Western Wall, along the streets of the modern city of Jerusalem, with its contemporary stone hotels and storefronts, almost all of which are closed on Shabbat. My father has stayed behind in the hotel to rest, and Akiva leads the way—me, my mother, my sister, Dahlia, and Akiva's children following behind. Akiva wears a gold caftan special for Shabbat and a crownlike *shtreimel,* the fur-trimmed hat that many Chasidic men wear. From the back, my brother looks like any ultra-Orthodox man. Only when I look past the hat and beard do I recognize him.

As we enter the walled Old City, with its narrow cobble-stoned alleyways opening into wide stone-lined plazas, we pass similarly garbed men, the subtle differences in hats or coats delineating their precise affiliations within ultra-Orthodoxy. Those who adhere to a particular sect dress the same as their fellow believers, as though God were the sort of parent who liked to put His children in matching attire.

We walk down the steps toward the Western Wall—once an outer wall to the Holy Temple that stood here and the only part to remain when it was destroyed by the Romans. As we approach the spot that is regarded as one of the holiest sites in the Jewish world, we split up, men and women. On the women's side, women in long skirts, hats, and wigs gather close to the front, weeping and whispering into the stones. Folded notes intended for God are wedged into the cracks, innumerable crinkled pleas, praises, and requests, a codex of human pain.

From the cart at the entrance to the women's section, Dahlia and I take prayer books creased and worn from use. Nearby, a uniformed woman is handing out scarves to cover those deemed immodestly dressed—cloaks of shame, I used to call them. We are safe, though. My skirt is long enough to pass, and Dahlia is dressed in long sleeves and an ankle-length skirt, taken from her back-closet selection of what she's dubbed her Israel clothes. Dahlia spent a year at the same women's yeshiva in Israel I did, but she stayed a second year, returning home more ardently religious than I had, deciding to go to the same Orthodox college my mother attended instead of to Columbia as planned. If she'd gotten married younger, perhaps she would have remained as devoutly religious, but during the years of being single, she has slowly evolved, nearer now to the Modern Orthodoxy of my parents.

Dahlia and I move as close to the wall as we can, slipping between praying women for a place at the front. In this spot, where I once felt the thrill of being at the epicenter of belief, I open the prayer book to the Shabbat-morning service. Pray, I was taught, even when you're not in the mood, and you will come to be in the mood. Though I rarely felt the passion visible in some of the women around me, who are swaying back and forth, their faces contorted with emotion as though beseeching a being who stood directly in front of them, I had once prayed dutifully. My lips moved, as was required, as I said every word. My knees bent at the appointed times. Often I had the sense of checking an obligation off a list over and over, the same words recited quickly every day, but sometimes, sometimes, I had been filled by a quiet, steadfast fervor—the words were not just written on a page but opened and admitted me inside.

Now I try to say those prayers; my eyes roll over them but to move my lips feels too false a display. Still, I try to feel something, anything. I think about those folded notes, prayers penned onto every free surface of paper and crammed into every space of this wall. I remind myself of the immense history of this space and try to be swayed by that, at least.

I try, I still try, but the gates of prayer remain firmly closed. It is the feeling of being locked out of a place that once felt like home. I hold the prayer book open in front of me but don't recite another word.

"Smell," urges an old woman who approaches Dahlia and me clasping bunches of mint and oregano. She holds the leaves to our faces and instructs us to make the blessing praising God who has created the varieties of spices.

Her face is pinched and grizzled. She is wearing a black dowager dress, her head covered in a scarf from which a few gray, wiry strands emerge. Her ankles, peeking out from the bottom of her dress, are swollen, trunks planted into the black leather ground of her shoes. If it weren't Shabbat, on which the use of money is prohibited, there would be a legion of similar women, palms upturned, asking for charity.

We do as she says, and the sprigs are surprisingly fragrant. Smiling, she looks us over and offers my sister (whose uncovered hair is a sign that she's not married) a blessing that she should find her *bashert* — the soulmate whom God has intended for her.

"She gave me a knowing look. I think she can tell I have a boyfriend," Dahlia whispers to me and we laugh. Even when so many other relationships feel strained and uncertain, this is one that remains close and steadfast.

"Are we ascribing supernatural powers to spice-bearing

women?" I whisper back, but I wonder why the woman didn't offer me a blessing as well. With my uncovered hair, I appear equally single. Maybe she is in possession of some magical power that enables her to see that I'm hardly a good beneficiary for her sort of blessing.

"You never know," Dahlia says.

In our hotel room, we've lain awake jet-lagged, talking about boyfriends, hers and mine, as though we were still the young sisters we once were, whispering late into the night. I talk of the excitement I feel about William, how when I'm with him, I have the constant sense of encountering someone strong and alive. And I tell her about my worry that we will prove too different. She talks about how it feels now, after all this time, to be regarded with eager expectancy, dangling on the brink of engagement to someone she met through a dating website that is (actually) called Saw You at Sinai, set up by one of the volunteer matchmakers who pair like with like. Since she graduated from college fifteen years ago, she has lived in apartments with various roommates, going out on blind dates set up by her friends and then, later, using the Orthodox dating sites where you classified yourself by your religious observance. *Do you plan to cover your hair? Do you wear pants? Would you date a woman who won't cover her hair? Would you send your future kids to co-ed schools? Would you let them watch TV?* Orthodox dating was like that kids' game of Concentration: flip over the squares until you found two that were identical.

Until this year, I'd played the role of older married sister, taking care of my kids and cooking dinner while talking to Dahlia on the phone about the exciting trips she was planning, six weeks exploring India and another trip backpacking in the

Rocky Mountains. When we talked about the men she was dating, I felt an underlayer of anxiety to our conversation, concern that it would become even harder for her to find the right person as she got older and the pool of eligible Orthodox men supposedly shrunk. Inside the Orthodox community, she constantly heard the message that to be single was the worst possible fate that could befall a girl, and though I tried not to let it show, I too worried that she might end up alone.

Why had it seemed so easy for me? I'd sometimes wondered as she described what didn't feel right about each relationship. "Do you think maybe you're just nervous?" I found myself asking her when she talked about the boyfriends who wished to marry her. I wanted her to find the right person, but a part of me wondered if she should just put aside her misgivings about these men and grab hold of any certainty while she could. I had barely dated anyone before meeting Aaron. I was twenty-two when we got engaged, twelve weeks after we started dating. I tried to feel lucky that in getting married so young, I didn't have to spend years in this uncertain state. I told myself I had escaped this need to reckon and wrestle. When I felt worried about my marriage, I consoled myself with the knowledge that I too could have ended up alone.

The spice-bearing woman is still hovering, and when she sees me looking at her, she finally offers me the same blessing — that I should find my *bashert,* my soulmate, speedily in our days. I know I'm supposed to thank her for the blessing but all I can do is smile tightly, wanting to ask her about the logical challenges my divorce poses to the concept of *bashert.* But most of all, I wonder what this weathered woman — half *bubby,* half witch — would say to this ending: You will find someone who is just like you, you will get engaged and follow the path, but you will be unhappy. You will fantasize of, and then pursue, escape. In the eyes of this blessing-bestowing woman, William would hardly qualify as a *bashert*. William, in Boston, has probably spent his Saturday biking or running or catching up on work. We've texted back and forth while I've been here, but it feels impossible to explain where I am. For him, this trip would have been a cultural experience, one that had little to do with who he is. It's hard to imagine him in Israel with my family—it feels like trying to drop an oversize figurine into a meticulously constructed diorama.

Before we meet my brother at the back of the courtyard, where we'll make the blessings over the wine he has brought along and eat the jelly doughnuts that are ubiquitous in Israel in these weeks leading up to Chanukah, I turn back to the spice-bearing woman.

I ask her in my Americanized Hebrew why she does this, gesturing to her bundle of spices. Standing right next to her now, I see that her eyes are watery and eerily pink, pools of pain.

So you will make a blessing, she tells me.

Yes, I say, I know. But *why* do you do it?

She holds out her hands, gestures up toward the stone wall that has seen civilizations come and go, yet has remained standing. *"Le-shem shamayim,"* she says. This, everything, is for the sake of heaven.

⁓

IN MY SENIOR year of college, Aaron and I were set up by two friends. "You're perfect for each other—you're exactly the same," my friend Elizabeth promised me when she and her boy-friend, who was Aaron's close friend, came up with the idea.

We were standing in the kitchen of my suite, which I shared with four other Orthodox women in a dorm called East Campus, dubbed "the Lower East Campus" for its hordes of Orthodox students who clustered on the low floors in order to minimize the flights of stairs we needed to walk up on Shabbat, when elevators were prohibited. I had made Shabbat dinner for a group of friends, as I did most weeks, and Elizabeth was helping me serve the chicken and kugels, our standard fare. She was wearing a long red velvet dress that hugged her body—even when she dressed modestly, she managed to look seductive. Elizabeth had converted to Orthodox Judaism when she was seventeen, becoming a devout member of the Orthodox community, though the first time I saw her, at afternoon prayers, I noticed the overly deliberate way she bowed at the required places. Even before I saw the small tattoo on her ankle, I knew she hadn't grown up Orthodox.

"She has a story," said one of my Orthodox friends, her eyebrows raised with suspicion.

The rest of us were presumed to be without any such story—a preordained straight line rather than a shape with turns and bends. I knew a few people who'd left Orthodoxy once they started college, and my curiosity about them was fueled by fear. How did they stop being who they already were? I didn't want to imagine myself ever ending up as they surely were, solitary figures who would now wander alone. I listened to the explanations offered about people like them; there was always a ready explanation. It wasn't that they had examined their belief and found it lacking. It wasn't that they wanted to choose their lives for themselves. Our belief was too absolute, too foolproof, for us to admit that someone else might see a few holes. People left because they had been led astray by temptation, lured by false ideas. People left only because they were depressed or because they came from abusive families or because their parents were divorced; they were unstable or defective or damaged in some way.

There were their opposites as well, those who started joining Shabbat dinners and wearing yarmulkes or long skirts until they had transformed themselves into one of us. I was curious about them as well: What made them want what we had? There were quiet whispers about possible problems these people were trying to leave behind, but that wasn't a sufficient explanation. Unlike those who left, people who became Orthodox had seen the truth —they came of sound mind and pure heart. They were proof of the meaninglessness of secular culture. They served as reassuring confirmations that we indeed held the truth.

"I felt God," Elizabeth declared when I broached the subject of how she knew she wanted to become Orthodox.

Though I nodded in agreement, I mostly felt envy that she seemed to possess such unwavering belief, envy that was followed by a wave of relief. If someone as sophisticated and smart as she chose this, then it had to be true, though she eventually grew disillusioned with Judaism and became an Evangelical Christian. By the time I met her, at the start of my senior year, I knew I wanted to be a writer. She too loved to write, and sometimes we shared our writing with each other, though she had far more experience than I did to draw on. "Write about Memphis," she advised me. "Write about what it was like to grow up in such a tight-knit world."

For our first blind date, Aaron and I met at the 116th Street gates of Columbia. He was sweet and gentle and soft-spoken, and I immediately felt I'd known him far longer than I actually had. The lines of connection were already in place. Two of my closest friends had gone to high school with him. Our fathers had gone to the same medical school. Our mothers had over-lapped at an Orthodox women's college. ("I think we were at his bris," my mother recalled when I told her his name.)

Before Aaron, I'd had no real relationships, just that one camp boyfriend, a few set-up dates with boys from Yeshiva University uptown, and a couple of flirtatious entanglements with Orthodox boys at Columbia, always under the guise of being just friends. We lived next door to one another, hung out in each other's rooms, sat on each other's beds, ignoring the way the air in the room sometimes became thicker and expectant. Follow every rule, I continued to admonish myself, even ones that some-times became more challenging by the minute. I assumed I was the only one to feel this pull of attraction—surely all the good Orthodox boys had conquered their evil inclinations. But if this was so, then why did we sit closer and closer, why did we allow only a sliver of air between us? Only occasionally did we suc-cumb to a few illicit kisses, which caused soul-searching and guilt-ridden promises to each other that we would never allow such an infraction of the rules to happen again. It confirmed what we had arrived knowing: You always had to be on guard. No matter how tightly you were secured, you were always in danger of falling.

Before Aaron, I was drawn to boys who were dark and stormy, who had poetic souls and moody dispositions. These aspects of myself made me nervous, but even so, I was pulled to the pleasure of uncovering the layers, down to the darkest, most complicated parts. But with Aaron, there were no hard edges; there was no wrestling, no fighting. We went out three times that week and three times the next week as well, to dinner, to play mini-golf, to a Shakespeare play in the Village. My roommates, well versed in the rules of Orthodox dating, had advised me that you were supposed to discuss, by the third date, where a relationship was going—as though there were various options for where this train might be headed, an Amtrak board of changing destinations, when really the only possible endpoint was marriage.

As we sat in the common area of my dorm one night, Aaron and I marveled at how similar we were—though both Orthodox, we weren't as rigid and dogmatic as some of our friends. If I felt sometimes that I was still a little unformed, he seemed the same way to me. Neither of us was especially forceful; we were both gentle and yielding and eager to please. We stayed up all night talking, and from the row of windows in the common area of our suite, we watched the sun rise over the East Side of Manhattan—pink and orange streaks in a blue-gray sky.

The next day, he came back to my dorm and handed me a rose that he'd concealed inside his winter coat.

"I really like you," he said.

"I really like you too," I said.

"You're going to marry him," Elizabeth predicted. I was twenty-two and the fact that I'd never before had a serious boyfriend didn't seem particularly problematic. As far as I could tell, there was little difference between a boyfriend and a husband. Never having been in love, I was overcome with exhilaration. I walked across campus and looked at the people I passed. Did they too know this feeling? Didn't everyone in love feel ready to burst from euphoria?

Every night, Aaron and I stayed up late talking in my dorm room, sitting next to each other on my bed but never touching. We were *shomer negiah* — literally, "guardians of the touch" — adhering to the prohibition against any physical contact until marriage. Outside the resident adviser's room a few doors down, a manila envelope offered condoms free for the taking, but in our room, the door was cracked open slightly so that we weren't technically in violation of another prohibition, this one against being alone in a room with a member of the opposite sex.

Follow every rule, I still told myself, but what about this spreading, bursting feeling that would not be contained — the part of life that did not want to stay within the confines of the law? Conquer it, subdue it, resist it, I had been taught, even though now, my body tingled with the feeling of proximity.

"Should we?" Aaron and I asked each other as we sat ever closer, a Zeno's paradox of desire. How close can you lean and not touch? For how long can one arm graze another and both of you pretend it hadn't happened?

"We shouldn't," we whispered, "we definitely shouldn't," yet his hand was tentatively on my face. We shouldn't, yet we kissed and then pulled guiltily away.

"Do you think badly of me now?" I asked.

"Of course not," he said, though we both worried that we

weren't who we aspired to be. I still carried a small scolding rabbi in my head, but I was growing accustomed to the idea that you could divide yourself as you did the rest of life, a line between allowed and forbidden, a separation between holy and profane. In one of my English literature classes, I'd read, in an Emily Dickinson poem, *Ourself behind ourself, concealed— / Should startle most,* and I'd felt like I was coming upon confirmation of a truth that I'd quietly known all along. Where every part of life was legislated—where even a gentle brush of arms, this sweet rousing of desire, was deemed bad—it was sometimes necessary to carve secret places inside yourself. You needed to harbor a private, second self.

A month later, during winter vacation, the dorm was mostly empty, just a few students who had stayed around as I had, trying to figure out what came next. Technically I'd already graduated—I had enough credits by the middle of my senior year and was planning to spend the upcoming semester in Israel, once again studying Jewish texts. I had applied to graduate programs in creative writing for the following year but didn't yet know if I'd get in. And if I did get in, I didn't know if my desire to become a writer was an impractical dream.

"You're going to go to Israel . . ." Aaron said playfully as we sat next to each other on my bed.

"Yes . . ." I said.

"And then you'll come back . . ."

"Yes . . ."

"And then there's August . . ." he said.

"August . . ." I repeated hopefully.

"Should we say it?"

Each word dangled. Each word, a path down which we took one more step. We could get engaged now, twelve weeks after our first date. We could get married eight months from now, in August.

It seemed so clear to me that this was the intended story of my life. It didn't occur to me that this was only one of the possibilities that could exist. Getting engaged so quickly was an essential part of the story, as though the speed itself confirmed that we were meant for each other. I felt the giddiness of love, but also of relief, as though before I were in danger and now I was pinned more securely to my world. Until now, I had worried that I would remain perpetually single, waiting for my life to begin. Orthodox women who didn't marry were doomed to wait and wait—our own version of a princess hidden in a tower—wait and wait for the husband who would open the doorway to everything else. Wait and wait, and if it didn't happen, then—the picture in my mind froze. If you didn't get married, there was nothing but a blank screen.

I told my parents we were planning to get engaged, and though I worried they would think twelve weeks of dating was too fast, they didn't object. I seemed so happy, so sure. The weekend before we made it official, we took the train to visit Aaron's parents in Boston. He had been nervous about telling them we were getting engaged and only snuck it in as an anxious aside at the end of a phone conversation. We might have been on the brink of engagement, but I felt like we were children, seeking permission for something we weren't old enough to do. They protested but then, to our relief, relented; they liked that they knew my parents, that I was by all accounts a good girl.

"You seem like someone who's always happy," Aaron said to me as the train neared Boston, and I worried about making a good impression on his family.

I wasn't sure if this was a wish or an observation but either way, I looked at him in surprise. No one had ever described me this way. Was it possible that he knew me so little? I felt a fleeting urge to press on the brakes and, to an enormous squeal of wheels and track, bring everything to a screeching halt. But I pushed the feeling away. *You're just nervous,* I soothed myself. *You're just adjusting to the idea of getting engaged.* I had no basis for comparison, but maybe this was how it felt sometimes when you were in love. And maybe he was right. I might have thought of myself as emotional, intense, often moody, but maybe he knew me better than I knew myself.

In Boston, we shopped for an engagement ring, eventually selecting a shining round diamond delicately set in antique platinum.

As we started planning the wedding, we began to fight. "Everyone fights during the engagement," my engaged and married friends reminded me. Alarmed at how our story of falling in love so quickly had become complicated by the press of family and obligation, I decided not to go to Israel for the semester. I wanted to be with him, I had a wedding to plan, but, most of all, I was worried that it had all happened too quickly—I had the same quiet urge to put all this on pause, maybe postpone the wedding until we got to know each other a little better. But once again I told myself I was just nervous. I grew used to crying every day. *The bride with the red-rimmed eyes,* I would sometimes think when I looked in the mirror, but I didn't let myself ask the questions that should have come after such an observation. To do so would have been to admit that the story I so badly wanted to be true was in danger of collapsing.

Instead, I planned the wedding and bought hats at sample sales in Brooklyn. I was planning to cover my hair in accordance with the Orthodox law that a married woman's hair should be for her husband's eyes alone. Neither my mother nor my future mother-in-law covered her hair. Laws like observing Shabbat or keeping kosher couldn't be broken no matter what, but some rules, like hair-covering, were regarded as, if not exactly optional, then still not always done. But in recent years, Orthodoxy had moved rightward, and practices that had previously fallen out of favor had returned. Stringencies, once the domain of ultra-Orthodoxy, had become accepted as the required norm in Modern Orthodoxy as well. Now Modern Orthodox young women like myself routinely covered their hair, especially if they wanted to be regarded as being serious about their observance. I didn't like the idea of covering another part of my body, but I accepted that I would do what was required of me. *You don't have to feel this way,* I reminded myself whenever I felt a surge of doubt. This was not about covering who I was — on the contrary, this was about displaying a sign that I was a married woman. This was a way to wear my belonging proudly on my head.

Of course I saw the conflict between Orthodoxy and feminism — it was hard to miss — but I wanted to be part of this burgeoning movement of Orthodox feminism that was increasingly talked about in the Orthodox community, among my peers, and in articles in the Jewish newspapers, some in favor, some decrying its growing influence. As I'd learned during my year in Israel, some of the laws could be reinterpreted so that women could take on scholarly and ritual roles. I could be one of the women who were pushing the rules as far as they could go. There still remained a gate at the end of the path, sealed shut and guarded, which I tried not to think about. Were these small changes a revolution or an appeasement? I sometimes asked myself but I had no good answer, only the feeling of relief that I could remain traditional while still thinking of myself as something of a radical. Contradictions would persist, but it was possible to live with competing beliefs.

I decided to get a fall — a sort of demi-wig that would clip to the top of my head and cover most of my hair. Because the front of my own hair would be showing, it was regarded as a more liberal approach. I consoled myself that I wasn't shopping for a wig as my right-wing counterparts might be. I was a feminist who was choosing to wear a fall. The difference between the two may have been a few inches of hair, but at the time, that small amount of space was sufficient to quiet my resistance.

"There's no way I can get the curls as tight as yours," warned Esther, the first wig maker I tried, as I sat in in her pink plastic salon chair in Borough Park. I was searching for a fall so curly that it would match my hair exactly.

A friend suggested I try the elusive Clairie, spoken about in reverential tones, renowned for using genuine Belgian hair, which, my friend claimed, was the most desirable for making a wig — sold to her, rumor had it, by Belgian prostitutes in need of cash.

I tracked Clairie down, feeling like I'd made contact with a celebrity, but couldn't get an appointment; she was too busy scouring the Belgian countryside for the perfect hair. Even if I had been able to meet her, she said she couldn't help me with a wig as curly as my own hair—apparently, there were no cash-strapped curly-haired prostitutes.

"Look on the bright side," said Suri, another wig maker in Brooklyn whose salon chair I sat in in a small back room of her house. "You can finally have straight hair. You can be anyone you want—a blonde, a redhead!"

She was decked out in a glamorous wig of long, straight blond hair that made her look part religious wife, part Hollywood starlet. It was tempting—my curls had always seemed too wild and unruly. When I was in high school, I'd tried, twice, to chemically straighten them, to no avail. The curls had reasserted themselves in a matter of days.

At her urging, I tried on a sampling of wigs, surveying the unrecognizable girl in the mirror. Was there a way, I wondered, to observe the laws and still look like myself? I didn't want to get married and lose myself entirely—I had decided that I wasn't going to change my last name, and I didn't want to alter my hair, everything about who I had once been.

I continued my search, trying someone in the theater district in Manhattan who made wigs for Broadway shows. When I walked into the small Midtown office for my appointment, the receptionist treated me with sympathy, assuming I was a cancer patient.

In the stylist's chair, John the wig maker, a short, balding man with a weathered face and a strong New York accent, took a long look at me. I worried I would have to explain why I, with a full head of hair, was in need of a wig, but this was New York and he already knew why.

"I can't get it that curly," John warned me. "But don't worry, I know what to do. All you Orthodox girls want your wigs to look better than your actual hair."

As he held small ponytail-like color swatches to my hair, he told me how he'd once had a customer who traveled to rural towns for business where he was nervous about wearing a yarmulke. John had crafted a small circle of dark hair that his client pinned to his own; he alone knew it was there. I gave up on the possibility of the fall being curly enough. All I wanted was for it to be so good that it rendered itself invisible. I had recently been accepted to Columbia's graduate program in creative writing, and I intended to sit in writing workshops where no one would detect the intricate world I wore on my head. Only those in the know would be able to decipher the coded message I wore, transmitting where I belonged.

At my bridal shower in Memphis, I sat displayed at the front of the room in a pink silk Laura Ashley dress — it wasn't the kind of dress I'd ever worn before but I'd bought it because it looked appropriately sweet and bridal. Along with the Pyrex sets and the blender and the meat and dairy cutting boards, my mother's friends gave me their cardinal pieces of marital advice: *Don't go to bed angry,* in block letters on a pink index card. *Don't criticize his mother. Don't keep score,* written on light blue and yellow cards. These women from the community, whose recipes were compiled in the synagogue sisterhood cookbooks, knew, without a doubt, the best way to make sponge cakes and brisket, and here was the recipe for a good marriage as well. Anger could destroy you. So could asking too much or pushing too hard. If those women had been handed notebooks instead of index cards, given days rather than minutes, and offered free rein and social immunity, I wondered, what might they have written to me and to all the other brides whom they sent off into their married lives armed only with paring knives and Pyrex?

In the dining room of a rabbi's wife, I, along with a dozen other engaged young women, sat around the plastic-covered dining-room table, learning the laws of Jewish family purity. We were all virgins, presumably, and we learned that after we had sex for the first time, we were in *niddah* — a state of impurity — and couldn't touch our husbands for the week or so afterward. Whenever we had our periods and for the seven days following, we couldn't touch our husbands — no sex, not a hug, not a handshake. Nor were we allowed to undress in front of our husbands at this time, or pass them a dish, or sleep in the same beds with them. For this reason, we needed not one marital bed but two twin beds, which we could push together when we were permitted to each other, separate when we were not. For seven days following our periods, we were to check ourselves for smudges or stains twice each day with small cloths that were sold at the mikvah — along with, for an extra few dollars, a flowered carrying pouch. On the day when we first believed ourselves to be clean, we were to leave the cloths inside us for thirty minutes, just to be sure.

I was supposed to do what with that cloth? The rules had always cloaked me like the long skirts I was supposed to wear, but by getting married, they were poised to enter my body as well.

I looked around the table at the other engaged young women, but no one had any visible reaction; they just continued to copy what the teacher said into their notebooks. *You don't have to feel that way,* the words like a long-standing prayer lodged inside me. *This is beautiful,* I told myself, hoping that if I said it enough times, I would start to believe it. Contrary to how it might appear, this was not an invasion of the most private sphere of my body. This was not an issue of a woman being deemed impure. Shape it and twist it, change it and smooth it—some sort of machine inside my head, skilled at reprocessing and reconfiguring any torn bits into a smooth whole in whose billowing folds I could still seek comfort. Quibble, if necessary, with some of the details, parse the interpretations, summon various rabbinic figures to bolster or support—I would do anything necessary so that inside me there did not form a small silent *no*.

I tried to focus on the photocopied calendar page that our teacher handed out, to understand the system she was explaining for how to know when sex was prohibited. It was forbidden not only for all the days of our periods and the seven days following, but on the night before we expected our periods; forbidden too on the night that was exactly a month after the date on which we'd last gotten our periods. It could be a little confusing, she conceded, and we shouldn't be shy about going to a rabbi with a question. Or be embarrassed to bring our stained cloths, or our panties, if need be, to a rabbi to see if we were permitted or prohibited.

For the final class, we met, together with our fiancés, with the rabbi to learn not only what was forbidden but what was allowed. Sex, which until now had been taboo, was ushered into polite company. It lay at the heart of all the rules about counting the days and checking our underwear. All rumors of prudishness to the contrary, it turned out that God wanted us to enjoy sex, as long as we had counted the days of our cycles, as long as we had checked ourselves internally, scrubbed and brushed and immersed ourselves in the mikvah's purifying waters. It was time to push from our minds all those former messages that desire was wrong. All at once, sex was right and it was wrong and it was good and it was bad. There were rabbinic opinions, we were taught, that prohibited sex in the light, sex during the day, sex anywhere but in the bedroom, sex any way but with the man on top, but it was permissible to rely on the most lenient of rabbinic positions that allowed anything consensual and pleasurable. I listened intently and, ever the good student, took careful notes. *Sex = allowed,* I wrote in my notebook, where I also had fragments of short stories, ideas for novels.

A few months before the wedding, Aaron and I were still fighting, mostly about family and the wedding, but those details were really stand-ins for larger issues between us. At the rise of any problem, he said he agreed with me, or maybe he didn't, I couldn't be sure. I felt muddled about what he really thought, then I felt bad for being upset, so I tried to mask what I felt until I felt muddled about what *I* really thought. When we were dating, it had felt blissfully uncomplicated. Now we belonged to parents and community, obligation and duty. What had happened to that story of falling in love so sweetly, so swiftly? Those twelve weeks that we'd known each other before getting engaged seemed like nothing now—in that short period, there hadn't even been time to have a fight.

I stayed focused on the wedding. I browsed the women's section of the Jewish bookstore, the equivalent of the feminine-hygiene aisle at the drugstore where books about marriage assured me that scrupulously following the laws of mikvah would keep my marriage fresh. Each month, when I went to the mikvah, the cleansing waters would almost restore me to my innocent bridal state, the night that followed like a recurring honeymoon. I picked up a lace-fronted book called *Dear Kallah,* a book addressed to brides like me that came highly recommended by the teacher of our class. Here in this sweet and well-meaning book was advice for how to create a blissful and tranquil home. We had found the life partners whom God sent to us to complete our souls; now our task was to carry out His work by ensuring that we built houses filled with peace and love and service of God. It all sounded nice enough, so why, as I leafed through the pages, did the easy prescriptions make me feel enraged? When I arrived at a chapter called "Thoughts to Banish," I wanted to scream. I wasn't married yet, but already happiness seemed far more complicated than the book's recipe. It sounded—could I let myself say this?—like a wishful fantasy. More than that— did I dare say what I really thought?—these easy promises sounded like lies.

A month before the wedding, I went to pick up the fall, which was stored on a towering shelf of other wigs, all in cardboard boxes bearing the names of current or former Broadway shows, mine inside one labeled *Beauty and the Beast.*

"Here's what you do," John said as he pulled out what looked like a small brown animal. He showed me how to arrange my hair to cover the seam between real and fake, how to attach the fall using the small clips, called wiggies, sewn to the mesh cap.

I practiced as he showed me. On my first attempt, it looked as though I'd recently undergone brain surgery and a part of my head had been left unsewn. After a few more tries, I managed to cover the gap, but because the fall was nowhere near as curly as my hair, it was immediately apparent which curls were mine. The fall lay atop my own hair, a halfhearted outer layer.

"Don't worry," John assured me, "it looks fine. Only you know what's real and what's not."

"I FEEL LIKE I'm in this alone," I said to Aaron on the phone one night as our fighting grew more intense. It was two weeks before the wedding, and I was home in Memphis, in my childhood bedroom.

"I don't understand what you mean," he said plaintively, making me feel bad for saying it. There was a soft-shelled innocence to him, a wide-eyed child so easily hurt.

I didn't know I felt that way until I said it, and even then, I didn't know what I meant; I just knew that when I was with him, the deepest parts remained untouched. I longed to know what he really thought and to be able to say what I really thought; to talk so that we uncovered the pieces of ourselves we didn't yet know. Yet I came away from our conversations with a feeling of having drilled into a wall only to see the plaster give way and crumble in my hands. This was a problem, I knew, but it still seemed hard to know how big of a problem. I'd heard stories about people who broke off their engagements, but that seemed a terrible fate, rendering you both damaged and alone.

"I'm sorry," I offered, learning early on that sometimes there was a choice between peace and honesty.

"I'm sorry too," he said.

When we hung up, I got out of bed and looked at the white lace dress hanging in my closet. I wanted to wear that dress. More than anything, I wanted to be that girl. My eyes were once again red from crying, and I knew from experience that they would be even redder and puffier in the morning. I put two spoons in the freezer, a trick I'd come across recently in the beauty section of a magazine. In the morning I'd place one cold spoon over each eye, a healing balm that I wished could soothe not just my eyes but all the nervous parts.

I counted the days. In the week leading up to the wedding, I checked myself with the small white cloths to ensure that there was no bleeding. A few nights before my wedding, I soaked in the tub, combed out the tangles in my hair, cut my nails, smoothed my calluses.

"Are you excited? Are you nervous?" my mother asked me as we walked into the mikvah, which was in the back of our synagogue, with a separate entrance to ensure privacy.

"Both," I said.

The only other time I'd been inside the mikvah was a few weeks before, when we'd immersed all the new dishes and wedding gifts in it—like women's bodies, utensils, pots, and plates had to be immersed before they could be used. This was the mikvah to which my mother went. Once a month, she would go out on an unnamed errand, and when she came home, her hair would be mysteriously wet, as though she alone had been caught in a rainstorm. By the time I was a teenager, I understood where she'd gone, but aware of the privacy that surrounded this ritual, I didn't say what I knew.

Inside, there was a bathroom with a shower and tub. In an adjacent room, there was the small pool—enough space for one person to stand comfortably with her arms outstretched. Above was a large round opening in the wall for the mikvah lady to watch through, to ensure that every part of the woman was fully under the water. In the bathroom, I showered again and forced a comb once more through my thick hair so that all the curls were disentangled. The comb ripped out strands of my hair but I wanted to follow the law precisely.

"I'm ready," I told the mikvah attendant, peeking out from the small room.

She looked me over for any dangling cuticles or stray hairs that would constitute a separation between my body and the water.

"Very good," she said.

I descended the steps. Here was the portal to adult life — once a girl, now a woman. I went under, hoping the water would rinse away any unease and uncertainty. I dunked twice more and said the blessing. Here was purity and here was holiness and here was a way to smooth out all those rough edges.

The next day, in the Peabody Hotel — a historic Southern landmark — a crowd of men danced around the mezzanine en route to the *b'dekkin* ceremony, always my favorite part of a wedding. Most of the tourists assembled in the lobby — there to watch the hotel's famed ducks march out of the fountain where they swam all day and get onto the elevator — had little idea about Judaism, let alone why a band of yarmulked men were singing and dancing. In one of the ballrooms, I sat in Venetian lace, flanked by my mother and mother-in-law, by my sister and sisters-in-law, by my row of bridesmaids in matching teal. As Aaron was danced to me by our college friends, approaching under a canopy of arms, all the arguing of the past few months seemed to disappear. A few minutes before, our mothers had stood together, taken a plate wrapped in a napkin, and broken it, the mark of our formal betrothal and a symbol of all that was unalterable in life: once broken, the plate could be glued together but never fully restored. Two male friends had signed the *ketubah,* the marriage contract, which, I had been taught, was designed to protect women's rights at a time when this was unheard of; though it might seem archaic to me now, I was supposed to regard this ancient document as groundbreaking. In it, the groom pledged to support, honor, and cherish his bride in accordance with the laws of Moses. The details of the acquisition of the bride were spelled out in Aramaic, along with the specifications for how many *zuzzim,* an ancient form of money, would need to be paid to me in the event of divorce — not because we would ever, God forbid, need these stipulations, but simply because the laws required this.

May God make you like Sarah, Rivka, Rachel, and Leah. May He bless you and keep you. May He shine His light upon you. These were the words my father offered with his hands resting gently on my head. Aaron's father and both my grandfathers also blessed me, like well-wishers saying goodbye to someone setting out on a journey. They stepped back and Aaron stood before me, his face close to mine, and we whispered that we loved each other, we were ready to get married, ready for whatever came next. He took a long look at me, symbolically checking, in the tradition of the biblical Jacob, who had been tricked into marrying the wrong sister, that he had the correct girl. We would make no such mistake. Certain that I was indeed the right one, he lowered the pearl-studded tulle veil over my face.

In accordance with the tradition that all brides are to be unadorned, equal in the eyes of God, I took off my engagement ring and gave it to my sister to hold, gave my pearl earrings and necklace to my friends, talismans that they would get married soon. I walked down the aisle on the arms of my parents, the veil casting the room in an ethereal white haze. Under the wedding canopy, which was supposed to symbolize the home we would build together, I circled Aaron seven times. My mother and mother-in-law held the train of my gown as, with my body, I symbolically built the walls of our house, as I affirmed that he would be at the center of my life. We stood beside each other and I swayed with quiet fervor. All that was good, and all that was true, and all that would happen to us, please let us remain protected and tightly held. After all the fighting and all the worry, please let this have been the right choice. Please let us be happy.

In accordance with Jewish law, I didn't say a word as I held out my hand and Aaron placed the ring on my finger, my silence my consent. Technically, he was acquiring me, but not really. We weren't bound by that literal meaning of these words; we would keep the laws, yet create a marriage in which we were equals. With his foot, he broke the glass—really a lightbulb that would shatter easily—wrapped in the caterer's thick white napkin so no one would be harmed by the slivers. A broken glass, because even in a time of joy, we remembered the destruction of the Holy Temple. A broken glass to remind us that both life and marriage were fragile.

The ceremony ended in a crush of hugs and mazel tovs. We were swept into the dancing circles, men with men, women with women. It was a celebration not only of our marriage but of everything we believed. I was handed a maypole and together Aaron and I stood on a chair in the center of the circle. With their arms outstretched toward us, our friends held on to pink and purple satin ribbons and danced around us. We were marrying not just each other but the community as well. I had never felt so loved, so securely within.

Near the end of the wedding, the men gathered on one side,

the women on the other, and as the groom did at every wedding we attended, Aaron sang the Aishet Chayil—a traditional song praising the ideal Jewish woman.

A woman of valor who can find? Her price is far above rubies. Her husband's heart trusts in her and he shall lack no fortune.

Our families came together and stood beside me. Our friends swayed back and forth in rows, singing along with the words that we all knew by heart.

She opens her mouth with wisdom and the teaching of kindness is on her tongue. Grace is false and beauty is vanity. A woman who fears God should be praised above all.

I was written into these verses, one of these women now. There would be no great adventure, but in this story, there was no need to journey to the places where you could get lost. I had followed the rules, had done what was expected of me—gone to Israel, then to college, and had fallen in love with someone like myself. I'd ventured outside but hadn't let it change who I was. At the end of the wedding, as our guests started to leave, we set off into the promised land of married life. I was in love with him. I was in love with the story.

⁓

THE HIGHLIGHT OF my niece's bat mitzvah party is an amen ceremony, a ritual that has become newly popular in Israel. At predominantly female gatherings, varieties of food are passed around and each woman makes the required blessing, followed by a chorus of amens. The goal is to make as many blessings as possible, then to add as many amens as possible, because every blessing, they say, opens the heavens; every amen rouses God.

Before the ceremony begins, the guests are asked to write down the Hebrew names of the people for whom we will pray. Some of these people are hoping for children, some for financial well-being, and some for a soulmate. The list of those in need of a soulmate is the longest.

"Are you adding your name too?" I ask Dahlia, who is writing down her friends' names on the page of those who are single.

"Of course," she says.

"Don't add mine," I say, and afraid that someone in this room already has, I check the list and am relieved to see that I'm not on there.

"Why not—you're a divorcée," she jokes.

"A divorcée," I repeat in an exaggerated tone, trying to imbue it with a scandalous feel. "Now you're more acceptable than I am," I tell her.

"No," she says softly. "At least you have kids. Being single is always worse. You don't know what it's like. Even now, you're not alone."

"It's true," I agree. "But there are different kinds of alone."

The room is filled with women, many of whom I've known my whole life. These women around me seem like the embodiment of goodness, the models for valorous wives who were selfless in their devotion to family and God. Women who, if they struggled, kept it hidden. *Don't you want to be as we are,* their siren song of certainty calls to me, *don't you want our happy homes, our beautiful families; don't you want our sense of purpose and most of all our faith that we are cradled in God's all-powerful hands?*

I feel stained, sour, riddled. I make strained conversation, deflecting any question about me with a rush of information about the kids, the safest subject behind which to hide. As far as I know, none of these women are aware that I'm no longer Orthodox, but my divorce is bad enough. I am now someone who needs to be fixed up on dates so that a suitable husband can be found, order to the kingdom restored. When I was getting dressed, I'd debated whether to wear a cardigan over my short-sleeved shirt and had brought it with me in case. Now I put it on.

When it's time for the ceremony to begin, small plates of food are passed around.

Blessed are You, God, King of the Universe, who creates the fruit of the tree, a woman says in Hebrew as she holds up an apple slice, and the women say amen.

Blessed are You, God, King of the Universe, who creates the varieties of grains, says one woman clutching a cracker, her face shaded by an enormous hat.

"Amen," the women say, resoundingly.

With their words, God no longer exists in the far-off plains of heaven. With each amen, He is here among them, capable of being swayed.

I feel lost, I text Ariel in between amens, hiding my phone in my purse. For her, seven hours earlier, it's technically still Shabbat, but because she isn't Orthodox, using the phone on this day isn't an issue for her.

Hold on to who you are, she writes back, and I study her words on the screen of my phone as though they can help locate me.

"Amen," I say along with everyone else but my voice sounds like it's coming from a place not inside me but beyond me. I wish

I could believe the gentle assurances that you can sway God with your prayers, that you can influence Him with your observance. To me, this feels like a magical proposition, an enchanted tale. I wish I could give myself over to the belief that there is a being who is watching our every move, a parent who will always come when we call. But I also know that wishing, wanting, doesn't make something true. The world offers its own refutations, which I hear loudest of all. Each time I hear a profession of certainty, the whisper *Not true* grows louder in my head.

Now it's my turn to make the blessing. A piece of apple is handed to me, and though I feel nervous — the words of this blessing, which I know by heart, might abandon me just when I need them — I hold it up like the women before me have done.

Blessed are You, God, King of the Universe, who creates the fruit of the tree, I say in Hebrew.

A chorus of amens in response to this blessing I have offered. I want to feel something, a small last stirring, a faint but still-present heartbeat of belief. But there is none. No rousing openness, no glimmer of possibility, nothing but a hard, unyielding silence.

This is an answer on its own.

You leave and you leave.

Cardigan on or off, it doesn't matter. I can't feel the belief that fills the people I love. It doesn't matter anymore what others believe. Outwardly you can try to match those around you, but you believe or not on your own.

THE NEXT DAY, at Mini Israel, a tourist-attraction model of the country, my brother and I walk together. "I need to talk to you," I'd told him on the phone before I arrived, but now I don't know what to say. All weekend, Akiva has purposefully met my eye, but it's been hard to look back with the same forthrightness.

"I'm not Orthodox anymore," I say and I finally meet his gaze. We take the winding pathway that leads tourists to replicas of famous Israel landmarks — the Bahai Hanging Gardens and the Jerusalem soccer stadium and the skyscrapers of Tel Aviv. The country, already small, is now traversable in a matter of minutes. His children tread like giants, one in Tiberias, another in Eilat.

He's not surprised. In his eyes, the path I've taken — from attending secular college and graduate school to becoming a novelist — has led me here. I am confirmation of the ultra-Orthodox belief that the outside world is indeed dangerous, that exposure to foreign ideas can harm you, that Orthodox feminism only paves the way out. It is for these reasons that he has chosen this cloistered life. Once, years ago, he posed this question: If you knew that half the wells in your neighborhood were polluted but didn't know which half, would you allow your children to drink from any of them?

"Don't think you can so easily walk away. A Jew can't divorce faith. It's not possible to do so. A Jew and faith are inextricably linked. When you don't feel it, that's when you cry out to God, that's when you scream," he says.

"I want to know what you believe," I say — not because I want to be swayed but to hear what it sounds like to live what you believe.

There is God, he tells me, and there is Torah. And there are mitzvot — the commandments — which we are required to do.

There is no greater joy he has ever experienced, he says, than to live in service of God.

"And what if you don't believe that?" I ask.

He pauses in rabbinic fashion, looking at me kindly from behind his small round glasses of the John Lennon variety.

"I can't prove it to you. I don't want to convince you. But to do mitzvot—this is the point. Be *mechalel* Shabbat—desecrate the Sabbath—or don't. But the reframing, the New Age interpretations of Judaism, this is *sheker,* this is falsehood."

"But what if you don't believe that?" I say again, feeling like a child who persists in asking a series of *why*s.

"To do an *averah*—a sin—it creates a *pgam,* a stain on the soul," he says. "Maybe you can no longer be the best judge of how you should live because of all the *pgam* on your soul." I feel like I'm at the doctor's, faced with an image of my internal organs riddled with disease.

I swallow hard at his words but welcome the honesty. From many in the Modern Orthodox world, I hear little talk of actual belief—instead, community is sanctified and extolled. I know this is important for him too, but it's a relief to hear someone speak of a belief that is unflinching.

In the distance, we can hear his kids yelling across this miniature model country that we have walked through several times during our conversation. His kids range in age from one to fourteen, the younger ones full of energy, the older ones growing into early adulthood, and I wonder if all of them will follow the path laid out for them. Surely for them, as for all of us, life will sometimes prove to be confusing.

"You can make yourself keep Shabbat and kosher, but you

can't make yourself believe. I've tried, and it's soul-deadening. You close up, you harden. You don't end up in the same place where you began — you're farther away for having tried to do it without belief," I say.

"Even then," he says, "you seek God."

You can believe and stay, or not believe and stay. In the end, the only choice is to stay.

"But —" I start.

"You're stuck," he observes, "you can't go left or right. The answer is to look up — toward God. Absence from God, the answer is God. Absence from belief, the answer is belief. Doubting God, ask God."

There's no secret panel to press on to release me. Outside of belief, he sees nothing but a black hole, but I am starting to see something else, a clearing, an open space. I know as never before: This is his story, the belief he has built his life on. It is not mine.

It's almost time for me to go to the airport and then back home to my kids, who are in a world that, from here, feels like a distant planet. He and his family will remain inside the life he has chosen.

However ironically, our conversation releases me. You can change your life and the lives of your children. You can live according to what you believe.

Part 2

Pizza

Bill's Pizza has oversize windows that open out to Beacon Street in the middle of Newton Centre. It is a few weeks after my return from Israel and the roads are covered with snow — outside, passersby peer in at this cozy restaurant scene. Josh is far too excited about this long-awaited outing to notice my trepidation at being here with him. I can't help but think about who might walk past and see us. I'm glad there's a long line — still time to ponder the theological implications of a cheese slice, still time to grab Josh and run.

As we wait, Josh eyes the toppings through the glass case. Every vegetable combination seems exotic, as do the speckled rounds of pepperoni. On the drive here, I'd told Josh there was one condition: we could order only vegetarian. In the codex of sins, plain cheese pizza is a misdemeanor, not a felony.

"One slice, please," Josh tells the man behind the counter.

"Actually, two slices," I add.

As we wait, I detect no signs of guilt on his face. My son is too young to know that food is as fraught as any other kind of plea-sure; he has not experienced the kosher-induced anxiety that in a new place, there might be nothing you could eat. For our hon-eymoon trip to Italy, Aaron and I had packed two kosher sala-mis, one in each of our knapsacks, and in every city we visited, we sliced them thinly with a plastic knife, afraid we'd run out of food before we made it to Venice, where we'd heard rumors of a kosher pasta restaurant. For us, there was nothing to eat in Rome, where, during August, the one kosher restaurant was closed; nothing in Florence, where we finished off the last of the salamis and, still hungry, drained jars of gefilte fish into the bidet of a *pensione*. The discovery of a kosher Häagen-Dazs in the Pi-azza della Signoria was as miraculous as the sight of Botticelli's *Birth of Venus* in the Uffizi nearby.

When Josh sees me watching him, a serious look comes over his face.

"I need to talk to you," he tells me, his voice hushed, his ex-pression earnest and intent. "Bend down," he says, and he whis-pers into my ear: "If one day I decide to eat pizza with meat on it, will you still like who I am?" he asks.

His face is unbearably solemn, his eyes trained on me as he awaits my reaction.

"Oh, Josh," I say, and as I look into his eyes, I feel my heart breaking open. Even at his young age, he knows the price to be paid for not following the rules.

This, more than anything, was the iron bar across the exit door—love was what tied you and kept you inside. Love was what you risked losing if you wanted to choose for yourself.

"Do you mind if I take off my hat?" I whispered to Aaron. We had been married for a little over a year and we were sitting at a reading at the KGB Bar in downtown Manhattan, a dimly lit room decorated with Russian memorabilia.

Every morning before I walked the six blocks to my graduate writing class, I stood in the bathroom of the apartment we'd moved into after our wedding, on 110th Street in Manhattan. I brushed, scrunched, and moussed the fake hair of my fall the same way I'd once played with my brush-hair doll, as I called it, a mounted plastic head of long blond hair that I'd braided and curled until, in a rash moment, I cut her bald.

I pulled some of my hair forward, clipped on the fall, then used my curls to cover the place where wig met hair.

"Can you come tell me if you see the line?" I called to Aaron from my spot in front of the mirror.

"I can barely see it," he told me when he joined me in the bathroom. "And only because I know it's there."

Wanting to be reassured, I looked in the mirror more closely. The fall might not have been a perfect match but there was a lot of hair, some dark brown, some reddish, some curly, some mere waves. How many people in my writing workshop would be looking for a nearly imperceptible seam along my head or would notice that the fake hair wasn't nearly as curly as the real hair? But no matter how hard I tried to convince myself that it was fine, I noticed how the outer layer of fake hair slowly separated from the underlayer of real hair. No assortment of bobby pins, no amount of spray or mousse could prevent this—despite all the coaxing and styling, my own hair would have nothing to do with this outside entity, my body rejecting this foreign object. Even worse, when I studied it carefully, I noticed the bump where the fall was attached to my head, a subtle glimpse of something rising from inside.

"It's too obvious," I said, and I ripped the fall off my head, then scrunched, curled, and attached it once again. Nearly a whole bottle of mousse, all in the name of God.

I started to say, "I hate this," but stopped myself. I didn't want to alarm Aaron with such an expression of discontent. I was supposed to feel that, with each bobby pin, I was securing our relationship. It was the early years of marriage, a sanctified time. If we'd lived in biblical days, Aaron wouldn't have been drafted to war during the first year to allow him to spend time rejoicing in me, his bride. For us now, it meant that we were supposed to think of this period as an extended honeymoon.

Only once the wig was close to undetectable would I leave for school, trying not to think about my hair and to focus instead on the novel I had started writing, about a woman who converts to Judaism and moves to the Orthodox community in Memphis. I knew that I was supposed to portray Orthodoxy in largely positive terms—any critical sentence could make people angry. Sometimes I read a few pages of what I'd written to my mother, and she'd laugh in appreciation, then worry what the communal fallout might be if it were ever published. I worried as well. Anything that did not uphold or affirm—could you think it? Could you say it? Even worse, did you dare write it?

Yet being a writer, I was learning, required a willingness to cast aside these restrictions. To write was to enter an underground that was rich and teeming—the world wasn't a single fluorescent-lit room but a house with corners and hallways and passageways to explore. *I lived in a small, small box in which I could barely breathe* read the opening to a classmate's novel in progress that we'd discussed that week. I'd put a check mark next to this sentence, then read it again, surprised by the power it had over me. I didn't think I felt that way, not really, but something stirred inside me. *I love this,* I scribbled in the margin, but what I wanted to write was *I'm afraid I am this.*

Walking six blocks up Broadway to the Columbia campus, I was distracted by the word *wig.* The sound of the wind: *Wig, wig.* The metal clips were supposed to be fail-proof but what would happen if my hair fell off in the middle of class? If someone were to ask why I covered my hair, I could explain why this ritual felt meaningful to other people, but the truth was that I did it because I wanted to be seen by my community as the type of woman who covered her hair. I'd once heard a story about an Orthodox woman who was taking a chemistry lab and her wig caught on fire. Rather than rip the wig from her head, she'd tried to put the fire out, allowing the wig to singe. A few days later, so this story went, she got a new wig and came to class with hair that showed no sign of having been burned, claiming to have found a magic serum that restored burned hair. When I first heard the story, before I was married, I thought she was crazy for not ripping the wig off her head—it was on fire, after all—but now I suspected I would have done the same.

In the small crowded bar where many of my classmates sat in groups, Aaron and I sat by ourselves. Constantly aware of how I wasn't like the rest of them—married and Orthodox and trying to hide a secret I wore in plain sight on my head—I was painfully shy. We had each ordered a Coke; the food wasn't kosher, and drinking was foreign to us. Even though I was twenty-five and living in New York City, this—a crowded bar—was a place to which I was a young and uncertain visitor. Tired of worrying about whether I'd secured the fall exactly right, I was wearing a black baseball hat, so unobtrusive that I hoped it could pass for some kind of halfhearted fashion statement. Aaron was wearing a baseball hat too, over his yarmulke, a socially acceptable method of disguise, though his hat was emblazoned with the logo for the Boston Red Sox, the team and the city for which he pined.

After our wedding, Aaron's parents had wanted us to move to Boston, even though I still had another two years of graduate school in New York. I didn't want to move; since our engagement, the relationship with them had been fraught, and I worried that if we lived close, conflicts with them would overwhelm our new independence. Marriage was supposed to confer adulthood, yet our life together often felt like an elaborate version of playing house, the hats I wore little different from the ones in the bag of dress-up clothes I'd had as a child.

"Is it normal to fight a lot?" I asked a friend who'd gotten married a year before I did, viewing her as wise older counsel. I tried not to think about how quickly Aaron and I had gotten engaged so I wouldn't feel the awful worry that I had married before I was ready.

"It's normal," she said and assured me that by the second year, when we really knew each other, everything would be much easier.

I tried to listen to the reading but the hat was pressing tightly against my forehead, the brim cutting across my view. I loosened the buckle and pulled it farther back on my head but the line of the hat still felt too constricting, as though my entire body were being compressed.

"Do you mind if I take off my hat?" I whispered again to Aaron, hoping no one nearby would hear me.

He looked at me in surprise. Though I'd complained about covering my hair, it never seemed possible that I would actually stop. He was sympathetic, but I knew that, unlike me, he didn't feel as if the edges of Orthodoxy could close in on him. My question felt dangerous, as though I were asking about lifting off the marriage itself for a few hours.

"If you want to," Aaron said nervously.

I took off the hat and lay it on the table, next to our refills of Coke. Viewed from this vantage point, the hat looked innocuous enough, hardly the vise I'd come to see it as.

"Do you think it's bad?" I asked him as I shook out my hair and felt like I could not only see more clearly, but breathe more easily as well.

"I'm fine with it," he said.

"Are you really?" I asked.

"I can see the difference in you," Aaron acknowledged.

When we left the reading, I put the hat back on and took his hand as we walked. The hat felt tighter, as though my head had grown larger, my hair thicker. *It's a slippery slope,* the rabbi still present in my mind warned. It would be only this one time, I decided. I would try harder to keep covering my hair, just as I prayed every morning before I left for class, cooked Shabbat meals every week, immersed myself in the mikvah each month. Doubt would be stamped out, like a small fire. More than anything, I wanted to be the person Aaron had married—still the girl he'd seen when he lifted the veil at our wedding.

"Is everything okay?" I asked as we got ready for bed. Our

apartment was a prewar building set back from the street with a wide courtyard and peeling green shutters, the façade arrayed with stone gargoyles set up like sentries to watch over the building's inhabitants.

"It's fine," he said, but even so, I wanted to apologize. I couldn't shake the feeling that I had endangered us — as though I'd tarnished the wedding photo that was displayed by our bedside. Any sin, I knew, wasn't mine alone — now that we were married, we represented each other. If I didn't cover my hair, Aaron was less religious just by being married to me. We had signed the *ketubah*, the official marriage contract, at our wedding, but I knew that another contract existed between us as well. In this unwritten document that was equally binding and unchangeable, we agreed that we would stay the same as we were now. We would always be Orthodox, not just observing the rules but living within the communal expectations. When we had kids, we would move to one of the nearby Modern Orthodox communities in Riverdale or Teaneck, as our married friends were starting to do. We would send our kids to the Modern Orthodox schools where our friends sent their kids. We were young, but the years ahead were already scripted.

A few months after I'd briefly removed my baseball hat, I was walking home from school, and, amid the crowds of pedestrians, I caught a reflection in the storefront mirror of a Love's drugstore. A girl in a T-shirt and long beige skirt. On her head, a matching beige hat with a floral decoration, her dark curls barely visible under the brim. She looked strikingly familiar but my mind did a double take.

For one moment, I didn't recognize this religious woman as myself.

People bustled around me, in a Manhattan hurry, but I stopped walking. I stared at my reflection. It was hard not to rip off the hat right there, not to strip down on Broadway to the person I sensed waiting below. A voice, stronger than I knew I had, whispered in my head: *This is not who you are.*

I CONTINUED TO COVER my hair but started wearing pants again. I reveled in the long-lost pleasure of jeans — they hugged my legs and made me feel powerful, capable of confidently striding anywhere. Was it this feeling, I wondered, that was actually the most forbidden part? When I was in college, wearing pants had seemed like a grave sin, but now at least I didn't have to worry that the Orthodox boys I liked wouldn't date me. I still worried about being judged by my community, but being married bestowed a level of immunity.

"It's just this one thing," I assured Aaron, who seemed to be okay with it, though I didn't know for sure.

One day, I came home to a message on the answering machine. I'd shown a finished draft of my novel to the literary agent for whom I'd interned one summer and had spent the past three weeks in a state of nervous anticipation waiting to hear from her. Every time the phone rang, I jumped.

"I'm calling to say that I read your book and I loved it," the agent said in the message.

Thrilled, I went to meet the agent without my hat or fall. I felt as though I'd never before walked outside so bare, as though I'd gone out without pants or a shirt, but I couldn't imagine talking to her about my novel while feeling so false and covered. I was still afraid of any negative reaction to my portrayal of Orthodoxy, yet in the three years that I'd been working on the book, I'd fallen in love with the feeling—rare, but there some-times—that I could find a way past the erected barriers; the words were not in my mind but actually in my hands, my fingers sprinting freely toward the fences.

After I met with the agent, Aaron and I went out to dinner to celebrate, my hair still uncovered.

"I'm going to stop covering my hair," I told him and looked into his eyes, wanting him to see all of me. I tried to tell myself that this was just one more slight adjustment so that I could bet-ter stay inside, but I understood that when you began listening to that quiet internal voice, it might grow louder.

"I guess it's okay," he said.

"Are you sure you don't mind?" I asked, as though I were squeezing him for some darker truth. He was trying to be com-fortable with what I had decided, but I recognized the anxiety in his smile.

"Do you think you're going to change any more?" he asked.

"I won't," I assured him, but I too was uneasy. It was too late to change. Once you were married, you were supposed to know who you were. Unsaid, but present between us, was the story we both knew—not about anyone specific but a general threat that the good girl could inexplicably morph into something unrecog-nizable, a Medusa-like creature whom the laws could not tame.

Once I stopped covering my hair, I felt like I could see more clearly, as though I'd started wearing glasses I badly needed. I made a pile of my everyday hats and gave them to a friend who was getting married, saving only the dressy ones I would still wear to synagogue on Shabbat, where there was no choice. I wasn't sure what to do with the fall. It seemed like some sort of body appendage that should be buried with ritual and ceremony or else an unwanted item set on the windowsill so that the city birds could carry it off and make, somewhere in Central Park, a nest crafted from genuine human hair.

My own hair was matted from being covered and had thinned at the front of my scalp. Since getting married, I'd paid little attention to my actual curls. In need of restoration, I went to a Manhattan salon that specialized in curly hair. Here, curls were treated as exotic, endangered creatures. Rather than straightened, curls were sculpted, gathered, cherished. Before I'd covered my hair, I might have been frustrated with the unruliness of my curls, but now they were an indispensable part of who I was.

That week, I invited a tableful of Shabbat guests, as I always did, baked challah, made chicken and vegetables and kugels and desserts. Before Shabbat started, I set up my silver candlesticks, and when it was time, I lit the candles, waving my hands three times in front of me as though ushering the light toward me. Placing my hands over my eyes, I whispered the blessing, adding a prayer for our families, as my mother did each week, as my grandmothers had done as well. In doing so, I was linking myself even more with them, as though I were lighting my candles not from a match but from their still-burning flames.

Together, Aaron and I went to the synagogue across the street from our apartment. In recent years, the congregation had dwindled to a few old members, but friends of ours had started a Friday-night service there that was spirited and soulful — part of a small transformation under way in Modern Orthodoxy to create more participatory services. Instead of the women being relegated to the balcony, a divider was placed down the middle of the mostly empty sanctuary, and the women were invited to sit downstairs, separate but at least a little more equal. From my spot in the newly made women's side, I watched as the people in the wooden pews around me began to sing, melodically, joyfully. There was no perfunctory performance of obligation, no hurrying through to get home quickly. *Sing unto God a new song. Sing unto the Lord all the earth,* we sang in Hebrew. Columbia students and professors and neighborhood families, retired men who had come here since they were young, elderly women who looked askance at these changes but eventually relented and sang as well. *Let the heavens be glad. Let the earth rejoice. Let the sea roar.* I sang along with the others. All these contradictions and places of constriction—they weren't all that mattered. There was this too. The words of the prayers, old and new, above me and inside me.

Then, with our friends assembled around the folding table we'd set up in the living room of our apartment, I brought out the food I'd spent all day making, using the platters we had received as wedding gifts, feeling as though I were serving a piece of myself. When I cooked and served Shabbat dinner, I was like all the other Orthodox women I knew.

One week, we were invited to Shabbat dinner by friends of ours who'd recently had a new baby. Their silver candlesticks were lined up on the white tablecloth, three candles burning, one for each member of their small family. This was a scene I'd imagined whenever I envisioned how my life was supposed to look.

"I think we're ready to have a family," I said to Aaron.

JOSH'S QUESTION HANGS over me. *Will you love me if I'm not like you? Will you love me if I choose something else?*

"Oh, Josh," I say again. As we get our slices of pizza — oversize triangles with sturdy crusts and thick layers of cheese — I begin a series of proclamations. "I will love you whoever you are. I will respect the choices you make. I will not be happy if you harm yourself or others, but the decisions will be yours."

He's looking at me with eyes wide open, wondering if he can believe me. He wants to give himself over to my reassurance, yet already, at the age of nine, he understands that, given the world to which he was born, it's a complicated proposition. All I can do is assure him that, in my love for him, there aren't edges past which he can't venture. My love for him is capacious enough for him to grow and change; it has ample space for whoever he wants to become.

"You're only at the start of figuring out who you're going to be. You don't have to be held back by what others think of you. You have the right, the need, to decide what you believe," I say, trusting that he will understand at least part of what I'm saying.

I'm in high gear, speechmaking mode, talking too fast, with far more passion and honesty than he expected. His eyes are open wide as he listens intently to me. Any moment he will change the subject, to the Patriots or the Red Sox. His eyes will drift to the ESPN-blaring TV attached to the wall behind us, but until then, I'm saying words that I'm starting to trust, offering sentences that are becoming truer in my own mind as I say them.

"This is the most delicious pizza in the world," he exclaims, though I've privately decided that I prefer the thin slices at Regina's in Boston's North End.

"Life," I continue on, wanting to impart this not just to Josh but to my younger self, "is about exploring and grappling and growing. You're allowed to change, even when it's painful. You're allowed to decide who you want to be."

Josh has sauce dotted at the corners of his mouth. He is savoring the slice.

The Underworld

The day looms. Another Day of Judgment. In one week, on December 20, the divorce will be entered. Ninety days from now it shall be sealed.

In the school parking lot, where I'm sitting in my car waiting, chronically early to pick up the boys, I talk on my cell phone to my lawyer. I'm glad that none of the mothers who are also talking on their phones in their parked cars—all of us an armored fleet—can hear what I'm saying. They know, of course, about the divorce, but the details of how exactly one becomes divorced seem mortifying, like something bloody that ought to remain out of sight.

Even when I get off the phone, I feel exhausted from constantly thinking about the divorce. There has been fighting, far too much of it, for the most part done via text and e-mail. We trade recriminations. The commodity most plentiful is anger. How, I wonder, had anyone gotten divorced before the advent of electronic communication? Did people write letters? Actually speak on the phone?

There is a knock on my car window, and I startle. It's another mother, a woman about my age, not someone I know well. Until now, we've had only a few passing conversations as we're picking up or dropping off kids.

"Can I talk to you?" she asks tentatively.

Even before she says anything more, I know what this will be about. The grocery-store shunnings are something to which I've become accustomed, but there are also women who seek me out. These are fellow mothers whom I know from the kids' schools or activities. On the outside, they give little away, but quietly, they bear their own unhappiness. For them, divorce is not an unfathomable choice but one they can imagine all too well. I now hear about marriages that are closed off or shut down, about fights and standoffs and means of escape. We are the undercover agents who live among the happily married.

It's freezing out, so we sit bundled in coats in my car. She tells me how she and her husband have struggled for years; she had been afraid to act but realized that she had been thinking about divorce for more than half of her marriage.

"I've lived for a long time with the knowledge that I don't love him anymore. I haven't told anyone else," she says. "I can barely bring myself to say the words."

Until now, other people's marriages have always been the great mystery, a sealed kingdom that few outsiders can enter. It was possible to gather a few clues here and there, but everyone was afraid to say too much. Because what if you revealed more than people really wanted to hear? It was okay to gripe about a husband who didn't know how to bathe the kids or dress them, but it was not okay to confide a deeper sadness—what if you said that in your marriage, you felt lonely, and then the others retreated to safer ground? Your admission might dangle alone.

But in divorce, the gates are thrown open. There is no more illusion left to uphold.

"How long did you feel this way?" she asks. "When did you first realize how unhappy you were?"

Though she also wants to know about practical matters such as child support and parenting plans, what she wants more is to hear someone say, *I felt that way too.*

"There was no one moment — it was a slow erosion. I didn't want to know for a very long time, not until I felt like I was erupting," I tell her, and even now, it's a relief to say this out loud. I have become warier, more self-protective over these past few months. From each non-hello, I'm reminded that in certain quarters, my story is incomprehensible.

"And then it was all I felt. I couldn't do anything else. I couldn't let myself stop, because I was afraid I would be talked into staying. I was afraid I would get scared and turn back."

As I tell her more, relief becomes visible on her face. I've hardly offered her a map for how to leave — I'm still finding my own way out, and even if I knew the path to the other side, each leaving requires its own map. The trail disappears behind you. But still, this is the starting point — to name what is messy and painful and true. To hear someone else admit the truth you might suspect but that stays buried nonetheless — that you're not the only one, that the outer versions are just that and beneath are stories you can only begin to imagine. With someone else's admission, a door cracks open, and there it is: the entryway to an underworld.

BUSY WAS THE best place to hide. We had a son now and I divided the days between taking care of Noam and writing. Aaron was working long hours at his law firm, but this, we told ourselves, was temporary.

My first novel came out when Noam was a baby. Just before the book was published, someone in Memphis got an advance copy and told people that it was not flattering to the community. This copy was apparently passed around, with all the "not nice" passages underlined. I was surprised by the angry reaction, though I shouldn't have been. I had known that to speak too honestly was to walk a dangerous line. My parents, who were entirely supportive of my book, had previously been viewed as troublemakers for disregarding the need to speak only good of the community and its institutions—this was a trait that apparently ran in the family. Though we were in possession of the right number of generations, to be truly inside required a willingness to subsume any errant idea or opinion.

"I read your book," said a member of the community, too genteel to go on to say what she thought of it, but I knew how to decipher the meaning of her tight smile.

"Who do you think you are?" asked a more forthright community member I ran into in the kosher frozen-yogurt store.

As a daughter of the community, you should give thanks, not offer criticism, read an indignant, chastising letter I received from a high-school classmate.

Despite the negative reaction, I knew this was still my world. There was more space within Orthodoxy, I was sure. It didn't have to be so narrow and unyielding. If I were a critic, it would be from the inside. During the question-and-answer period at the end of a book talk, I was always asked: "Are you still Orthodox?" Always that word *still,* and always my same response. "I'm a liberal, feminist, pluralist Modern Orthodox Jew— whatever that means," I said, playing it for laughs instead of giving the longer, more complicated answer: I was Orthodox, even though I sometimes doubted. I was Orthodox, even though I sometimes chafed. It seemed less a statement of what I believed than a truth of who I was—its language, its rhythms, its customs, all part of me. Its weaknesses, its battlegrounds, its shortcomings, part of me as well. If I had attempted a longer answer, I would have said that I was willing to live with the contradictions and the tensions. I would have said that I didn't think I would ever leave this tenuous, unresolved position. I would have said: My parents and my siblings and my husband and my son are all inside. I would have said: This is my only version of home.

Now that I had a child, there was also less time to question what I believed. My son was my devotion. When he was born, we were going to a synagogue that met once a week in the basement of a youth hostel and fell on the liberal edge of Orthodoxy. Women were carefully given more roles in the service so long as these changes could be justified within an interpretation of Jewish law. The people who attended, mostly graduate students and young professionals, were interested in creating a religiously observant but left-leaning community. It was a break from the more established, organized structures of Orthodox life, but as Noam got older, we decided we needed some of that—at least some other kids and a play group. We started to attend one of the large Orthodox synagogues in our Manhattan neighborhood, where I sat in the women's balcony, looking down at the men in dark suits and yarmulkes, the view I had when, as a teenager, I had visited the U.S. Senate and peered down at the lawmakers from the gallery above. I still sometimes felt that low burn of resistance but I tried not to think about it. I had been taught that children needed to know exactly who they were. By becoming a mother, maybe I had to surrender the part of myself that questioned. I clipped on Noam's yarmulke. I didn't want to raise a child who wouldn't belong in his own world.

When Josh was born, four years later, I was finishing a second book, about two Orthodox families whose children marry. In my work, I continued to explore the boundaries of Orthodoxy, but in my life, I had come up with a way to stay inside. I would try not to focus on those parts of Orthodoxy that I disagreed with. I would craft a smaller segment in which I could live, one remaining sliver while a larger swath was washed away. Compartmentalizing was a way to remain within. Disengagement, I was realizing, could be a comfortable place to rest. I would keep kosher, observe Shabbat, go to the mikvah, follow all the laws about which there could be no discussion. I didn't need to be moved by these rituals so long as I continued to do them. I no longer made a point of regularly studying Jewish texts as I once had. I stopped praying every morning — not a deliberate decision but a practice that slowly fell away. I didn't go to synagogue every week, not because I was making any kind of statement but because I was staying home with my children. In Jewish newspapers, I read increasingly of intramural squabbles in the Orthodox community over women's roles and gay rights and the dangerous influence of the outside world, the battle lines drawn, rabbis more stringently patrolling the borders lest any outliers try to pass themselves off as Orthodox. I didn't agree with the positions espoused by many of the Orthodox rabbis, nor with the angry tones that they employed to enforce their views. These were presumably the leaders of my world, but they didn't have to speak for me.

Underneath this disengagement, lurking quietly, was a larger question: Did I believe in it? I had no clear-cut answer, but Orthodoxy, I was told, was not about belief but about actions. It didn't matter what I believed as long as I continued to observe and belong. If the threads of belief began to fray, community was the net that kept you from falling. God was the prerequisite, presumably, for the religion, but sometimes He seemed like an embarrassing parent of whom it was better not to speak too often. Actual belief seemed like a small line in the fine print of the membership forms. How hard is it, the man selling the grand all-inclusive package seems to say, to leave those questions unasked and bask in the rest of what we have to offer?

"Are you coming home?" I asked Aaron over the phone late one night, long after I had put both boys to bed.

"Soon," he said with an air of having been beaten down by the taskmaster partners at his law firm. He was doing the best he could, he told me; there was nothing he could do differently.

I fell asleep, then woke at two in the morning to discover that he hadn't come home yet.

"Are you still there?" I said over the phone in a groggy haze.

"It won't always be like this," he promised. I had been with the boys all day, not a moment to myself, yet I felt alone. But all I needed to do was try harder — to do everything for the kids and our home, to allow him to work as long and as late as he needed. *Try, try, try* — the word that kept me wound, in constant motion.

"COULD YOU SEE YOURSELF living in Boston?" Aaron asked me one night as walked together down Broadway.

It was a Saturday night after Shabbat had ended, and we had gotten a babysitter so we could actually talk to each other. We walked with no particular destination in mind, one of our favorite things to do in the city — just walk, taking in the people, the stores, the lights coming from the apartment buildings, as beautiful to me as any constellation of stars. I felt the urgency to enjoy the city while we still could — with a small apartment and two kids, I knew that sooner or later, we would have to move away.

At his question, I stopped walking. The expression on his face was plaintive. No matter how much we both loved New York, Boston was his home.

"I know we're going to eventually move," I said to him as we continued downtown, "but I don't know if I'm ready yet."

I tried to imagine piloting my children not in a stroller but a minivan. In the city, I could hold out a little longer against what I knew lay in wait. Memphis still felt like home, the place I would always be from, but New York had become the place I most wanted to be. Every day, with the boys in the stroller, I walked down Broadway feeling the pleasure that something unexpected could always happen. More important, here I could be Orthodox but feel anonymous. It was the opposite of Memphis, where the eyes of the community were always upon you. For this reason, I didn't want to move to a suburban Orthodox community like most everyone we knew had done and go to the same synagogue everyone else did and send our kids to the same schools and then to the same camps. Aaron and I had looked at a map and, with one broad gesture (unfairly, we knew), ruled out all of New Jersey, all of Long Island, all of Westchester — not the cities and towns themselves but the Orthodox communities, which were all we saw on a map anyway. Not wanting to be pioneers, we could go to only a handful of places, only to the discovered Orthodox world.

"I don't want to if you don't want to," he said. "It was just an idea."

I softened. "Would you have better hours in Boston?" I asked.

"Definitely," he promised, and I heard the desperation at how much he hated his job.

We went out to dinner for his birthday. It was our favorite restaurant, a gourmet kosher steakhouse where the best compliment you could give was that you'd never know it was kosher. After we ate, I handed Aaron a small box.

Inside was a silver-and-blue mezuzah to hang in the house we would live in in Boston. I couldn't wrap the whole of Boston for him as I wished I could, but I hoped that Boston would be, if not a cure-all, then at least a chance to fix what I had started to worry was in danger of cracking. I felt an unease below the surface, an anxious echo to my sentences, a slivered crescent of something lurking behind. I no longer believed that the parchment inside the mezuzah would actually protect us, but it could serve as a symbol of my attempt to make Boston our home.

On our last day in New York, I went back inside our empty apartment for one final look. At the sight of the bare rooms, I started to sob. I didn't want to move. But it was too late to feel this way. This was what we needed to do. I splashed cold water on my face and went outside.

We strapped the kids into the back of a Volvo station wagon, our first car, and we drove to our new home, a blue-shuttered white Cape house that was in the Orthodox community in Newton, Massachusetts. Housing prices there were astronomical, Jewish day-school tuitions equally so, but if you were Modern Orthodox, this was what you did. We joined one of the Orthodox synagogues and went every week. We sent Noam to the Orthodox day school where Aaron had gone. We didn't have to ask ourselves where we would fit in. A place was already carved out for us, our social life entirely intertwined with our religious one. I invited members of our synagogue over for elaborate Shabbat meals—a huge amount of work, but this was both the price to pay for belonging and its reward. All so that our children could grow up encased inside a community. All so that we wouldn't be alone.

WE'D BEEN LIVING in Boston for almost a year when my agent called to warn me that an essay criticizing a group of authors who'd written about Orthodoxy was slated to appear in the *New York Times Book Review* the following weekend. It was about a year after the publication of my second novel, and in the essay, a newly Orthodox writer called out me and a few other authors for being critical of Orthodoxy—and even worse, for presumably pretending to be Orthodox in the first place. She described her own recent transformation to Orthodoxy and her recognition that this way of life was good and beautiful. To be inside, she said, was to see it this way. If you didn't see it this way, you were really not Orthodox. I was accused of being negative, of writing characters who'd wrestled, doubted, and strayed, whereas real Orthodox Jews, this writer claimed, did not engage in such activities. In my novel, I had depicted a religious young man who, caught between desire and loyalty to the law, tentatively hugged his fiancée, but according to this essayist, everyone knew a man like this would never succumb to desire—he would probably not feel it in the first place.

How dare you say I'm not Orthodox? I e-mailed the author of the piece angrily (one of those moments when I should have been made to take ten deep breaths before pressing Send). I listed my credentials for her: I had spent my entire life inside this world. I kept strictly kosher. I went to the mikvah every month. I attended synagogue every week. My husband and sons wore yarmulkes wherever they went. That would show her! If observance was what Orthodoxy required of me, I had dutifully complied. I imagined the *Times* would now be forced to issue a retraction—after a careful investigation into my closet, my kitchen, and my bedroom, the editors turned religious judges would certify that I was, in fact, Orthodox, as claimed.

The week after the essay came out, I stood on the women's side of our synagogue in Newton, where I still felt like a newcomer, and sensed the question marks in people's eyes—as though under my camouflaging hat there lurked an impostor. I picked up Noam from school, and as he came out, in a yarmulke and tzitzit—the required ritual white fringes, which hung outside his sweatpants—I felt exposed. Unlike my son, I was clearly questionable. I read a piece a rabbi published in a Jewish newspaper attacking me for an essay I'd written in response to the *Times* critique; it was as though one of the small figures that had lived in my head all these years had come to life and taken up pen and paper. As I cooked for Shabbat, I read blog posts that parsed just how Orthodox I really was. I read an angry missive from a woman who demanded that I label my novels as fictional representations that bore no relationship to anything that actually happened in Orthodoxy.

You must have just had a bad experience, said one of the e-mails I received—a common trope, I'd come to realize, to explain anyone who didn't see the world as you did.

Most people would discuss their questions with a rabbi. You decided to write a book, read an angry e-mail from a woman who identified herself as a friend of my cousin.

I understood, and often felt, the anxiety about how we appeared to those on the outside—the sense that no one could really understand what it meant to live in this way—but I had believed that there was room for portrayals that showed the varieties of experience within Orthodoxy. I had wanted to reckon with the ways people lived not only within the sanctioned positions of the law but inside all the human possibilities between. I had wanted to write about the small transgressions and religious compromises people make and yet remain inside—that wily inner sphere that surely existed here as it did everywhere. But apparently, here there was no doubting, no desiring, no wandering, no wondering. Just a single shelf of sanctioned stories—stories of compliance and cohesion. Orthodox Jews went to synagogue. Orthodox Jews had Shabbat dinner with their families. Orthodox Jews were good and content. There was no other story.

Each month, I tallied the days of my period. I checked my underwear for any signs of blood. With small white cloths, I inspected myself for staining and counted out the days that I was clean. Then I went to the mikvah in Brighton, a fifteen-minute drive from my house. We had been in Boston for a few years by now, but it was still hard for me to drive in what felt like an unfamiliar city. Despite the hope we'd both felt when we left New York, Aaron continued to work long hours, and I had given up believing that the underlayer of unease might lessen. All I could do, I decided, was try to accept that this was how it would always be. I longed to be back in New York, where I had walked everywhere, my eyes ravenously taking in the buildings around me and the bustle of people. After barely driving for all the years I'd lived in Manhattan, the car was now my primary means of transportation. Though I'd driven on the highway as a teenager, I'd let too much time go by without doing so, and now I was afraid. I limited the places I went, plotting out routes carefully, avoiding those areas where it felt too hard to drive. I told few people about my fear, making up excuses for why I couldn't go certain places. More than anything else I did, driving was how I knew I wasn't from here. Bostonian drivers were a different breed than the deferential Memphian ones; in Memphis, the only time you honked was when you were passing a friend and wanted to say hello. Though I'd always had a terrible sense of direction, I'd foolishly decided not to buy a GPS, preferring to study the maps, trying to take hold of the city in my mind, to grasp its turns before I got in the car and had to navigate this place that I was sure would never feel like home.

With the mikvah, I had no choice about going. There was an appointed night and an appointed time and I went as I was required to. I studied the map and nervously set out. One night, I drove there as I had every month, but traffic was heavier than usual. My cheeks burned and I gripped the steering wheel tightly. I didn't want to always be this way. Though it was hard to envision how my fear might ever lift, I promised myself that I would get over this by the time I turned forty. I was thirty-four then, so it felt far enough in the future as to seem unimaginable.

It wasn't only driving there that I didn't like. That night, and every time I went, all I wanted to do was get in and out as quickly as I could. I soaked in the tub, showered, pumice-stoned my heels, trimmed my nails, and reminded myself that this ritual was beautiful. In the mikvah, there was no safe spot of disengagement. The laws were written across my body. Out of the shower, I started to work on my hair, which had grown past my shoulders, and tried to convince myself that this act lay at the heart of what it meant to be a Jewish woman. It was dangerous to admit that I didn't necessarily think this was true — even one's own self couldn't be trusted with such treachery.

Once I completed the list of required preparations, I called to let the mikvah lady know I was ready, and in a white terry-cloth bathrobe, I came out of the room. I loosened the robe and she checked my back for any stray hairs that would constitute a separation between my body and the water. Once my back had passed inspection, she motioned for me to hold out my hands so that she could examine them for any hangnails or remnants of nail polish. She checked my toenails, making sure they too had been clipped and scrubbed.

The privacy of this place was essential but when she checked my body, it wasn't just her eyes on me but the eyes of the community, the eyes of the rabbis, the eyes of God. Everywhere you were supposed to be covered, yet as an Orthodox woman, you were always subject to inspection. When we still lived in New York, I had occasional spotting between periods, so sometimes I had to put off going to the mikvah (you couldn't go until you had had no bleeding for a certain number of days). I was trying to get pregnant at the time, and since you couldn't have sex with your husband until after you'd been to the mikvah, I grew concerned that we were missing the time when I was ovulating. Some Orthodox women, I knew, struggled with this for years, unable to get pregnant because the laws prevented them from having sex when they were most fertile. Ask a rabbi; this was what I had been taught. I called our synagogue and talked to the assistant rabbi, who told me to bring over the stained cloths with which I'd checked myself. I went to his office in the synagogue, where I stood hesitantly in the doorway, not sure just how embarrassed to be. He appeared uncomfortable as well — he probably wanted to look at those smeared cloths as little as I wanted to show them — but in the alleyway outside, he held them to the sunlight and squinted at the stains as though he were a doctor making a diagnosis. Finally he decided that I was indeed permissible.

"Can you comb your hair a little better?" the mikvah lady in Boston asked me, taking my curls in her hand and shaking her head in dismay.

I was surprised — she'd never before said much to me, only picked a few hairs off my back or motioned to a hangnail I needed to snip. Long ago, I'd been taught that each time I immersed myself, I would be like some incarnation of an innocent bride once again. Maybe that was what it was supposed to feel like, but at her request to comb my hair better, all I wanted to do was put my clothes back on and get in my car and head in the opposite direction of Newton, into the lights of the city of Boston, where I was also afraid to drive.

Not knowing what else to do, I went back into the small bathroom, held the comb to my hair, and looked in the mirror.

Do you believe in it? I asked myself.

Orthodoxy wasn't about belief, it was about observance, I fought back.

Do you believe God cares about you combing your hair?

It was part of a system; it wasn't about just this one rule but all of them.

But do you believe in it?

You didn't have to believe; you just had to observe.

But do you?

It was a question I thought I had buried sufficiently, and it was alarming to hear — a once-mischievous old friend now returning to make serious trouble.

I looked at my hair. My quiet unease broke open. It didn't matter what she'd asked. I wasn't going to comb it again.

"I can't," I told the attendant when I emerged from the room a second time.

She raised her eyebrows in confusion, as though what I'd said made no sense.

"I can't," I said again. Nothing in my life felt as certain as this one sentence.

She gave a small, perturbed shake of her head and quickly inspected the rest of me without pointing out any other area where I had fallen short of the rules. Maybe she saw the resoluteness in my eyes. Maybe she was calculating that the sin would be on my ledger, not hers. Maybe I would be inspected more thoroughly in the future, the mikvah equivalent of a no-fly list.

With resigned approval, she stood watch as I walked down the steps into the mikvah. I went under the water, my fists loosely clenched, my eyes lightly closed. I came up and crossed my arms over my chest as I made the blessing praising God, King of the Universe, who commanded us to immerse. The water might have been there to cleanse me, or purify me, or maybe it was supposed to remind me that life could flow freely like a river or a stream, but as I dunked twice more, I was sure of one thing: It wasn't possible to change my life. I might have been young, but it was far too late. I was pinned in place like the bugs in the collection I'd had to amass for my sixth-grade science class. I'd caught spiders and beetles and moths in a glass jar and placed a cotton ball soaked with nail-polish remover inside. I'd watched, horrified and fascinated, as they flittered and scurried then slowed, their legs no longer moving, their wings no longer flapping. When they were dead, I carefully emptied them onto a Styrofoam board and stuck a pin through each hard body.

The water washed over me. I would continue trying, as I always did, but even so, I hoped that one small part of me was shielded, one spot of tangled hair, perhaps, where the water couldn't penetrate.

"Kosher," the mikvah attendant pronounced. "Kosher."

A YEAR LATER, I gave birth to my daughter. For a girl, there is no equivalent to a Shalom Zachor, the traditional celebration welcoming a son on the first Friday night after his birth; no ceremony on the eighth day as there is for a boy, his circumcision marking God's covenant with the Jewish people—or at least, His covenant with Jewish men. I was glad I didn't have to witness another circumcision. At the ceremony for each boy, I'd waited, in horror, for the deed to be over. This was what countless Jewish mothers before me had done, and only fleeting in my mind was the question, *Is there a choice?*

I wanted to do something, though, to mark the birth of our daughter. A week after she was born, we had a Simchat Bat, a celebration for the birth of a daughter, a tradition that had become increasingly popular in the Modern Orthodox community. At the ceremony, I talked about how Layla was named for my father's mother, who had died unexpectedly when I was fifteen. In the weeks after, my grandfather had come to stay with us in Memphis and sat in the backyard staring out at nothing, tears silently rolling down his cheeks. That he had loved her deeply was something I hadn't needed to be told — it was evident to me, even as a child, in the way he helped her make dinner, cutting the vegetables for their meals; in the way, when she was older and it was hard for her to bend over, he painted her toenails for her. Before any of this, she had been a Phi Beta Kappa from Duke; she didn't get married until her early thirties, when she returned to Hampton, Virginia, where she worked in her parents' store and met the new young single rabbi in her hometown synagogue. Like my maternal grandmother, she became Orthodox when she got married. In naming Layla after her great-grandmother, we were tying her to tradition, our own version of the blessing we would bestow upon her every Friday night: May God make you like Sarah, Rivka, Rachel, and Leah.

As my daughter nursed, I ran my hands over her tiny legs and silken cheeks, marveling at the mystery of such a small creature, the fact that inside her head, a world was awakening. Looking at her blue-green eyes and fuzz-dusting of blond hair was like waiting for a picture to come more fully into focus. So far, little had been imprinted on her but each moment, even right now, was shaping who she would become. It felt too late for me, but was I going to offer her words that would stick in my mouth as I tried to say them? Orthodoxy, or at least our small corner of it, had continued to evolve, changes forged by women I admired. Maybe my daughter wouldn't have to feel the inequalities and the constraints as viscerally as I did. But even then, would I have to teach her the tactics I used to remain inside? *Don't say what you really think. Don't name what you really feel. It's not what it sounds like. It's not what it really means.* I didn't want her to feel that she had to tuck away any dissenting part of herself. I didn't want her to feel that the only choice was to live with an endless sense of obligation and contradiction. *Try not to be bothered by things that make you seethe. Try not to feel exhausted from walking against an ever-present tide, the current pulling your body, the sand slipping away beneath your feet.*

I touched the indentation under her nose—the legend I'd been taught was that a baby in the womb is taught the entire Torah, then, before birth, an angel slaps the baby's face, causing the infant to forget what he or she has learned and leaving this mark. Was it already determined who my daughter would become, this world encoded inside her, its rules a submerged memory, a hazy blueprint?

My daughter slept and she woke and she continued to nurse. "Be happy," I whispered in her small soft ear. "Be free."

⁓

My phone rings as I'm sitting in my car in the school parking lot, early again, waiting to pick up the kids. This time it's my sister Dahlia calling.

"I'm getting engaged," she tells me.

"Mazel tov," I say, thrilled for her.

Her voice is filled with excitement, but at the age of thirty-seven, after so many years of being on her own, she finds it hard to take this step without some nervousness as well. It occurs to me that we won't both be married at the same time. At my wedding, when she was newly returned from her second year of studying in Israel, I would never have imagined she would be so long unmarried, but then, I couldn't have imagined how any of this would turn out.

Over the next few weeks, Dahlia and I discuss arrangements for her wedding—she and her fiancé have decided to get married in Israel in May. We also discuss my divorce, so our conversations veer from wedding menus and invitations to parenting plans and lawyers' fees.

"Does my divorce scare you?" I ask her.

"Of course it does," she says. "There's no way to know for sure."

To someone newly engaged, am I the best person or the worst to give marital advice?

"I remember how nervous you were when you got engaged," she tells me, recounting how, in the weeks leading up to my wedding, I had cried to her on the phone, worried about the constant fighting between Aaron and me, but neither she nor I had known what to do. It seemed like a fixed rule: I was a bride, therefore I was happy. There was no way to make the reality conform to what we both believed to be true, and both of us were too young and unpracticed to know what to do with any apparent contradiction.

"I was twenty-two. I'd barely had a boyfriend before that. I was scared out of my mind—but I was even more afraid that if

I didn't get married then, I'd end up single forever. I thought that was the worst thing that could happen. I had no idea how to be alone."

"Of course I feel nervous," she says. "But I know that this is what I want. This is what I'm choosing."

In her voice, there is confidence and a sense of calm. She sounds happier than I've ever heard her. I think back to the different people she dated and the pain she suffered when a relationship didn't work. I think back to her descriptions of what it felt like to have the word *single* emblazoned on you, as though it were a deformity. All those times when I stood in my married-couple's house and listened to her, I'd let myself believe that not getting married was the worst possible outcome in life. But she had a strength that I hadn't possessed — she hadn't allowed others to convince her to do something she knew wasn't right for her, nor had she tried to convince herself. I am filled with happiness for her now. Despite the pain of relationships that didn't work out, despite the years of pressure and uncertainty, she waited — not just until she found the right person, but until she became the person she most wanted to be.

⁓

"Do you want to do something a little crazy?" my friend Dena asked me when Layla was almost two years old. Our lives mirrored each other's; we went to the same synagogue, had the same observances and patterns of the week. We invited each other for Shabbat meals, sat next to each other in synagogue, traded recipes and details of our lives.

To my surprise, she wanted me to go with her to Crystal Lake late one night and be the equivalent of the mikvah attendant as she immersed. She said she couldn't bring herself to go to the Brighton mikvah where she usually went.

Going to the lake did sound a little crazy, but in a good way. Immersing oneself in a natural body of water was hardly a trespass against religious laws—I had been raised on countless stories of the devout women who walked on the most frigid of nights across the harshest landscapes of Russia to immerse themselves in the icy Black Sea. On vacation once with no mikvah nearby, I had no choice but to immerse myself in the Atlantic Ocean. I went to the beach early in the morning—though you were supposed to go to the mikvah only at night, I had made this compromise because the thought of being naked in the ocean at night seemed too scary. Aaron stood on the beach watching me as I swam out, removed my bathing suit, and quickly dunked under the water, hoping no one else would see what I was doing. But these outdoor mikvahs were regarded as options of last resort. In suburban Newton, with an established mikvah nearby, this excursion to Crystal Lake would surely have raised a few eyebrows. I understood, though, why Dena wanted to go to the lake. Since the time I hadn't combed my hair well enough to please the mikvah attendant, I too no longer wanted to go to that mikvah and instead had started to go to a new nondenominational mikvah in Newton whose mission was to reinvent this ancient ritual and make it relevant and accessible to all Jews. It described itself as a place to mark not just the end of one's period but any rite of passage. Instead of inspecting me, the mikvah guide dimmed the lights and asked me how she could help make my experience more meaningful. The first time I heard this question, it caught me by surprise; so focused on fulfilling my obligation, I had given little thought to what I wanted this to mean. I went there each month for several years, even after an e-mail was sent to members of our congregation saying it didn't meet the standards of the Orthodox community. Even by complying with the rules, you could be rebelling. One more small transgression, one more air hole I was punching in the top of this box.

Once it was dark, Dena and I drove in her minivan to the lake, which had once been called Baptist Pond and used by a local church. She had brought a flashlight, and tripping, clutching each other's hands, and laughing, we walked to the edge of the water. We wondered what anyone who saw us would imagine we were up to. Swimming in the lake was prohibited by local ordinance, but there were rumors of swimmers who defied the rules and swam the length of the lake at night. Perhaps anyone who caught sight of us would mistake us for one of these stealthy night swimmers.

Standing on the shore, Dena and I talked about our marriages, one admission allowing for another. Neither of us was in any rush to get home. Out here, not under the eyes of inspection, not inside the official organized structures, it was easier to speak honestly. I told her about the novel I had been working on for a few years now, set in New York City, which I still longed for, about husbands and wives who were increasingly estranged. I hadn't set out to write about this but somehow had found myself in this fictional terrain and it scared me. Even though I always assured Aaron that of course I wasn't writing about us, I had come to understand that it was more complicated than just that. I told Dena how I constantly tried not to be bothered by the issues between Aaron and me—issues that included the division of responsibilities, religious differences, family, and the difficulty of creating emotional intimacy. We couldn't talk openly about the problems, so the only way around them was to act as if they weren't there, though this only exacerbated that underlayer of unease that I'd long felt. I'd started to think about the two of us going to couples therapy and I had collected a few names, but I hadn't done anything else about it. "I'm done," I sometimes told Aaron when the issues erupted into a fight, but the words vanished as soon as they hit the air, as though I'd never uttered them at all. When I talked to my mother on the phone, I confided in her about my marriage, but later told her I had just been upset and didn't mean what I said. Sometimes I cried to Dahlia, who was a therapist and therefore, I reasoned, wouldn't mind if I stopped pretending that everything was fine.

"What are you going to do about it?" Dahlia asked me.

"*Do?* I was planning to ruminate about it for the rest of my life," I said, only partially joking.

"People who are unable to make small changes sometimes end up making big changes," she warned me. I was intrigued by the possibility that change might one day happen to me but couldn't imagine it was something I would ever bring about. I was hardly the kind of person who would upend her life — I didn't know what that kind of person looked like, but I was sure she didn't look like me.

Across the lake, a train rumbled by. A few late-night walkers strode past us, in pairs or with dogs. Somewhere nearby there was the laughter of teenagers. Dena stripped down to her bathing suit and handed me her glasses and wedding ring. We looked at each other and laughed again. "Local Mothers Arrested for Skinny-Dipping in Crystal Lake," I imagined the headlines of the *Newton TAB*. "Orthodox Women Cited for Naked Water Ritual." I could barely see her as she walked out and crouched down so that the water covered her shoulders, then she wriggled out of her bathing suit and went under.

In a few months, this summer would end, and once again, there would be the start of the new Jewish year. No matter what feeble protests I launched, I knew that I would once again stand in my in-laws' synagogue on Rosh Hashanah and pull my hat over my face to try to cover what I felt.

Dena emerged from the lake and wrapped a towel around herself. After she dried off and put her clothes on, we got back in her minivan and she dropped me off at home. I had put the kids to bed before I left, and Aaron was at the dining-room table, working and trying not to fall asleep. Words played loudly in my head—my marriage didn't fill me, it wasn't enough—but they needed to be hidden at all costs, concealed weapons that endangered us all. Upstairs, I checked on my three sleeping children. If the word *divorce* ever dared to crest in my mind, the sight of the three of them sleeping unsuspectingly was enough to push it away.

I went to our bedroom, where I lay awake in one of the two twin beds that were pushed together or not according to the prescriptions of the law. It was hard to fall asleep, but when I lay awake, dangerous thoughts unfurled. If I thought about my marriage, I felt the spread of sadness. If I thought about religion, I felt a burn of frustration. Fantasy was the only escape. It could be enough, couldn't it, to live inside your mind? I spooled backward in time to the time before we got engaged and constructed different versions of my life. What if I weren't Orthodox? What if I hadn't gotten married so young? I could try to blame Orthodoxy for my choices, but really, I knew I had only myself to blame. I hadn't listened to that voice inside me that doubted whether marrying Aaron was the right choice. I had wanted to keep my eyes closed and force the reality to match the story I held in my head.

The next month, when it was time for me to go to the mikvah, I went to the lake. With Dena standing watch by the edge of the water, I waded out. The water was still cold, even though it was the end of summer. I slipped off my bathing suit and went completely under. Dena could hardly see I was here, let alone know whether my hair had been sufficiently combed. Alone in the water, my body made ripples that floated across the still surface. I lay on my back, took in the moon, which was low and full, and the sky lit with stars, a consolation for the loneliness lurking inside me. I felt more at ease being naked out here than I had in any of the indoor mikvahs I'd used. I didn't think of myself as someone who would be moved by a lake, by a night sky, yet for the first time, I felt some softness and easing amid all those callused places. If there was any sliver of meaning, any sense of God's presence, it lay in the feeling of being away from the rules, away from the official eyes.

ALMOST A YEAR LATER, I was invited to participate in the Orthodox Forum, a group of approximately one hundred rabbis and Jewish communal leaders selected annually to discuss an issue of relevance to Modern Orthodoxy. In past years, they had debated personal autonomy and rabbinic authority, and relationships between traditional and nontraditional Jews. This year the topic was Orthodoxy and Culture, and I, along with several other Orthodox artists, was asked to describe how my religious and artistic lives meshed.

Sitting at my desk in the alcove office off our living room, which I considered my small refuge, I answered the questions that had been sent to me, a welcome break from working on my long-unfinished third novel—no longer a book but a maze in which I was endlessly wandering. The more I wrote about marital unhappiness, the more stuck I became. I couldn't finish the book because I was afraid of the ending I might discover.

Behind me were all the books I loved, the novels and memoirs and volumes of poetry—these books were my refuge as well, as though the pages were green fields or night skies. On the other side of the wide entryway, in the living room, were the shelves of religious books, the volumes of Talmud and the Bibles, the works of biblical commentaries, books detailing the laws of the holidays.

Did I consider myself an Orthodox writer?

How did my Orthodoxy affect my work?

Did I think there was a conflict between being an artist and being Orthodox?

I was happy to take part in this interview—it seemed remarkable enough that these rabbis were engaging with the role of culture in religious life. Trying to sound reassuring, I said that I used Jewish sources in my writing, that our tradition encouraged questioning. Art didn't seek to threaten Orthodoxy. There was no reason for the rabbis to be afraid—art meant no harm; it came in peace.

I wrote this even though the words *allowed* and *forbidden, appropriate* and *inappropriate, nice* and *not nice* continued to battle inside me. I had wanted to believe that I would live my small quiet life but allow my mind to roam. You didn't have to live boldly as long as you could write this way. But could you write of doubt that gnawed through you; could you write of loneliness;

could you talk of wanting to escape and still go to synagogue each week and act as though you knew nothing of such feelings? Could you write of other people's urges to break free but keep your own always concealed?

A few months after I turned in my response, I was sent a copy of my answers along with all the others, which, like mine, downplayed the potential conflicts between being an artist and being Orthodox. I reread my initial responses and hated myself for the falseness. I e-mailed the interviewer to say I wanted to revise my answers. I couldn't be one more person who covered the truth in order to belong, couldn't be one more person who pretended so that others had to pretend as well.

I sat down at my desk. The words rushed out of me. There was a conflict, a terrible one. To write required freedom, but I didn't think you could create freely with the admonitions of Orthodoxy looking over your shoulder. Did you have to show your rabbi any potentially controversial scene and ask whether it was permissible — here, too, were you subject to inspection? What did it mean to write knowing you'd be viewed suspiciously by your community if you pushed past the comfort zone? What about stories that didn't confirm the official public version of Orthodoxy — what about stories that wanted to challenge or subvert? Even though what I'd written didn't overtly cross any line — there was no attack against Orthodox doctrine, no open disavowal of the rules — I knew that I had become willing to walk closer to the edge.

"I know what I'm supposed to say, but I hate writing something I don't believe," I told Aaron. I showed him my new responses as I debated whether to send them. By now, the uncertainty I used to see in his eyes had started to look like fear

—not just of what I was saying but of who I was becoming. By growing into a stronger version of myself, I was endangering us.

"I don't know if I can stay inside much longer," I said softly to Aaron. I still carried the residual sense that I was bad to feel this way, but I was exhausted from cloaking what I really thought, for fear of being too much of myself. Now when I confided in my mother, the words *I'm done* erupted out of me, but I couldn't possibly mean anything by it. "I'm done," I still said to Aaron when we fought, but I told myself I didn't mean that either. I had stood in synagogue on Rosh Hashanah the prior year and pulled my hat low over my face so I could continue to hide, felt like I was shrinking myself into smaller and smaller boxes, felt as if my head, my whole body, was being compressed. All this, yet I did nothing. Nothing could change, not me, not him, not the laws around us, not the feeling between us. The story we had once told about how we, so young and so innocent, had fallen in love now felt like a cautionary tale.

"I know, but I want to be Orthodox anyway," Aaron said pleadingly.

I hit Send on my e-mail before I could stop myself.

Would you be willing to speak at the conference? one of the organizers asked me in an e-mail a few weeks after I'd sent in my revised responses. He was appreciative of my willingness to be so honest and I agreed to come—I didn't want to feel that the only way to remain inside was to hide what I thought. There were Orthodox writers, of course, who didn't feel the conflict as I did, but I could no longer say what I didn't believe. If I was going to stand before this group, I was going to say what I really thought —even to do this seemed a transgression. And yet it seemed so clear to me, so true and necessary, to say out loud that here and everywhere, people lived and loved and doubted and despaired; people strayed and people wandered and people believed and people did not. All protestations of contentment to the contrary, this lay inside Orthodoxy as well. This was my personal truth, but this was also one of the truths of this world.

The conference was held at Yeshiva University in New York City, in a hall that happened to be housing the student art show. Behind the speaker's podium, a large banner proclaimed THINK OUTSIDE THE BOX. Waiting for my turn, I observed the other women in the room, the minority by far. I looked around—I was the only woman not covering her hair. Out of respect, I had worn a skirt, but I couldn't make myself put on a hat.

I'd given so many book talks that I could usually speak before a crowd without trepidation, but this time I was nervous. It was too late to turn back—the rabbis had my responses in front of them, so I summarized what I'd written. I quoted Cynthia Ozick that to be a novelist was "to seize unrestraint and freedom, even demonic freedom, imagination with its reins cut loose." By the time I finished speaking, the mood in the room had tightened. A slew of hands awaited me. In a closed world, the borders had to be protected, but sometimes the invaders came from within.

Was I saying rabbinic authority did not apply to me?

Was I saying I didn't believe that fiction needed to fall within the acceptable norms of Orthodoxy?

Was I denying that every art form came with its own limitations? Was I saying that there could be no boundaries at all?

Should we not concede that, based on what I was saying, all was lost—there was no possibility of art and religion coexisting, and we should all just go home?

I looked out at them, rabbis from synagogues in which I had

prayed, from schools that I had attended. These men were the deciders and enforcers of the law, and they were right to be bothered by what I was saying. I didn't believe in their ultimate power. I wouldn't submit my artistic freedom to their rules.

I find what Tova Mirvis is saying to be incredible, one rabbi said.

Praise! I thought. *Acceptance!*

Then he continued on. A doctor has to ask a rabbi. A lawyer has to ask a rabbi. An accountant has to ask a rabbi. But not Tova Mirvis. If you wanted to run a brothel just because you had a talent for it, would that be okay as well?

There was a chuckle and a small gasp of surprise. I grew calmer. As though I'd rehearsed this moment, I spoke in a voice long in coming with words that had slowly collected. I spoke, at last, with what felt like all of myself.

What about the messy reality of people's lives that differed from the mandated story? What about stories that claimed that people didn't always know, didn't always believe, didn't always observe; stories about people who weren't always content, about marriages that weren't always happy, about children who didn't always follow the path?

What about art that wasn't interested in making people see the beauty of Orthodoxy?

What about art that could unsettle you, change you, unleash you?

I knew that in a highly codified world, the inner life posed a threat. I knew that these rabbis' mission was to keep people inside the bounds of the laws. They didn't believe there were other good or true ways to live, didn't want their children or their students or their congregants to think that there was a legitimate choice to be made. I understood it, of course—I too had lived it. There was openness, up to a point. A measure of freedom, until you arrived at the border. There could be questions, as long as you accepted the answers given. There could be some sort of journey as long as you returned safely home in the end. There could be art, as long as it didn't pry open too many doors. There could be stories, as long as they didn't offer a viable other way.

"You can't create freely if you're always aware of where the borders of permissibility lie," I said.

"We can't tell our kids 'Think outside the box' as a slogan but not really mean it," I said, gesturing to the words on the royal-blue felt banner behind me. Pad the box, decorate it, disguise it, enlarge it—but no matter how small it felt, bend arm over leg over neck to remain squarely within it.

This moment, standing in front of this room of rabbis, was the last time that I considered myself still inside. *No,* every part of me knew. *No,* I didn't believe in the same God whose will they invoked with such certainty and *no,* I wasn't willing to write in accordance with their rules, and *no,* I didn't believe, really believe, their rules contained the ultimate truth, and *no,* I didn't want to create the same kind of enclosures, and *no,* their limits weren't ones I was willing to accept, and *no,* I didn't want to teach my children to heed these lines, and *no,* it wasn't just about writing honestly and freely, it was about living honestly and freely, and *no,* I couldn't keep trying to tuck away this feeling, and *no,* I was no longer willing to follow without believing, and *no,* I was no longer willing to pretend in order to belong.

THE NEXT SHABBAT, we finished dinner; the blue-and-white china dishes waited to be cleared, the remnants of soup and roasted vegetables needed to be parceled into containers and put into the fridge where the light was taped shut so it didn't turn on when I opened the door. The candles burned low and flickered before sizzling softly and leaving a trace smell of burn. When I'd lit them a few hours before, I thought, as I always did, about my mother and grandmothers, who had also done this every week. I had no idea if any of them ever felt the way I did, only that they had lived and raised their families as part of this world. If I were to leave, would I be ceding my connection to them as well; would they have ceased to claim me as their own?

All through dinner, Aaron had looked worried; he knew something was wrong but didn't ask what it was. I'd told him about the Orthodox Forum, but we'd both assumed that I would back down, as I always did. I might be upset, but it was impossible that I would ever act on those feelings. This was one of the truths of our marriage. I don't think either of us thought I would ever do anything about what I felt. We both believed that I was too afraid. But the feeling of standing before all those rabbis at the Orthodox Forum replayed continuously in my head. There, I hadn't hidden what I thought, and now it felt hard to do so anywhere. I couldn't sit at the Shabbat table, not this night, not any night, if I had to pretend.

I went upstairs to the bathroom, my phone smuggled in the pocket of my sweatshirt. Even with the door closed, I could hear the kids talking and running around, the bedtime routine waiting to be done, all of them in need of me to keep the night in motion. Somewhere buried in the basement was a one-time favorite toy of the kids, a set of plastic gears on a magnetized board, all of them needing to be in contact with the middle gear, the sole one turned by battery power. Watching the kids assemble the gears so that each of them was connected to that center gear, I'd always felt a sense of kinship: that one gear couldn't stop moving without the rest of them coming to a stop as well.

In a few minutes, I would go back downstairs, but right now, I made sure the bathroom door was locked. I stared at my phone. Could I actually break a rule of Shabbat, or would the forces of taboo and guilt, if not actual belief, hold me back? And if that failed, maybe the entwined loyalty to my marriage would keep me inside.

But *no,* I knew even more strongly now. *No,* I would no longer pretend. *No,* I could no longer hide myself away.

I turned on my phone—my first official desecration of Shabbat.

One sentence played in my mind, and this time I wasn't as afraid.

I do not believe it is true.

For the first time, I could face those words without flinching.

I can no longer live a life I don't believe in.

One sentence set free another sentence.

My marriage works only if I am willing to hide away the truest parts of myself.

My marriage works only as long as I agree not to grow.

I sat quietly with these words and allowed them to fill me with a sadness so large I felt like I could walk around inside it. Everything I was supposed to believe was cracking, a world I had wanted to think was vast and true suddenly small and breakable, a glass-domed object I held in my dangerous hands. My marriage and my Orthodoxy had been intertwined from the start. Leaving one would make it possible to leave the other.

It was terrible to think this, and it would be even more terrible to act on it, but I had arrived nonetheless at this moment of knowing. Until now, those words *I'm done* had been one more fantasy I didn't have to act on. They hadn't moved me toward action but consoled me and kept me inside. *Nothing can change,* my mantra of so many years. *Nothing can change.* All this time, I saw it as a prison, a curse, but I hadn't realized that it was also a crutch, an excuse, a prayer. Change felt as alarming as anything I might have done — so afraid of falling, so afraid of finding myself severed from all that was secure. All this time, I'd preferred to stay unhappy rather than take a chance on what was unknown.

I flushed the toilet to cover any sound that might escape the pink-tiled walls of the bathroom. I checked my e-mail, went on Facebook, read the *New York Times.* This might have seemed like an insignificant trespass, but if you were stitched inside by so many small rules, maybe you needed to undo them one at a time. I knew that leaving didn't happen with a single transgression, but if nothing else, it was a declaration to myself.

I felt oddly calm. This doubt had been here for so many years and now it emerged with a force that surprised me — this, the price to be paid for all those years lying in wait. I sat a while longer, flushed the toilet again to cover my prolonged absence, leaned my forehead against the cool tile of the wall. In the years in which I'd lain awake plotting escapes, I'd imagined some dramatic moment of departure. But sometimes leaving happens more quietly, not with any grand proclamations but with a single, still action.

"DO YOU BELIEVE the marriage to be irreparable?" the harried, black-robed judge asks as Aaron and I stand before her and our marriage is officially brought to an end.

It's a little late for this question and the ones that perfunctorily follow.

"Is there any reasonable chance of reconciliation?"

"Have you entered this agreement of your own free will?"

Yes. No. Yes. A few more questions, a cursory glance at the agreement, and it's over. There is still a ninety-day waiting period before we will be officially divorced, but that's only a formality. We walk out of the courtroom, Aaron and me and our group of lawyers, to the mezzanine, where we awkwardly confer over how we will transfer the outstanding credit card debts.

It's over and it feels like it will never be over. You can leave a marriage but you can never leave a divorce.

For one quick moment before we both depart from the courthouse, Aaron and I look at each other. All I want to do is avert my eyes but all I can do is keep staring. Here finally is the sadness I had long feared, but after all these months, it's a little easier to face. There is no choice, anyway — the sorrow stands in my path, no passage granted until I can cross through it to the other side. The anger has been a fire that raged and burned; it was a fuel pack strapped to my back, propelling me out. The sadness was the smoke that hovered afterward. After all the fighting and all the accusations and all the terrible anger, the sadness coats the barest of facts. It surrounds the truest of sentences. Once we were married, and now we are not.

The Freedom Trail

It's a Daddy Shabbat," I tell Layla.

When Aaron arrives to pick up the kids, I hug Noam and Josh goodbye and lift Layla over the snow that has been piled by the curb for weeks now. Not wearing a coat, I shiver as I buckle Layla into his car and whisper that I love her and will see her on Sunday.

"I always miss you," she says into my ear.

"I always miss you," I whisper back as my heart clenches. Here is the pain, the price still to be paid.

It's getting close to Shabbat by the time they drive off. On the weeknights when they go to Aaron's house, a longing for them sweeps over me, but even more so now, before Shabbat, when there will be no way to reach them. For this one day, I feel as if my children—my parents and sister too—are sealed off. With phone use forbidden, they are out of range, as though they are, or I am, in the farthest reaches of the wilderness.

When I go back inside, I don't light the candles. I haven't

bought challah. Without the kids, there is no Shabbat. I'm still unaccustomed to being in the house when they're not here, and I quickly gather my things to leave as well. Before I go, I dart into each of the kids' bedrooms and begin what has started to feel like my own ritual. I straighten their rooms and make their beds, a guilt offering and a wish to create order. Then, when everything is in place, I turn off the lights and gently pull shut the doors to their rooms.

I DRIVE TO William's apartment, a few minutes away. The street he lives on is heavy with traffic, as it is on most nights at this hour. Though I drive on Shabbat whenever I'm not with the kids, I'm still aware of the routes I take, wary of being seen. But now, alongside the fear there is also relief — seemingly so simple yet still immense to me, the fact that I'm not trapped inside my house, not stranded inside my own life. I can get into my car and drive. On this day, the automobile feels newly invented.

I let myself in and wait for William to come home from work. In his apartment, there are no traces of my kids or the past to fill me with longing, only pictures of his children, whom I've yet to meet, and a recent picture of the two of us, arms around each other, smiling. When I am in this apartment, I slip out of one self and into another — every time I walk in, I feel like I'm arriving somewhere new, but like a modern city in an old land, it sits on the ruins of what came before.

"Where do you want to go?" William asks when he gets home from work, energetic and eager to shake me from my lingering melancholy over missing the kids.

"Up," he says playfully to me as I lie on the couch. "Up, up, up."

We decide to take advantage of the night and go to the North End, the old Italian neighborhood downtown. Boston still feels like a place I'm getting to know — I've spent nearly a decade in Newton but I've rarely ventured into Boston itself. For all the years we'd lived here, I'd thought of Boston as a place that belonged to Aaron.

William drives through Coolidge Corner, the epicenter of the Brookline Orthodox community. On these four or five blocks, where there are several kosher restaurants, a kosher bakery, a kosher butcher store, two Jewish bookstores, and an Orthodox synagogue, people are walking home from synagogue, on their way to Shabbat dinners. I'm both inside the car and outside, looking at myself through multiple sets of eyes. It feels possible we might pass an old version of me walking as well.

"Did you have to go this way?" I ask William, half joking, and I tell him about a friend whose family drove on Shabbat but didn't want their religious neighbors to see; if the neighbors were outside when they drove past, they all crouched down — from the outside, it must have appeared as though the car piloted itself or was guided along its forbidden Shabbat journey by a phantom crew.

Though I feel the urge, I don't let myself duck. All that can happen, I remind myself, is that someone I know will see something about me that is now true. In William's car, on this night, here I am. This Camry of his can drive us not only to a new place but to a new time — not Shabbat but a regular Friday night.

William turns and we are in Brighton, another heavily Orthodox neighborhood, where the right-wing Orthodox inhabitants are easily recognizable by their dress, the men a parade of black and white, the women in long skirts and head coverings.

To them we are probably just another passing car, part of the outside world that exists in a different plane of reality. If they see me staring from the passenger-side window, they probably assume it's because I view them as exotic. There's no way they could know the opposite is true.

At a red light, two wigged women pushing baby carriages cross in front of our car.

"Is that what you used to look like?" William teases me.

"That's right-wing Orthodoxy. It's different from Modern Orthodoxy," I correct him.

"Modern Orthodoxy," he jokes. "Is that like liberal fascism?"

"Stop," I say, laughing even as I protest, playing, as always, the role of diligent explainer, still trying to teach him about the differences among the various groups and the various rules and various ways around the rules, how, for example, these women can push strollers because of the *eruv* that wraps the neighborhood, the symbolic thread that turns this street into private property.

"So God came down and said that if you tie a string around the neighborhood, it's okay to carry, and otherwise it's too much work?"

"It's all part of a larger system," I say, but every explanation I offer him yields another question. He can see it only from the outside.

"There are so many rules. If you follow them by rote, do you ever have to think about what it really means to be good?" he asks.

"Of course you do," I say quickly, but then I pause, knowing it's more complicated. His question burrows into me. Here lies the heart of it—not what he is asking but its opposite. When you're inside, good is a word that automatically belongs to you. When you leave, it's a word you surrender at the gate. Despite the very meaning of my name, being good is something to which I can no longer lay claim. Until now, I've still been asking the questions of my former world, just from the opposite side. Do I still observe? Do I not? Am I bad? Am I good? My answers might have slowly started to change, but these questions still form a tightly woven grid. I'd held on to them even once I'd left, because I didn't yet know what would take their place. Absent the rules, what gives shape to your life? In the unscripted world, what does it mean to be good?

We are almost downtown now, driving past the Public Garden and the Boston Common and the rows of old buildings all lit at night, this vast city full of life in which I've yet to take part. All the hard truths I'm supposed to know rush at me. I wanted freedom, and here it is — not the freedom of escape, not the freedom of fantasy, but a freedom that is confusing and daunting and complicated. In this freedom, there are no preordained questions, no easy answers, no ready definitions. No assurances of truth, no endless castigations about badness, but also no ready promises of goodness.

You leave and you leave again.

My life won't look the way I'd once imagined. One more separation from that image that has been so long fixed in my mind. *End this,* I tell myself. *End the vision of how it's supposed to look. End the urge to rebuild what you have already knocked down. Do not require others to believe as you do. Do not be someone who looks continually back at the place you have left.*

"I know it's time to stop thinking about what I've left. I need to decide what I believe now and then live it," I say.

"Maybe you need to ask yourself what you're still so afraid of," he says.

⸺

A FEW WEEKS after I sat in the bathroom and broke Shabbat for the first time, Aaron and I finally started couples therapy. I could no longer force myself to believe in our story. I was ready to admit the problems, yet in my heart, I was already gone.

Though I was consumed by a dread of what I would unleash if I overturned our lives, another set of questions had started to consume me. What if I continued to tuck myself away? What if I lived without growing or changing or speaking freely? I'd always tortured myself with the emotional cost of leaving, but now I felt tortured with the price to be paid for staying.

Contrary to what I had wanted to believe, there was no way to make it through unscathed. I didn't want the kids to grow up with the anger that now coated the house, didn't want them to harbor an underground kind of awareness that everything was not as it appeared. I didn't want to be a mother who had to parent with the truest parts suppressed, who had to constantly restrain herself in order to stay within.

Once a week, in the therapist's office, Aaron and I fought about the pileup of issues between us — there were many, both his and mine. We agreed about neither the state of our marriage nor the reasons for its unraveling. We presented different versions to the therapist, as though we'd both come here to discuss the problems we were having with some other set of errant spouses. Orthodoxy was one of these issues, but our differences there had only laid bare the larger problem. We had no way to talk honestly about anything that was hard. Together, we were not able to forge deeper, for fear of what we might find.

"I feel like I'm in a box. I'm not allowed to change. I'm not allowed to grow," I said while the therapist looked from me to Aaron. The therapist was like a fair-minded parent intent on ensuring that neither child felt the other was being favored, and it occurred to me how often Aaron and I had sat like children before others, awaiting judgment, awaiting instructions, awaiting permission, awaiting rules so that we could earn praise, so that we could remain safe, so that we never had to grow up.

As the conversation veered back and forth, I stared at the books lined up on the shelves next to me: *The Crucible, Paradise Lost.* How, I wondered, did the therapist decide which books to keep here — were these supposed to be symbolic? Instead of fighting one more pointless round, I wanted to enter these pages, write myself into these sentences, and become part of their stories. I had always believed that unexpected plot twists, life-altering epiphanies, and dramatic changes happened only to characters, never to someone like me.

No matter where our conversations in therapy began, they always wound their way back to the subject of Orthodoxy, because that seemed to be the most resolvable problem. If the problem was simply Orthodoxy, an easy solution might be proposed. I wouldn't have to be fully Orthodox; a small hole in the dense fabric of our lives could be cut. Realizing that my religious discontent wasn't going to recede this time, Aaron had started urging me to attend an egalitarian service that met nearby while he took the kids to the Orthodox synagogue we had always attended. On my own, I could make small changes, as long as I promised that the rest of the family would remain the same. I knew I should be grateful for this concession, and maybe years ago, before my feelings had been eroded by all the unresolved issues, this small change would have worked, but now the problem was so much larger. I knew that fundamentally we believed, and wanted, different things. I knew, more importantly, that there wasn't sufficient space within our marriage, or within Orthodoxy, to accommodate this.

Orthodoxy was the life he wanted and the truth in which he believed. If you believed in those rules, you had a life built of tradition and ritual, richly populated with family and community. But if you didn't believe, then those same structures could be a prison. You could stay by carving out private spaces for yourself, but even then, you always had to be aware of the gap between who you were and who you were supposed to be. I didn't want to live any longer in this tucked, crouched position. More than anything, I wanted to write bravely. I wanted to speak openly. I wanted to live freely.

"You don't have to feel that way," Aaron would say repeatedly in the weeks that followed as the fighting that had been so long compressed became fiercer. We fought terribly, with the door to our bedroom closed, hoping the kids, who were supposed to be asleep, couldn't hear us. All those years of avoidance had led us here; the problems between us had not disappeared, as I'd wished they would. They had simply been lying in wait, growing darker and more dangerous.

"But I do feel that way," I said.

"You won't try," he said.

I breathed in this word, *try*. It tore through my body, exploded inside me.

"All these years, I've done nothing but try," I said.

"You've changed," he accused me.

I fell silent. I couldn't argue with this. I had changed.

IN SEARCH OF A WAY to ease the constriction I felt in every part of my body, I went back to my book. I still felt lost inside it and was still afraid of the storyline's resolution, but I started to remember what I had most loved about writing: the feeling that my hands contained the words, that my fingers could sprint across the keys like runners who didn't look behind them, who didn't slow down when others called to them.

Before the Orthodox Forum, I'd been haunted by a fear that every sentence might earn me condemnation. Now the naysaying rabbinical figures in my mind were gone. I reminded myself of what I knew but had shied away from, that in writing, and in life, there came those moments when you had to allow everything to break open.

On the nights that Aaron came home early, I tried to get the kids settled so I could go out to readings and hear other writers talk about their books. The tension at home was unbearable. I said I was done more forcefully now, but it still meant nothing, just a word to utter when you couldn't say anything else. My life might have felt unbearably restrained but the bookstores were portals to something larger — all these stories, all these subjects you could learn about, all the places you could go. Even just being out at night felt like a respite, the streets seemingly different from the ones I drove through on my carpool loops.

At one of these readings at a bookstore that I loved in Newton, I recognized someone I knew sitting a few rows in front of me. It was William, a physician I'd seen a few years before. After the reading, I went up to him and reintroduced myself. We talked and I told him I was a writer and he told me that he'd started to work on a novel. Medicine was his love, he said, but writing was something he'd always wanted to try. He asked me if I'd be willing to talk with him about how to write a novel, and I said I'd be happy to help him.

EVERY WEEK, Ariel and I got together for coffee. We lived a mile away from each other and had become friends soon after I moved to Boston. Our kids were in the same Jewish nursery school, but what we shared, more than the mommy routines, was the fact of being writers. Like me, she had written two novels and was working on a third. Every day, we both dropped our kids off at school and tried to enter our fictional universes, then sealed them off when it was time to pick up the children.

In the café, we bent toward each other. We had the same long dark curly hair, so similar that we were sometimes mistaken for sisters. She offered me some of the muffin she was eating but I said no—I was hungry but though I had broken Shabbat, I wasn't ready to openly break the rules about keeping kosher, at least not while sitting in the window of this coffee shop. I told her about couples therapy and how I felt, increasingly, that the goal was for me to be talked out of what I felt. A successful session would be one in which I agreed to try not to be myself.

As we talked, I watched her eat—an act that for her was innocuous and for me would have been a sin. For her, Jewishness had nothing to do with whether she ate this muffin. Unlike me, with my family's six generations in Memphis and my all-Orthodox world, she was from a family of mostly secular Holocaust survivors. For her, Judaism was about history and memory and trying to sort out what it all added up to. It made me sad to realize that my experience of Judaism had become reduced to whether or not I followed the rules.

With each bite she took, my feeling grew larger. Not everywhere in the Jewish world did you have to live according to ideas you didn't agree with, offer explanations for observances you didn't believe in.

Until I got to know Ariel, most of my closest friends had been Orthodox, and I'd worried that she might not be able to understand the particulars of my world. I'd worried, too, that she *would* understand — that if I said too much, and if she understood the meaning of what I was saying, there would be no turning back. But now, sitting over my coffee at our small café table, I started speaking and didn't stop.

I told her I broke Shabbat secretly every week now while locked in the bathroom. I told her of the internal debate that ceaselessly raged, one part of me trying to bend and twist the other part into believing something. I said that even though it had been years since I had stopped wearing the fall, I felt like I was still covered.

"I know that I can't stay inside," I said.

"I've always wondered why the rules didn't bother you more," she admitted. "I told myself that there was must be something about Orthodoxy I didn't understand," she said. "Tova, I couldn't live the way you do."

"The rules *have* bothered me terribly. I've always been afraid how much they bother me. But I don't want to be afraid anymore and I don't want to keep pretending."

"What will happen when you stop pretending?" Ariel asked.

I knew without having to think about it. I had always known. "Everything will fall apart," I said.

I TOOK THE T to the Boston Athenaeum, a private library in downtown Boston, to meet William to talk about his book. The building was across from the monumental gold-domed State House, but the Athenaeum was a monument in itself. Even the impressive, imposing stone façade gave little hint of the wonders inside—past the security desk, a private domain of dark polished-wood floors, decorated, arched ceilings, gilt-framed portraits on the walls, and everywhere, floor-to-ceiling built-in shelves of books old and new. The rooms were completely silent —any cough or rustle was met with an indignant stare. I imagined losing myself in the stacks of books or camping out on the small balcony that overlooked a Colonial-era graveyard—anything to avoid going home.

William showed me the pages he had written, a medical drama, and I gave him what advice I could. When we left the Athenaeum, we walked across the Boston Common. All this open space in the midst of the city, reminiscent of Central Park in New York, which I'd always loved. On the other side lay the Public Garden with its flowers and iron footbridge spanning a man-made lake where, in the spring, you could take rides on the famous swan boats; growing up, I'd seen pictures of them in books. Why, I wondered, did I so rarely come into Boston? Why had I forgotten that this beautiful city was so close by?

"Aren't you cold?" I asked William. He had short sleeves on, though it was chilly in Boston. Winter was long over by now, but the weather continued to be damp and cool—the lack of a real spring was one thing I still held against this city.

"I didn't wear a coat all winter," he told me and his voice cracked. "My fifteen-year-old son spent this past winter in Utah, in the middle of nowhere, freezing. I didn't want to be warm when I knew he was cold." For years, he told me as we walked, his son had suffered from debilitating anxiety, and William had spent much of the past decade caring for him. When he didn't know how to help his son, he said he would get in his car and drive, ending up in the parking lot of the grocery store near his house, where he would cry. He had tried everything, and not knowing what else to do, he had decided, a few months earlier, to send him to a wilderness-therapy program in Utah.

"More than anything, I've wanted to heal my son. But I know that he needs to learn that he can survive on his own. The antidote for anxiety is independence. He needs to see his own strength," he said. "Still, I miss him terribly. I think about him all day long."

I had no answer for this. We walked in silence.

"So what about your book?" he asked me.

"I'll finish it one day," I said lightly, because I didn't like to talk about how ashamed I was that after all these years, it remained undone, how afraid I'd been of what I was writing.

"What holds you back from finishing?" he asked me.

"Oh, kids," I said. "Not enough time." Then, as though my conversation with Ariel had unlocked a gate I couldn't close, I decided to say what I really felt. I told him how I'd always wanted to believe that my book was fiction—it was all just fiction—but I had become increasingly aware of how much of my own feelings I was writing.

"You have to be willing to write what scares you," I said, to him and to myself.

AT OUR FAVORITE CAFÉ, Ariel and I bent our heads together and whispered. This time I shared her almond croissant.

"Welcome to the dark side," she said and we both laughed. "Is this your first nonkosher food?" she asked me.

"One of the first. It depends how strict you want to be."

"What was it?" she asked.

"Sushi—but I'm not sure if that really counts." I told her how the year before I'd bought sushi that was not officially kosher at the grocery store, though, because it was uncooked, a lot of Orthodox people ate it anyway.

"It's the gateway food," I told her.

With the avocado roll deftly tucked under some other groceries in my shopping cart at Whole Foods, I didn't believe I was really doing something wrong, but even so, I had worried who might see me, as though I had bought contraband drugs. For so long, this was what I had worried about, I realized—who would see me, what they would think. A sin not against God but against community. Back then, still intent on remaining inside, I had eaten the sushi quickly in my car, hardly enjoying it, and threw the container away in a garbage can not my own.

"I could bring you bacon cookies," she joked.

But suddenly I wasn't laughing. "I don't know how to leave," I said.

She turned serious as well. "I think you're already doing it. I know you still feel stuck but from the outside, it looks like you're starting to move."

I nodded. I felt it too. I knew that the slow accumulation had finally reached its tipping point. All those air holes I had punched had finally made an opening so wide that I could climb through.

"It's possible," she said, "that the next half of your life might look very different from the first."

I startled at her bold pronouncement, but it shocked me to realize that she was right. More important, I wanted her to be right.

I MET WILLIAM again at the Athenaeum, where we both worked on our books. The first time I'd come here, I'd realized this could be a place where I might finish my book. The prospect of leaving Newton every once in a while felt liberating. The quiet in this library felt startling. In this transcendent space, I felt myself shed some of the years of accumulated worry and I wrote a little more freely.

After a few hours of writing, we left the library. I'd been so immersed in my novel that I felt like I had to blink myself back to reality.

As we walked out onto Beacon Street, we talked and he told me that his son going to Utah was only one of the changes taking place in his life. He said that he was getting divorced.

"How did you know you needed to do it?" I couldn't help but ask.

"It's very painful, but it's been years in coming. I'm just trying to do the best I can for everyone now," he told me.

I felt like I couldn't talk about the precarious state of my own marriage but marveled at anyone who knew how to act, even when it was painful or hard.

Weeks later, after another writing session at the Athenaeum in which I was thrilled with the progress I'd begun to make on my book, William and I walked out together. He was turning toward his car when he asked me where I'd parked.

"I took the T," I told him.

"I can give you a ride home," he said.

In his car, I decided to confide in him. "I'm afraid to drive downtown," I said and told him how, when I was a teenager, I'd driven easily everywhere, how the summer I graduated from high school, two friends and I took a six-hour road trip from Memphis to New Orleans. Blasting Bryan Adams on the tape deck, guzzling Diet Coke, and eating Twizzlers, we took turns at the wheel, driving south through Mississippi and into Louisiana. We had a map in the glove compartment and instructions handwritten on a light blue index card. We went over the bridge that crossed Lake Pontchartrain, twenty-three miles long, and felt like we were traversing not a lake but the entire ocean.

But ever since we'd moved to Boston, I said, almost seven years before, I'd been afraid of driving in many parts of the city, but the highway most of all. I told him about my terrible sense of direction and my fear of getting lost. I told him what happened one time when I'd had to drive to Cambridge to pick up Aaron from a meeting. This was an area I usually avoided, and before setting out with the kids in the back seat, I'd studied the map, looking for the easiest way. But despite the directions I wrote out for myself, a street I'd planned to drive down was one-way in the wrong direction. I turned sharply and the next street was unfamiliar. Up ahead, it looked like Memorial Drive or maybe Storrow Drive, but it didn't matter which, because both were highways, or close enough. There was no way off this road, no turn I could see in the dark. NO STOPPING, NO STANDING, read the signs along the road. I might have been a novelist and a mother who could make dinner while folding the laundry while nursing a baby, but I was lost. The cars behind me honked mercilessly. The kids grew silent, aware that something was wrong. I clutched the steering wheel, my face prickling and hot. We were only a few blocks from where I was supposed to get Aaron, but all I could do was pull over, call him, and ask him to walk over to us.

It was hard to admit all of this — it felt shameful to be afraid of something so mundane. I often thought of the promise I'd made to myself, that I would overcome this fear by the time I turned forty, but the milestone that had once seemed like centuries in the future was now a year away and I was no closer. To be forty and not be able to drive on the highway — it brought to mind stories of veiled women forbidden to drive or stunted shutins. To be forty, it seemed to me, was the last chance to finally become an adult.

"I can go with you on the highway," William offered.

"Maybe one day," I said.

"You don't just have to write the things that scare you. Sometimes you have to do the things that scare you too."

It was a sentence as shocking, as radical, as any I'd ever heard.

Before I had a chance to protest, he pulled over by the side of the road.

"Now?" I asked.

"Why not?"

"You're not afraid to let me drive your car?" I asked.

"You know how to drive. There's no reason why you can't do this."

I had a storehouse of reasons for why I couldn't drive on the highway, but he was so calm, so sure I could do this, that I got behind the wheel. I drove through the Back Bay, with its labyrinth of one-way streets, down Beacon, and through Kenmore Square, where lanes merged into one another and streets crossed at will. I clutched the steering wheel and drove far too slowly, annoying those behind me, who loudly honked their displeasure. I kept driving toward Newton, and we reached an entry ramp for the Mass. Pike.

"I can't do this," I said even as I was starting up the ramp.

"You can, you already know how," he reminded me.

"No, really." My mouth had grown so dry that I could barely get out the words.

Until now, he hadn't realized just how afraid I was. He took hold of the wheel, and together we merged onto the highway, my hands shaking, my eyes tearing, my ears prickling with heat.

"I'm afraid the person behind me minds that I'm going so slowly," I said.

"Don't look in the rearview mirror. Don't think about the person behind you," he said.

Cars whizzed by me, but I kept going, driving past one exit, then another. All the parts of the city that had seemed closed off, yet here were the signs for them. Nothing could change, yet I was driving on the highway, driving next to this man, this not-my-husband man. Nothing can change, yet I was behind the wheel picking up speed, traveling sixty-five miles an hour, which the day before would have seemed as likely as traveling at the speed of light. My head contained its own highway and I was hurtling faster now toward an endpoint that I knew lay somewhere in the distance but that I hadn't known how to reach.

For so many years, I had been afraid of my own feelings, afraid of my unhappiness, afraid of change, but also afraid of traveling to new places, afraid of riding a bike, afraid of anything in which I would move too fast, in which I might careen and fall. It had never occurred to me that when the time came, I might actually welcome the sensation of falling — the rush of air, the feeling that my unencumbered body was awake and alert. I'd never imagined a falling in which I stopped wanting to remain safe at all cost, when I didn't want to grab hold of any last secure spot or didn't worry about where and how I would land.

When I got off the Mass. Pike, I was crying with exhilaration and relief. Having become accustomed to the feeling of speed, I had to force myself to slow down on the city streets.

"I'm tired of being so afraid," I said.

EVERY TIME I sat down in front of my computer, the words escaped as they never had before, sentences unfurling. I wrote at the Athenaeum, wrote in the small alcove off the living room, wrote in the middle of the night when the kids were asleep. I felt like the lights inside me, which had previously been dimmed in order to preserve power, were being switched back on. I continued to go to readings, eager to shake myself from my quiet pose. In prior drafts of my novel, I'd been afraid to have characters who acted on what they felt. I tried to have characters believe it was enough to be free inside their minds while in the rest of their lives they agreed to remain discontent and enclosed. It was a lie, and I knew it now.

I finished a new draft of the novel, which I printed out and left on my desk. I didn't know what time it was when I awoke that night and realized Aaron was standing over me holding the manuscript in his hand. I startled when I saw him there, afraid of any potential conversation we might have. By this point, we barely exchanged more than a sentence unless it was to fight. I felt as sealed off, as tightly pressed, as I ever had, though some days I wondered if all this compression might create a fierce dense spot inside me that would not yield. Again that morning, I'd told him that I was done, yet the word *done* seemed to exist in a cordoned-off section of the dictionary, detached and inaccessible to all else. We still went to couples therapy, though pointlessly, it seemed to me—I was desperate to move toward some kind of separation and sometimes I was sure I detected in the therapist's pained expression a similar desperate wish to escape from us and our furious fights about who was good, who was bad, who was innocent, and who was to blame.

"The couples in this novel all seem so disconnected from each other," Aaron said to me in the dark of our bedroom. For the first time in a while, his voice didn't sound angry, just unbearably sad, as if he were finally seeing what I saw.

I couldn't back away from what I'd written. I wanted to console him and apologize to him and also flee from him. Impossible as it was, I wished there was some way to end this peacefully, to say that this was as far as we had been able to go together. I wished, also impossibly, that I could protect what had once been sweet and innocent between us, then slip quietly away.

"I can't be married to you," I said.

I cried as I said it, but inside this sentence, there was nowhere to hide.

ONE NIGHT, after a terrible fight when I continued to insist that I meant what I said and Aaron continued to believe that I didn't, I left the house and got into the car. After years of always being at home, now all I wanted was to be outside. I drove slowly down the quiet street, all our neighbors securely inside their houses—no sign of disarray, but the safety seemed threatened, as though intruders had been set loose. At home, every word was sharp-edged and slivered, as though all the glass there had broken and now we walked across the dangerous shards.

I was trying not to call or text William, aware that his life was in its own state of painful upheaval. I knew no one could serve as my guide out, but I was thinking about him more than I should have been. I knew that my feelings for him were growing, that he was no longer someone I thought of as just a friend. I tried to push this away as I did with every thought that scared me. But there was no more hiding from myself. I took care of the kids, cooked dinner, did the laundry as always. My body remained at home, but my mind had taken flight. Before this, I hadn't been able to summon another vision of how my life might look. But now I was starting to imagine another possibility.

I drove past the Newton library, past our synagogue, past friends' houses. I circled the center of town, two intersecting streets with a church on one side, a Starbucks on the other. By ten o'clock, the stores were all closed. I circled back to Crystal Lake and drove down Beacon, toward the entrance ramp for I-95.

I merged onto the highway with the same shaking hands and red prickling ears. If there was ever a time my body spoke to me louder than the ruminations of my mind, it was now. *Do it. Go.* The cars were coming up quickly behind me, a barrage of lights. I felt the old startle of panic. *Pick your spot, make a decision, and start moving,* I heard in my head, some more confident version of myself. *You confuse other drivers when you're tentative. They can't tell what you intend to do.*

I merged, as afraid as I'd ever been. Even though Newton had appeared quiet and asleep, the highway was crowded with cars—there were always people who needed to get away. I opened the windows; the air rushed in and my hair blew wildly. I didn't know what would come next, but at least I was on the highway, driving, driving. I changed lanes, I got off the highway, I merged back on. Something was going to change only because I had decided to change it.

⌒

WILLIAM AND I arrive in the North End now on this Friday night. The kids are at Aaron's house celebrating Shabbat as we once did all together, but for me now, a new day has sprung into existence, like those dreams I used to have in which I opened a door in our house and discovered, to my great surprise, a vast extra room. So this is what Friday night looks like. William and I wander along streets that are windy and narrow, paved in cobblestone, lit with gas lamps. The brick buildings twinkle with lights.

We wait in the long line outside Regina's Pizzeria. Over the past few months, we've eaten our way through Boston. I want to sample everything, hungry not only for the food but for the choices.

At a Thai restaurant in Coolidge Corner that was both cheap and delicious, in sight of the kosher Chinese place and the Jewish bookstores, William held out a forkful of pad thai.

"It's delicious," I said.

"Soon I'll stop eating like this. It's only because it's still new," I said at an Indian buffet where I tried to limit myself to just two vegetable pakoras and seconds of only the sag paneer. William held out a forkful of chicken tikka masala but here I did say no.

"I'm a vegetarian," I reminded him.

"Wouldn't it be nice to look at a menu and eat whatever you want?" he asked me.

"Just to be here feels radical enough," I said.

"Do you think you're just used to being restricted?"

I'd thought about it. I'd been a vegetarian for five years, since seeing one too many videos about slaughterhouses and too often feeling the need to tell myself that the burger or piece of chicken I was eating wasn't what it actually was. It was the same time as I was starting to recognize how deadened the rest of my beliefs were, how I didn't find the rules of keeping kosher meaningful, though I complied with their every detail.

"I hold on to it because it's something I actually believe in," I said.

When there's a free table at Regina's, we squeeze our way into the crowded dark space that is decorated with framed pictures of local celebrities who have eaten here.

"Are you hungry?" William asks me.

"Starving," I say.

The pizza is thin-crusted and gooey, and in order to eat it without it falling apart, I hold it with both of my hands and hurry it into my mouth. I devour one slice after another. Still hungry, we go into Mike's Pastry, which is famous, though I hadn't heard of it until recently. People crowd the street outside. A line stretches out the door — shopping-bag-laden tourists wearing newly purchased Boston gear, eager to declare their allegiance, noisy college students bustling in large groups, old Italian women with ink-black-dyed hair and their dark-eyed husbands. Inside, in glass-fronted display cases, there are containers of tiramisu and peaked white meringues; rows of small pink-and-green-layered cakes; cream puffs; and cannolis, plain and covered in chocolate, dipped in powdered sugar, their ends dotted with chocolate chips, their insides filled with sweet ricotta cheese or mousse or raspberry cream. The women behind the counter speak to one another in Italian as they package pastries into white bakery boxes that they expertly tie up with the red-and-white string that hangs from rolls attached to the ceiling.

William holds up a chocolate chip cannoli for me, and I bite into the crunch of shell, then the sweet surprise of ricotta. It's the most delicious thing I've ever eaten. I motion for William to try some too, but instead he feeds me another bite. That Chasidic story, it turned out, was wrong. You can partake, and you can enjoy.

We dodge patches of ice along the sidewalk, which in the summer, William tells me, will be filled with people attending the weekly Italian festivals, the image of the Madonna paraded high, the porcelain figure covered with the dollar-bill offerings of the devout in search of healing and salvation. As we walk, my leg brushes against William's; his arm is around me, pulling me toward him. He stops, takes my face in his hands, and kisses me. We start walking again and it feels possible to stay out all night long, explore every neighborhood in this city.

In the small bench-lined park, underneath the statue honoring Paul Revere and his midnight ride, we sit. Behind us is the Old North Church, where the famous one-if-by-land, two-if-by-sea lanterns hung. The white spire is bathed in golden light and from where we're sitting, it looks as though Paul Revere is leaving behind the brightly illuminated world and setting out into the dark unknown of his midnight ride.

Snow is falling lightly as we walk along the famed Freedom Trail, past Paul Revere's house and Faneuil Hall and the Old State House. Surrounded by this blend of old and new buildings and by these bodies of water and these bridges and, everywhere, the twinkling of so many lights, I relent in my conviction that this city isn't mine.

Jump

"White-water rafting on the Pacuare River!" William says when I meet him for dinner.

I hear his excitement, but even so, I can't help myself: "Is it safe?" I ask.

"No!" he says with a smile.

William and I are going to Costa Rica in February, a dream vacation. It's an odd-number year, so according to the finalized separation agreement, December vacation is my time with the kids, the February school break is Aaron's. He is taking them on vacation and I'm thrilled, of course, to be able to go to Costa Rica with William, but the prospect of being away from the kids for a week feels scary. I concoct torturous stories of all the ways they won't return, or I won't. Before the divorce, I would have marveled at this amount of time to myself, but now I feel only the fear, entirely unfounded as it is, that Aaron will take them and never return; they will cease to be mine.

It's not only my fears about the kids. The list of all that I'm afraid of follows me still. As much as I want to believe that I've banished my fear, I know that it needs to be conquered not once, but again and again. Travel has always been one of the things that scared me—I like browsing the travel guides in the bookstore and constructing an itinerary, but fear overtakes me as soon as I start to pack for a trip. When Dahlia told me stories of backpacking or parasailing or kayaking, I reminded myself that she was the adventurous sister. I didn't see the point of traveling only in order to be scared.

I decide not to tell William about my urge to stay home, preferably in a fetal position, until the week of vacation passes and the kids safely return. Instead, I Google pictures of Costa Rica and stare at the green-and-yellow-beaked toucans with black bodies and bright blue tufts of feathers, more like fanciful imaginary creatures a child would draw than anything that exists in real life. A desire stronger than fear comes over me. I want to see this bird not caged in a zoo, not drawn on the front of a cereal box, but outside, in the wild.

In preparation for the rafting as well as the hiking we have planned, I browse Eastern Mountain Sports, where it's easy to feel outdoorsy. Here, it doesn't matter that until now, hiking has belonged to the category of activities (like exercise) that I only wanted to want to do. There had been a few halfhearted attempts to take the kids hiking when they were younger but I had no good answer to the question: What about walking is supposed to be fun? My family was not meant for the outdoors—on a rare canoe trip we took on the Wolf River in Tennessee, the water level was so low we got precariously stuck on branches and made our way to the end only because, as my mother tells it, an old man in a motorboat passed by and assured us that we were almost there. "It was Elijah," my mother still swears—the prophet who supposedly roams the earth, takes on various forms, and makes appearances at the most fortuitous of moments.

I take a pile of clothing with me into the dressing room, hiking gear for the most extreme of locales.

"Hiker. Adventure seeker," I say as I stand in front of the mirror. My reflection—which is complete with a pair of quick-dry zip-off hiking pants and purple rafting sandals—looks back and I try not to laugh at the new person I'm pretending to be. But maybe the only way to become her is to act as though I already am her; instead of waiting to feel less afraid, start out and trust that the rest of me will follow.

～

"I'm leaving my marriage," I'd told my mother as I talked to her on the phone from my car parked alongside Crystal Lake. To say this to her felt like leaping past all that was safe and known between us. I'd said I was done so many times before, but now it was different—not just how I felt but what I intended to do. I felt a ferocity unlike anything I had ever experienced, as though in order to act, I needed to tear down the borders of my own self. All this time I had been held in by fear. Now I was propelled by a fear of inaction.

My mother sharply drew in her breath. She was sad but not surprised, having heard for years of my unhappiness. My story tumbled out between sobs. Until now this was a story I'd known only about other people, never one that might be about me. Even as I said it to her, I was still surprised that I was talking about my own life.

In a quick encapsulated version, she repeated what I'd said

to my father, who'd come up beside her. I steeled myself for the possibility that she would try to talk me down, that my father would get on the phone and speak to me in the rare stern tone he'd used when I was a little girl in trouble.

"We love you," my father said, his voice cracking with emotion.

"We are here for you," my mother said, a phrase I clung to, the most beautiful words a parent can utter. Later she told me that she and my father had stayed up all night in worry—this, the part of parenthood that never ends.

By now, I had started sleeping on the couch in the basement, where I awoke, disoriented, every morning. My dreams and my life had the same hazy unreal cast. The kids were aware that something was wrong even if they didn't yet know what it was. Layla joined me in the basement, sleeping on top of me on the couch. Josh started to sleep down there too, in the extra bed that had once been part of a guest room.

I took off my wedding ring, placed it in a box inside another box, and put it on a shelf high in my closet. I'd stopped wearing my engagement ring a few months before, when I'd been sitting on the bed with Layla, looked down at my hand, and discovered that the diamond in the center of my ring was gone. I'd stared at the empty prongs as though I'd imagined or willed this, knowing that if it were a detail I'd read in a novel, I'd have drawn a line through it and written *Too obvious*.

Watching my frantic search, Layla looked around and saw a glimmer on the bedspread. "Is this the shiny bead you're looking for?" she asked, holding out her palm.

I took it from her, closed it in my hand and her in my arms.

Now, without either ring, my finger looked naked. All that

remained were the indentations the bands had carved into my skin.

"YOU LOOK DIFFERENT," Ariel said as we sat together, whispering. By now we had graduated from coffee and croissants to a full nonkosher lunch.

I glanced at her in surprise, assuming I appeared stressed, exhausted, awful.

"Stronger," she said. "More sure."

I held on to her words, hoping they were true. In my body, I had a strange summoning sensation, as though an outer layer had been sloughed off. I didn't feel smaller, just distilled and true.

I looked at Ariel. I knew she could understand what felt so complicated and unsure. This was a friendship that would help see me across. Even if you were preparing to step off the edge of the world, there would always be the few who'd remain beside you. Sometimes you didn't need a community, just a true close friend. She knew about my friendship with William, but now I told her that I felt something more for him. I didn't know what would happen between us — and I knew that this would only make what was already so painful and fraught even more so. But I was so used to pushing away what I felt; I didn't want to do it again. This was never how I had imagined my story might turn out, but making one change set in motion so many others — as though once you took the lid off an ordered life, all sorts of possibilities sprang loose.

WE MET WITH a mediator. We hired lawyers. There was no salvaging anything. In the end, with lawyers involved, it was wrenching and it was liberating and it felt impossible that this was my life even as it felt like everything that happened until now had been leading me toward this moment.

"I didn't say what I really thought for the last sixteen years and I'm going to start now," Aaron said angrily as we sat across from each other in a lawyer's conference room, and this hurt more than all the other accusations. It confirmed my sense that the most important parts between us had always been left unsaid.

The anger was terrible, his and mine. It blanketed us both. After a lifetime of trying to be good at all costs, in the end, I could only assume the mantle of bad. He railed at me as though I had become an unrecognizable creature. Now I held nothing back as well, angry that my experience all these years couldn't be heard or accepted, much less understood. We tore at each other as though only one of us could emerge intact.

In the end, the anger made it easier to go. The sadness would have wrapped around me, held me longer inside.

I walked the few blocks to Crystal Lake, where I sat on a bench and cried, not worrying who would see me. I'd spent the morning meeting with my lawyer. There were multiple therapists now, his, mine, and ours. The end was set in motion — a long list of what needed to be done in order to actually leave. But out here, I thought only about the water and the trees and my tears, not the sprawling houses behind me, not the town full of people I knew, not the web of connections that had held me inside.

I dialed William's number.

"Where are you?" he asked.

"Crystal Lake."

Half an hour later, I looked up and he was standing next to me. I was crying so hard I hadn't heard him coming.

We looked out at the lake, at the trees that encircled it, and at each other, both of our faces solemn and drawn. There was still the haze of unreality to all of it—when I woke each morning, I still believed that this was a wishful dream or harrowing nightmare, both at once.

"I will be here for you," William said to me and cupped his hands together as though his fingers could actually form a net. I saw the look of pain on his face and knew he understood.

I cupped my hands too and placed them inside his. I might no longer be good—that was a word lost now inside the wreckage—but I hoped that at least I might be able to live true.

I cried for this ending and all the endings rapidly piling up. William held me as I sobbed. The path out was forged in pain. And on the other side of that, there were no promises and no guarantees. He had the end of his own marriage still to grapple with, as well as his ever-present worries about his son. I was on the brink of a multitude of changes all at once. There was no way to know how we would fit together when I wasn't sure yet who I was becoming. It was still a skyscraper I stood on, and he was a small figure below. But more than this, I knew I needed to be able to catch myself. Having William here made it easier to leave, but no matter what he offered, I still had to jump off alone and live through the fall.

Now, on our first day in Costa Rica, we hike near the famous Arenal Volcano, on a national park trail that takes us across a series of hanging bridges. As we hike, we scan the trees in the hope that what seems like a flower or leaf will rustle, caw, and fly. We jump at any sign of movement, but the density of wildlife—the monkeys in trees, the birds on branches — remains largely out of sight.

At the end of the hike, in which the only animals we've come across are a pack of fire ants that bite our legs, our guide calls us over.

"Look," he says and points to a patch of trees closest to the restaurant and parking lot.

Coming from the branches, there is a rousing scream: a family of howler monkeys, two adults and a baby, scurrying along a branch. At first we're enthralled, but we later grow suspicious at how close these animals are to the most crowded spot of the park. Did the staff feed them, entice them here to make the tourists feel they'd gotten their money's worth? The possibility makes these monkeys seem counterfeit, little different than if we'd seen them caged in a zoo.

The next day, we are picked up at our hotel at five in the morning, and we travel by van over bumpy country roads. Along the shores of the Pacuare River, we get a crash course in how to paddle. Hoping my new rafting sandals lend me an air of competency, I gamely strap on my life jacket and helmet.

"Don't be afraid," says Alejandro, our guide and a member of the Costa Rican national rafting team. He's able to see through to the other side of the supposedly practical questions I ask and knows I'm really wondering about all the ways you can overturn, fall out, and die.

Also on our raft are four sisters whose names all begin with the letter *L*. "The four sisters from Ell," they call themselves. Each year, the four of them take a trip together. They've been to Africa, where they went on safari, and to the Amazon, where they hiked and kayaked. As they recount their trips, telling us of one adventure after another, I consider asking them, *Are you ever afraid?,* but what I really want to know is whether they will take me under their wing.

On our first day of rafting, we are setting out for an eco-lodge that is four hours away and accessible only by river. Our guide is perched at the back of the raft, reading the river, which winds through the tropical rainforest; the water is green, the trees greener. As we float along with our small caravan of rafts, I scan either side of us for any flash of movement, any rustling of life. I want to see anything, but a toucan most of all. It's good this is supposed to be the easiest part of the river, because I keep forgetting to paddle. In the distance, there is the scream of more howler monkeys. Hummingbirds whiz by; kingfishers hover above the water; butterflies that are brown on one side, electric blue on the other, flutter past, but no toucan.

"They are not nice birds," Alejandro tells us, without saying why. But it doesn't matter. I can't be dissuaded from scanning and hoping.

"There's a class-three rapid coming up," Alejandro warns us.

Because it's not yet the rainy season, the water level is low and rocks jut out ominously from the river.

"Lean in," he says sharply right before we hit one of the rocks.

I lean into the boat, paddle harder and faster, and am pulled and pushed and turned and hurtled. Instead of shrinking in fear, my body feels coiled and taut. There is no loop of thought, no spool of worry, nothing but my arms paddling furiously, my legs bracing my body in the raft.

When we reach our eco-lodge, the midpoint of our trip, where we will spend two days before rafting the rest of the way, we eat a lunch of avocados and mangoes and fish and tropical drinks the same bright shade of pink as the heliconia flowers that bloom everywhere. Instead of giving in to the temptation to lounge in the hammocks outside our hut, William and I hike through the rainforest to a waterfall. I look up while I walk, still scanning the endless canvas of green. Every rustle, every crackle of branches, offers possibility. For the guides, the sounds of the forest are all recognizable. Just as they can read the river, they know to whom the screams and caws belong. Out here, nothing is simply itself. A dash of color on a fallen tree trunk turns out to be elaborately decorated circus mushrooms. Twigs become intricate walking-stick bugs. The ground moves—green leaves carried by unseen battalions of ants.

Stopping short next to me, William silently grabs my arm and points.

In a tree a few feet from us, sitting in one of the branches, there is a toucan, black-feathered and yellow-beaked. The shape of its beak makes it looked immensely pleased with itself, smiling, almost sneering, at some private joke. The yellow is so rich, nearly fluorescent, it seems to be made from plastic. If the toucan is aware of our presence, it matters little. We are simply a few more creatures in this dense forest.

My eyes can't open wide enough. All this green feels like a silent rebuttal. Out here in this wild forest draped in growth, there is none of that sense of enclosure, none of that deadened, callused feeling. Inside this rainforest that cannot be tamed or controlled, so much life is constantly changing and rustling and cawing and growing. Out here, the only eyes watching are the hundreds of species that we can't see, the ones that at night will light this forest with dots of iridescence. When I'm away from the strictures and structures, it feels abundantly clear that there cannot be just one way—no rule book I'm supposed to be following. Out here, the tightness inside my body loosens. The word *good* seems irrelevant. The grip of *bad* gives way. All those rules that have for so long pressed on me are like the light from a star that's burned out, the last flicker of something that once existed.

With a croaking scream, a flash of yellow, and the spreading of black wings, the toucan is gone.

Our room has a thatched roof and an outdoor shower surrounded by a stone wall on top of which birds of paradise flowers bloom. When I shower, I look down and discover that I'm not alone. On the floor is a lizard the exact shade of tan as the stone. Instead of screaming and fleeing, as most of my body wants to do, I stay in the shower. I wash my hair as the lizard watches me.

When I come out of the shower, the lizard still in there, William and I lie together under the white cotton bedspread. Outside, the river rushes, the water slamming against the hard rock. My arms and legs are mosquito-bitten and sunburned. Every part of my body aches from the exertion of the day. William reaches for me and I for him. Between us, it is a tangled love, all urgency and elation and escape, and I want to partake of it all, this feeling that we are riding the current between us, deeper into the wilds.

The mosquito net drapes over us, a gauzy canopy. We listen

to the caws and buzz and shrieks of the forest's night world waking. When I close my eyes I have the sensation that I am still on the river, rushing downstream.

BEFORE WE LEAVE COSTA RICA, we head off for the required ziplining outing, at a tourist trap that bills itself as the longest, scariest one in the country. We sign up for the full package, including lunch and a souvenir DVD of our adventures. It's early in the day, cool and damp, and with only our light sweatshirts, we shiver as we're strapped into our ropes, harnesses, and helmets. After a quick lesson, we set off into the cloud forest.

Ziplining is scary only for the first run, and then only if you let yourself think of all the ways there are to fall. After that, the ride along each rope is a controlled glide through the trees. A few more lines take us deeper into the forest, and we stop at the side of a cliff overlooking a vast green valley. A cable is embedded in the ground, and the guides begin to hook my line to it.

I shake my head no — this is still the word that arrives first. But before I can say anything else, the word *yes* crests inside me. I stand at the edge of a cliff and do as the guide instructs me.

"Jump," he says.

My legs won't obey. Starting to count, I promise myself that I'll do it by the time I reach ten. But my feet are still planted — there seems no way they will ever let go of the ground. I begin counting again, but before I know I'm doing it, my legs take me by surprise and I'm jumping out and the guide's hands are pushing me hard so that I swing out, Tarzan-style, over the canyon. I rush forward until I reach the apex, at which point I seem to freeze for a moment, then soar back. The guide pushes me out again, and this time my eyes are open, taking in all the varieties of green and a sky as much below me as above.

I know I'm strapped to this cable and have to do nothing, not even hold on. We're hardly brave explorers and this is hardly the Amazon or Mount Everest. When we return to the starting point, tourist-filled buses will be arriving. We will eat our prepaid lunch of rice and beans and pick up our souvenir DVD. But if there's anything I want to wrap up and take home with me, it's this sensation of soaring. There comes, in that moment, a glimmer of what it feels like to be free.

Part 3

Other People, Other Worlds

"Can we bake hamantaschen?" Layla asks me on the morning of Purim, a holiday that falls at the beginning of March and that she has been learning about in nursery school. Though a minor holiday, it's one of the kids' favorites, a boisterous celebration of the deliverance of the ancient Jews in Persia from the evil Haman. It comes complete with costumes and baskets of treats, including this triangular, filled cookie reminiscent of the three-cornered hat worn by the villain of the story.

At her question, I pause, threatened for a moment by hamantaschen. For all my leaving, I worry I could still be swept back inside.

Even so, I stand on a chair to reach my selection of kosher cookbooks, which have remained all year on the highest shelf in the kitchen. I flip through the pages of the one I'd used the most, the spiral binding coming apart, the pages stiff and sticky. At the back, in the section labeled *Traditional Food,* is my one-time favorite hamantaschen recipe.

As I'd done with each of the boys, Layla and I make the

dough. After it has chilled, we roll the dough out on the table and use mugs to cut circles, as my mother taught me. Inside each circle, we drop a spoonful of apricot jelly or chocolate chips, as Layla prefers. I call the boys in to join us, and Noam and Josh oblige, filling a few circles and folding them into triangles.

With the four of us together in the kitchen, I remember how much I once enjoyed doing this—baking these cookies as I had as a child, assembling them into small packages that we decorated, then delivering them around the neighborhood to family and friends, coming home to find an accumulation of these packages on our doorstep as well. In this moment, it feels clear to me: I still want to participate in this tradition with my children. Surely freeing yourself means being able to choose what to let go of as well as what to keep. By leaving, I don't have to leave it all.

"Should we go?" I ask the kids when the hamantaschen are almost done baking. I'd tentatively made a reservation for the Purim party at our former synagogue. As wary as I am about going, I don't want the kids to feel entirely cut off from the way it used to be. I wonder if I can ignore the discomfort of being around those who don't speak to me so we can be occasional visitors to our former world.

With the kids, I drive to the synagogue that once was the epicenter of our family life. I try to gauge their moods as we walk in—for Josh and Layla, I suspect that this is just a place we used to go to, but I wonder if Noam looks longingly at where we used to go, if he feels, as I do, that in some alternate existence, this is where we still could belong.

The mood inside is festive; scores of kids are dressed in costumes, as are many of the adults. There is a clown twisting balloon animals and a makeup artist applying face paint to a long line of kids. Milling around are all the people I'd once known — time travel does indeed exist, and on this day when life is supposed to be topsy-turvy, I've found my way back to my former life.

Making hamantaschen was one thing, but as soon as we walk in, I realize it was a mistake to have come. My body instantly knows where it is — I instinctively cross my arms in front of my chest, my fingers tightly grasping my arms. I feel uncomfortable inside my own body, as though nothing of me is correctly attached. There is no way for me to return in this partial way. In a tight-knit community, you're either inside or out. I can partake of some of the customs and rituals, but not those that require me to be wholly inside.

Some people are friendly and I'm grateful for this — I feel as though they're purposely reaching across the barrier that surrounds me, and I return their greeting, genuinely glad to see them. But all too often, I turn and face the shunners and snubbers, the ladies and gentlemen of the awkward withheld hellos. The man who once lived near us and who now seems to regard my presence here as impossible, as though I have returned from the dead; a woman who says with narrowed eyes and clenched teeth, "Nice to see you," in a voice that lets me know she means it is anything but nice.

Behind these responses, I know, there are many reasons. Getting divorced, leaving Orthodoxy — there was plenty of fodder in that alone. And it was easy too, I assume, for gossips to claim that William's appearance in my life led to the demise of my marriage, when in fact it was the opposite. I don't know what has been said by whom, what people have presumed to know and share. All I can do now is let go of thinking about how my story is viewed by others.

This too has become part of what it has meant to leave, and it has changed me, making me feel preemptively sealed off when I run into someone I used to know. To protect myself, I know I can close ranks inside myself, craft a smaller circle in which to hold tightly to my own story. But I don't want to have left only to feel clenched once again. The other possibility, hard as it is to act on, is to know that just as I have my own story, so too do each of these people who walk past—even the denial of a story is a story. All these other people, all with their own myriad forms of sadness and fear, their marriages with their thwarted desires and wishful hopes, their children with their own hidden questions and private struggles. No way to know how our stories brush up against the rawest parts of someone else's. No way to gauge how little we know of the insides of other people's lives.

I still feel the loss of some of these friendships—but my earlier anger has softened and now it's mostly just sadness that there exists this additional stark line between then and now. But if these small moments of shunning are the price for being myself, I'm willing to pay it.

I get food for the kids but I don't feel like eating. I stand off to the side, watching the festivities. Until now, I've seen these community members as oversize figures who populate the entire known world. But this is one small land, and the people inside it occupy a smaller sliver.

"It's good to see you," says one man with whom I used to be friendly and he looks me warmly in the eye. "I mean it. Don't be a stranger."

I smile back, appreciative of his gesture and happy to see him as well, but despite his kindness, I know that a stranger is exactly what I am. The word comes as a relief. One more reminder. This is no longer my world.

We leave early. I don't belong here. It's a sentence that once would have filled me with fear, but now it's simply a statement of fact. It turns out that there is no cliff at the edge of the earth, no never-ending black hole in which you would endlessly float. There are other people, other worlds.

WHEN WE GET BACK to our house, a package is waiting for us in the breezeway — a shopping bag filled with Hershey's Kisses and chocolate chip cookies and also a hot-pink hula hoop, which is hardly a typical Purim item but is a welcome addition.

"It's from William," I tell the kids when I look at the card that is tucked inside.

"You have a boyfriend," Layla teases.

William has started to come over when the kids are here. He first came on a Sunday night a few weeks ago, with ice cream. The kids were excited when I told them he was stopping by, but even so, I played detective to every expression that passed across their faces. To my relief, they were surprisingly at ease with him. The boys discussed sports with him, while Layla climbed on his shoulders and asked for a ride. For all of my worry, the kids seem better able to accommodate what is new and changing.

Come over for hamantaschen, I text William and he does. We all sit on the couch and eat.

"I still like Halloween better," Josh decides.

Layla considers the issues before nodding. "You get more candy," she agrees.

"Does this count as celebrating a Jewish holiday with you?" William whispers in my ear.

"I'll give you partial credit," I say.

"I'll take it," he says and we laugh. As our lives become increasingly intertwined, we will continue to wrestle with the ways we are different. When it comes to religion, he will join me sometimes, remain separate other times. But I know that there is room for this, between us and around us. He doesn't have to be who I am. I don't have to be who he is. To be free, I'm learning, is to allow others to be free as well.

We finish off the hamantaschen, then eat the chocolate too. The kids and William play hallway basketball on the net that hangs from the pantry door. William lifts Layla so she can dunk the ball. Noam gives William a high-five when he makes a shot. The kids are comfortable with him, energized by his exuberance. There is something almost childlike about William— playing with the kids is not an act but something that comes naturally to him. He pays careful attention to everything they say, not just pretending to be engaged but handing over all of himself.

I cheer them on, then take a shot from the kitchen, and the kids laugh as I miss badly and the ball ends up in the bathroom. The game is wild and festive and fun, and when I look at them, my three children and William, I know that I belong to this.

"Do I have to go to school?" Josh asks me the next morning and every morning when I wake him. Fourth grade feels like an impossibility for him. I console him by telling him that it's springtime, he has to make it just a few more months. But no matter what I say, he doesn't want to go.

"I hate the Jewish stuff," he says as we near the school.

Not just at school but everywhere, he is chafing, refusing. There are those who are upset about his continued refusal to wear a yarmulke—this still feels like a change that cannot be accepted. If he doesn't follow this path, then it's someone's fault —mine, obviously. If I don't teach my children to be Orthodox, I have supposedly failed as a parent. If I don't show them the one true way, I'm at fault when inevitably they end up lost.

After Josh has a particularly bad day at school, I go into the garage and pump air into the tires of his bicycle, a hand-me-down from Noam that has sat unused for a few years. I'd taught Noam to ride a bike but hadn't yet taught Josh because there never seemed to be enough time. Now that he's turned ten, he's embarrassed not to know how, but it's harder because he's become afraid.

The week before, William and I went on a Saturday afternoon to Falmouth, on Cape Cod, where we rented bikes. "It's been a long time since I've been on a bike," I said nervously to the man at the rental shop and asked about the exact course of the path and how crowded it would be. Like driving, riding a bike was a fear that had snuck up on me when I let too many years pass without doing it. The last time I'd been on a bike was when I was in graduate school and Aaron and I had rented bikes on a weekend trip to Montauk, at the tip of Long Island. On that rented bike, which was a little too big for me, I'd no longer felt sure of myself. Unsteady, I shied away from biking up a huge hill, afraid I would career out of control down the other side. After that, my fear had solidified and grown.

"You'll remember. It's like riding a bike," the man at the rental place joked as he selected a bike and helmet for me.

He was right. I did remember. William and I biked through the main streets of Falmouth, past seafood restaurants and souvenir shops. Each time a car went by, I slowed down and my heart sped up. *Just how close are they, can they hit us, will I fall into their path?* My fear was riding alongside me, but I continued anyway. At first William led the way but he urged me to go ahead and I did, onto the Shining Sea Bikeway, past salt marshes that opened finally into an expansive view of the ocean.

"You can do it," I tell Josh now as I summon all my optimistic good cheer and say that William offered to meet us in the empty parking lot of the local public school and teach him.

"I'm too tired," he says.

"It'll be fun," I coax him, trying to betray none of the urgency I feel. Suddenly, Josh learning how to ride a bike is more important than anything else.

"I don't want to learn. It's boring," he says with wilting bravado.

"I was afraid to ride a bike," I tell him.

Josh looks at me intently as I tell him how I had always ridden a bike as a kid but became afraid when I was older and that recently I'd tried it, even though I was afraid, and now I no longer am.

"Will you try?" I ask, and this time he agrees.

I load his bike and Layla's into the back of my car and we drive to the parking lot where William is waiting. As Layla makes circles around the lot with her training wheels, William teaches Josh to glide slowly down a slight incline so that he can see what it feels like to balance.

"Don't worry about the pedals, and don't worry about going

fast," William tells Josh, whose forehead is furrowed in concentration.

William is so confident that Josh can learn to ride that Josh begins to feel confident as well. As William calls out encouragement, his voice remains steady and unrushed—the days ahead are open spaces and we can stay here for as long as is needed. He has the patience of a man who has done this before; with his son and two daughters, he has stood watching a child who was unable to imagine that he or she would ever be able to do this, yet knowing that there will be a moment—it will seem like magic—when balancing became possible.

Josh tries to glide and he falters; he gets frustrated and wobbles. But again and again, he positions his bike at the top of the incline and sets off, hoping this will be the time he gets it. His face is set in fierce determination. I'm glad he's not looking at me, unsure what combination of fear and hopefulness he might detect in my expression. With each lap he's slowly making, I want to yell to him about courage and liberation. I want to tell him that sometimes the things you come to late, after a struggle, are the ones you appreciate most. More than anything, I want him to feel the exhilaration that comes from taking yourself by surprise.

After a little more wobbling, Josh finds his balance. He puts his feet on the pedals and rides across the parking lot.

Passover

Will it feel lonely?" my mother worries, referring to our small Passover seder in Memphis. It's just my parents, the kids, and me — it's an odd-number year so the kids are with me for the seders. My sister is in Israel with my brother and his family; her fiancé is with his family, the last Passover he and my sister will spend apart before they get married. The crowded, cousin-laden family seders of my childhood no longer exist, except in our minds — the vision of how this night is supposed to look.

We are in the kitchen, of course. The turkey, with its matzo-meal stuffing, is in the oven. I've made the matzo balls, rolling them in my hands and boiling them in hot water seasoned with a few ladles of soup. My mother beats egg whites into a froth for sponge cake. This might be the festival of freedom, but the weeks before are a time of enslavement. The already strict rules for keeping kosher are made infinitely stricter. The rules have multiplied, spawned new categories and subsets. My parents' kitchen is in a locked-down state, nothing admitted without first being screened at the door. In my kitchen at home, I'd made my own efforts—got rid of the prohibited food, covered the counters, cleaned the oven, pulled out the few dishes I had that were used only during this one week. I stockpiled matzo and jelly candies for when we return home so I can feed them to the kids in lieu of forbidden pasta and cereal. All of this not out of a sense of religious obligation but for the sake of people I love.

Next on our list to make is my grandmother's mayonnaise—not only a kosher-for-Passover recipe but a family heirloom that my grandmother learned from her own mother, who made it year-round. "It has how many eggs?" my father the cardiologist asked in an undertone when my grandmother unveiled the finished jar at the table and we spread it sparingly on matzo, knowing better than to waste any drop of this delicacy that we hoped would last all eight days. The mayonnaise was always discussed with great reverence at the seder table, as if it were a piece of herself my grandmother was passing around. For her, not having grown up Orthodox, I think that when she looked out at us, her all-Orthodox family, she felt like she fully belonged inside this world she had chosen.

I pull out the eggs. In the scrubbed-clean refrigerator, three dozen are stacked in cartons, another dozen already gone into the matzo balls and sponge cakes, but on this holiday of no leaven, you can't risk running out of eggs. Earlier in the day I'd made a trip to the supermarket, where the kosher-for-Passover aisles are stocked with macaroons and jars of gefilte fish floating in jellied broth. A week before the holiday, the grocery store usually starts running low on certain items—this year it's tomato sauce and pareve margarine, so we've rationed out the one precious stick my mother borrowed from a neighbor. On the way back to my parents' house, I'd detoured through the neighborhoods I'd known since I was a child, past the Hebrew Academy that I attended, past the houses of former friends and relatives. It occurred to me how little of this city I actually knew —little of its music, none of its food. It wasn't even Memphis I longed for, just the sense that there was a place I was rooted and held. Now, Memphis is no longer the place that feels like home —the sentence reassembles, and Memphis becomes a place that once felt like home. On the map that existed inside my head, its name was always marked in bold letters, my long-standing capital. Now, on the eve of this holiday of Exodus, it becomes a small city among many others.

"Do you think we're doing this right?" my mother asks as we crack and separate the eggs.

I peer into the bowl, trying to envision how this liquid mixture will congeal into a substance that resembles mayonnaise.

"I hope so," I say.

A few Passovers before, my grandmother, mother, and I gathered by the Mixmaster. "Watch first," my grandmother said and demonstrated the proper way to pour in the lemon juice, sugar, salt, and paprika, and then—and only then—add the egg yolks. "You're pouring in the oil way too fast. You have to do it just like I say or the eggs and oil will separate," she chided my mother, who wasn't as exacting as she was. In my family, all the best conversations and the most fraught interactions take place in the kitchen. Under the surface of how to fold and pour, they were debating who knows best, and am I still needed, and is there enough room to be myself, and am I the same or different from who you wanted me to be?

This year, my grandparents are away for the holiday, in Florida at an all-inclusive kosher-for-Passover hotel, a rare late-life luxury, so if there is to be mayonnaise on the seder table, it's up to us to make it.

"What will you do for the last days of Pesach?" my mother asks about the restricted days on which the kids will be with Aaron and we (they) don't write, don't drive, don't turn on lights.

On the Passover CD that is blaring from the living room, freedom is sung and extolled. Freedom, freedom, freedom—a word usually greeted with suspicion in this world. On the stove in front of me, the matzo balls have been boiling and are now ready. Though I'm not supposed to—eating any form of matzo before the seder itself is forbidden, likened by the Talmud to a man who sleeps with his bride on the night before the wedding —I filch a matzo ball and devour it whole.

"I want you to be able to tell me things," my mother says. "I feel you holding back."

"I'm not going to observe those days," I say. "You know that when I'm not with the kids, I don't do Shabbat. I drive, I bike, I hike, I write." I keep going, each word a tiny key unlocking one more tiny door. I had once thought that others could unlock these doors for you, but over this year, I've come to realize that no one can offer freedom to you. It's yours to choose and to claim.

"It's no longer my world. I feel like I've started to live somewhere else," I say.

She knows this, of course, yet to openly name it is to allow the differences between us to become cemented in place. I still feel her discomfort with what I'm saying, yet she is listening to me, her face as gentle as it always is, and open and loving and kind—not approval but the beginning of acceptance. It is among the hardest of concepts to wrap your mind around— that this child who once took shape inside your body is now a separate being, with her own mind, her own beliefs. My mother and I meet each other's eyes and I feel her creating room inside herself for this new version of me as well.

In the backyard, where the kids and I go to take a break from the preparations, we once again pile into the hammock. It's early April, and the azalea bushes are in bloom, along with the lacy white dogwood trees. Spring is the prettiest time of the year to be in Memphis, when the blazing summer days still seem like misremembered exaggerations.

The school year is winding down, and each of the kids is on the cusp of change. In another few weeks, Layla will finish the small nursery school she has loved. In the fall, she will start kindergarten at the school the boys have attended, though next year, they won't be there.

Noam will graduate from this school and plans to go to a pluralist Jewish high school instead of the all-Orthodox high school where, until a few years ago, we had assumed he would go. But the pluralism of his elementary school has become part of his Orthodoxy. He observes the rules, but he doesn't feel that his is the only way. He doesn't want to impose his beliefs on others. For him to choose this high school is to know that he will navigate these religious differences at home and at school, always having to think about how to hold on to what he believes while at the same time make room for what others believe.

Josh too is on the verge of something new—his unhappiness at school has made it clear that he won't go back there next year. Aaron and I aren't yet sure where he'll go instead, whether to public school or another local Jewish school. For the past few months there has been a fragile peace between Aaron and me, but this conversation, or anything to do with religion, has the power to rupture that. We've exchanged a few e-mails but mostly we avoid any potentially difficult discussion. I'm not sure yet what I think is best, still sad that Josh won't remain in a school I have loved. I know it isn't just a question about where Josh will go to school next year, but a larger one that goes to the heart of what it means to be a parent. How to differentiate between something you love and something your child loves. How to find the balance between teaching your children what you want for them and helping your children discover who they are and what they want. How to separate who you are from who they are going to become.

I look at my three kids, snuggling in next to me, then jockeying for better spaces, threatening to knock one another out of the hammock, which sways and tilts at all this shifting weight. But before any of us are thrown overboard, there is a quick reshuffling and rearranging so that we all still fit inside. One change, I know now, leads to so many other changes—with no overarching system or set of rules to which we all belong, we are always shifting into new spaces. All of this is now part of their stories as well, stories that come with bends and turns, areas of fracturing and inconsistencies. In place of the complete protection I once so badly wanted to give them, I can instead offer them my honesty —a more complex vision of the world as I see it. When they were babies, and I read all the right books and tried to follow all the rules, I also bought the expert-recommended black-and-white toys that I displayed on any surface their eyes might pass over. Then, black and white were supposed to be the only colors they could see, but now I trust that my kids can understand a world that comes in a multitude of shades, dizzying and beautiful at once.

Despite the worry and the rush, we are ready. The seder will take place in the living room, on the sectional sofa, which has been taken apart and reconfigured to make a circle. Wineglasses are set on TV trays, the seder plate placed on the coffee table. We dress in colorful robes from the costume bag my siblings and I played with as children.

"It's time," my mother says.

"Do I have to come?" Josh asks me when I call the kids to the table.

I look at his face—he is afraid I'm going to force him.

"What if you come to the first part of the seder, then you can leave when you need a break?" I suggest and gratefully he agrees.

The three kids are here and ready to begin. My parents are here and so am I. On the table in front of us is the seder plate with its sprigs of parsley, its shank bone, and hard-boiled egg. Next to it, scarves my mother will use as props for the Bibliodrama she has planned. On the table too are the various Haggadahs my parents have collected over the years, the most basic version with the script for this night written in Hebrew on one side of the page, the English translation on the other. Volumes as well with rabbinic commentaries both classical and modern. There are newer, nontraditional ones too: a feminist seder and an experiential seder and even a vegetarian seder. Some of them hew closely to the original text, while others take those words as the starting point and use them to create something new.

Alongside these books is the volume my father has assembled. For the past few weeks, he has looked for Passover essays and articles that are personally meaningful to him; he seeks out voices of moderation, voices that are not excessively rule-based, that espouse openness and that pull from art and literature and science. He has printed out multiple copies, and from these he has assembled binders labeled *Mirvis Family Seder,* one for each of us, companions to the official booklets. Inside these binders is the version of Orthodoxy in which he believes.

We sing the order of the night, a tune which reminds me of being a little girl in a new dress that, because of the season, came with an Easter bonnet, which I wore as well. It reminds me of being so studious that I took to heart my teachers' promise that for each word of the seder we recited, we would receive divine credit for a separate good deed. Now, for me, there is no counting up good deeds, no worrying about ingesting every crumb of required matzo. It's not the same seder I used to attend but an alternate one being written in the margins. There is room for the pleasure of being here with my family, telling the story we have been imparting for generations. I am still part of this story, and the story remains part of me as well — its language, its rhythms, its customs all have shaped who I am. To the rabbi who once issued the warning about partaking but not enjoying, and to the wayward yeshiva student who tried to go, I want to offer my own ending: When participation no longer feels like it might be mistaken for capitulation, when there is acceptance of who you have chosen to become — then it's possible to return and enjoy parts of what you've left. Not every leave-taking had to be absolute and entire. Orthodoxy can remain my childhood home, a place I visit but where I no longer live.

We turn the pages. We dip parsley into salt water. We break

the middle matzo. We arrive at the Four Questions, where we encourage our children to ask what is different about this night. We reach the passage describing the four sons, among them the wise one who asks a question that includes himself as part of the story, the evil one who looks at it and dares to state that this tradition no longer belongs to him.

"If you were a slave in Egypt, what job would you have?" my mother asks.

We would be bricklayers, laundresses, cooks. We would build pyramids, lay roads.

"Can you name a time," my mother asks, "when you felt enslaved? Can you tell us about a time when you felt free?"

We act out the story, run wildly around the house. Josh joins in, grabbing a robe that he tosses over his head and chasing after Noam.

"Let my people go," my father proclaims, our makeshift Moses.

"No, no, no, I will not let them go," bellows Layla, our Pharaoh, in a clear, strong voice that is emerging more all the time now.

But the people stand up to Pharaoh regardless. They are ready to set out on this journey—even though once they are in the desert, they will lament how it was better for them in Egypt. They couldn't make the transformation from slavery to freedom. When we learned about this in school, the desert Jews were depicted as a foolish, ungrateful lot—how could they bemoan such a painful past? Back then, I had yet to understand that leave-takings are slow and painful and carry their own losses, that you can miss even what you needed to leave.

The seder moves forward, and now we are up to the ever-popular Ten Plagues. We pull out the plague bag, a burlap sack containing small rubber frogs, black plastic lice, a cow who keels over when a button is pressed. All this so Pharaoh will say, "Yes, I will set you free." All this so that we could set out on the slow journey toward something new. Leaving has always been a part of the story. So has passing through the uncertain spaces between fixed realms.

It's getting late — we're hours still from matzo balls and gefilte fish and the equivalent of Thanksgiving dinner my mother has prepared, even further from the moment when my father will search for the piece of matzo the kids have stolen and hidden and for which he will offer presents in order to assure its safe return. On this night, we are supposed to feel as though we too left Egypt, to see our own journeys as part of this story — not a closed, fixed tale but one that expands to include each of us.

On this night I too am reminded of my own moment of leave-taking. Almost a year has passed since I stood waiting before that panel of rabbis, my hands cupped in front of me.

The ceremony took place once Aaron and I were no longer living in the same house. I was busy getting the house ready to be put on the market. We had divided the time with the kids, divided the furniture, begun the task of dividing any assets — all these tasks necessary to separate our lives. In my inbox one morning, along with missives from the lawyers and updates from the real estate agent and ongoing exchanges with the therapists, there was a poem called "The Journey," by Mary Oliver, sent to me by the editor who, a few weeks earlier, had bought my novel, which I'd finally completed.

There would come a time when you had to set out, the poem reminded me, even when it was difficult and uncertain. Eventually, you began to find your own path. After reading the poem once, I read it every day, sometimes multiple times, until I knew it by heart, until I could sing it to myself like a soothing lullaby or else follow it like the only kind of instruction manual that could guide me through. Soon there was an offer on the house. I found a place nearby to rent. I packed with the urgency of someone who was fleeing. I started with the books, which were the easiest for me and Aaron to divide up. I turned to the toys and sorted into piles what would go to his house and what to mine, then I went through the kitchen, the linens, the pictures on the walls, disassembling in a few weeks what had taken sixteen years to put together. I packed up our bedroom where our two twin beds were pushed permanently apart, like the beds of innocent children. I collected the hats I still wore to synagogue and added them to the give-away pile. I heaped letters and photos into boxes that I knew I wouldn't look at for a long time. I cried as I packed, burned through with guilt. But there would eventually be another way to live, the poem reminded me as I recited it again to myself. In the now almost empty bedroom, I left a copy of this poem on our dresser, hoping Aaron would read it. Where I'd failed to make myself understood, I hoped the poet's words might make it clear.

I'd driven to the meeting with the rabbis as raw and as brittle as I'd ever been. "Bring a friend," the rabbi of my synagogue advised me when he called to ascertain my identity. "You should have someone with you for moral support," said an acquaintance who'd received a *get* the prior year and had found the ceremony to be impersonal and demeaning. I thought about asking Ariel to come with me or about having my mother fly up to Boston to stand with me. She and my father had walked me down the white-sheathed aisle at my wedding. Then, I had been accompanied by every approving message that this was what I was supposed to do. But I didn't want to rely on anyone else for my strength. The divorce was a decision I had arrived at on my own. This aisle, I needed to walk alone.

I stood in front of the rabbis, awaiting the piece of paper. The colloquial word for it was a *get,* but the biblical term for this document was *sefer kritut* — a book of termination, a book of rending, a book of separation. Here, on the piece of parchment before me, the words were meticulously parsed, legislated, and scripted, but despite any protestation to the contrary, there was always another story, a longer and more complicated version waiting to be written.

With a sharp, deliberate movement, the rabbi dropped the folded paper into my hands. I played the role as I'd been directed. I clasped the document tightly between my hands and brought it to my chest, demonstrating that I was taking full possession. With the rabbis watching, I ceremoniously turned and walked from the room. As the door closed behind me, the divorce took effect.

On the other side of the door, alone, I took a deep breath. I was free now to craft another story for myself, one that I could eventually take hold of in my cupped and waiting hands.

I was summoned back inside. One of the rabbis took the piece of parchment from me and drew an *X* over it and tore it up — another legalistic move so that no one could ever examine the document and find an error, which could be used to declare that we were in fact still married. Then I was apprised of my new status in Jewish law as a divorcée and informed of all the new laws that went along with this—as far as the rabbis knew, I would remain Orthodox. I was told that I couldn't be alone in a room with my former husband. I wasn't allowed to drive alone in a car with him between cities or live in the same apartment building. I wasn't allowed to remarry for ninety days. When I was allowed to remarry, I was not permitted to marry a man of the ancient priestly caste.

I listened politely but looked at the rabbis differently now, not as men who stood in authority over me, but as people I once knew. Now on the other side of it, I regarded this room of rabbis with something like nostalgia, something like the feeling that comes from looking back at a receding shoreline once you've finally set sail.

I was about to leave when the head of the rabbinical court looked me in the eye. I steeled myself for judgment and rebuke. Instead, he told me a story.

The Temple altar, the Talmud says, weeps when a man divorces his wife. When a revered rabbi got divorced, his students came to him and asked: "How can this be? Does our tradition not teach that the altar weeps over a divorce?"

The rabbi looked at his students. "Better the altar should weep than should I."

Now the head of the court told me, kindly, "It's a new beginning. Don't look back. Go forth, become the person you need to be."

I was surprised and moved by the sympathy in his voice. All these rigid rules, all these minute and unyielding laws. Yet here too was the recognition of human pain; here too was an acceptance of human experience. It was this wisdom from my tradition that I wanted to hold on to, even as I was leaving so much behind.

Before I left, as they did at the end of my wedding, as they did at the conclusion of divorce ceremonies hundreds of years ago, the rabbis wished me a mazel tov.

Shelter in Place

We are safe at home when we hear the news. Noam finds out first, from a text message from a friend, and he comes into the living room to tell us that the Boston Marathon has been bombed.

Every year, on Patriots' Day — the third Monday in April — the marathon passes a mile from our house, and every year we stand along the sidewalks, marveling at the scores of runners, the ones who seem to glide effortlessly, the ones who by this point along Heartbreak Hill look beaten and worn. Now, horrified, we are glued to the TV.

"There was an explosion at the finish line," I explain to Josh and Layla, feeling the protective urge to make it sound as innocuous as possible, yet I watch their faces cloud as they come to recognize the magnitude of what has happened.

For the past few weeks leading up to the marathon, the carriage road along Commonwealth Avenue and the path beside the Charles River have been crowded with runners. As spring makes its cautious approach, I have tried to be outside whenever possible — walking downtown near Trinity Church, a famous landmark whose arches and towers seem to belong more in a fairy tale of castles and witch houses than in the middle of a modern busy city; along the Esplanade, where, in the summertime, kayaks and sailboats will pass by; or closer to home, sitting by Crystal Lake and the Chestnut Hill Reservoir, where runners make their laps. Somehow, somewhere, in the past few months, Boston has become the place where I feel most at home—not the rooted feeling that my grandmother expressed, that where you live is where you must live, but the happenstance feeling of a transplant who knows that things change, that people move on and away. It is a city that reminds me we don't always arrive where we once intended to go.

The days after the bombing pass in a state of anxiety and sadness. At the end of the week, early in the morning, my phone buzzes with news that school is canceled—that all of Boston is canceled. Shelter in place, we are told, as though this is just an odd sort of snow day. But nothing feels remotely normal. There has been a shooting and a carjacking and a gunfight with the police, and one of the suspected bombers has been killed and one is still on the loose in the town where Noam and Josh go to school.

I'm at William's, the kids are with Aaron, and all I want to do is go scoop the kids up, bring them home, and cook for them and feed them and hold them. Instead, Noam and I text back and forth, trading tidbits of information. At Aaron's house, they are doing the same thing that William and I are doing, that everyone I know is doing: watching the news.

It's Friday, and so just before sundown, when we have waited all day with a sense of imminent expectation, I leave William's apartment and drive home. The streets are empty of cars, as though the Shabbat prohibitions soon to descend apply temporarily to everyone. Because it's my weekend with the kids, Aaron and I agree that he will bring the kids to me before sundown or it will be too late for him to drive.

When the kids come home, I hug them tightly. I want to huddle with the three of them inside this house that, after nearly a year, is now cluttered with books and toys and pictures of the kids that make it feel like home.

I start the Shabbat preparations, assembling a meal of pasta and vegetables from what we have. As pots boil on the stove, as dishes are cooking in the oven, I remember something else I need to do.

"The light in the refrigerator," Noam had said to me two weeks before, at the end of the last Shabbat we were all here. "Do you think you can unscrew it for next Shabbat?"

By opening the door to the fridge, he was causing the light to go on. It was a prohibition that I'd become haphazard about — one of the many small acts of observance that once were givens and now need to be purposefully recalled.

"I'm glad you told me," I said.

"Do you mind doing it?" he asked.

"Of course not. You can always tell me. You know that, right?" I say.

I reach my hand to the back of the fridge and feel around for the bulb. It's hard to get hold of and too hot to touch, but I'm determined to unscrew it. I'm doing this, and other actions like it, to help Noam be part of this world that he is choosing. And doing so comes not only in the broad strokes and large proclamations about love and respect but in each of the minute actions

—not just God, not just sin, lay in the details, but love lived there too. This is one of the lessons of my former world, one I want to hold on to as well.

The bulb remains stuck, and finally, in fear of burning my fingers, I grab a dishtowel and cover my hand with it as I pull —too hard, though, breaking the bulb in the process. The base of the lightbulb remains inside but the glass cracks and breaks.

"Good news and bad news," I tell Noam as I'm cleaning up the slivers of glass and he is passing through the kitchen on the way to his room, preparing to turn off his devices and enter into his stricter version of Shabbat. "The bulb is out, except I shattered it trying to do it."

"That's one way to handle it," he says.

He's laughing but his gratitude is written on his face. I've never admired my son more than I do right now as I watch him navigate the contradictory, compromise-filled landscape that's hard for many people much older than him.

It's the kind of moment that will recur in many guises in our family. Even when we're tired of it, we will revisit the conversation about how best to live with different beliefs and practices, all in the same house, as part of the same family. For me, moments like this are a reminder that when I feel that rise of difference—with children, with family, with all those whom I love —the best answer is to look at the person on the other side more fully, listen more openly. Rather than placing a wedge, these conversations can pull you closer—they let you see, really see, who someone else is.

There are still a few minutes to go before candle lighting, and we are gathered around the TV. Finally, there is news. Just as it's time to light candles, we hear of the arrest and the fact that it's over.

William arrives and watches as I gather the kids and light the Shabbat candles, waving the light toward me, covering my eyes, silently reciting my own words of gratitude for my children and their safety. I don't know if I can still think of this as a prayer, but I close my eyes, and this wish, this hope, whatever it is, overflows from me. That line of connection, with my mother and grandmothers, and the women before them too, can still be mine to claim if I want it. It wasn't monolithic to begin with, never a line of sameness as far as the eye could see. Both my grandmothers had changed course from what had come before, had set out in search of something else. Each of us was always a new and diverging link.

At the table, I sing "Shalom Aleichem," welcoming the proverbial Shabbat angels into our house. One at a time, from oldest to youngest, I place my hands lightly on each kid's head and bless them as I was blessed each week. I fill a cup with grape juice and recite the blessings. Without the sense of obligation and restriction, there is room for me to consider what I want these blessings to mean. Still in the state of no-longer-being, I'm not yet sure. This is something I will begin to build anew, but for now, these acts form a connection between then and now. William sits quietly as I make the prayers, as I pass around the grape juice and slices of challah. I know the words are foreign to him and will remain so, but he sits beside me as I hold on to rituals and reminders that will remain mine.

It's not a Shabbat like the one in which I was raised, not a Shabbat that is without its painful complications, but we've become more accustomed to the uncertainty that remains when you cease to follow a rule book; no one way but lots of ways, each with its benefits and losses. I still miss being part of a community —the one to which I no longer belong is a place inside me that I sometimes peer in at, all the houses lined up in rows, candles lit in the windows. Inside this freedom, there is still a loneliness. There are other kinds of communities, I know, that I can eventually build for myself—smaller maybe, less all-encompassing, ones in which I won't have to cede my independence in order to belong.

But now, I have this day with the people I love. As I look at the Shabbat candles, I think, as I still do sometimes, of the angels who are supposedly peering in my window. I can't erase them entirely, but I can exchange them for another pair who come not as inspectors or outside arbiters of whether our night is good or bad. These angels are gentle and forgiving and care only that this is a house of love.

After dinner, William goes home and Noam goes to sleep— newly arriving at the age when going to bed early has become a treat. I kiss him good night, and Josh gets into my bed, along with Layla, who is still there every night. I know that by now I should be making an attempt to move her back into her own bed, but she sees through my halfhearted efforts, able to sense that I'm as unready as she is.

"What if we were near the finish line?" Josh asks as we all huddle together.

"I would have grabbed you and run," I say, imagining myself a maternal version of Wonder Woman who is fast and strong enough to carry them in her arms for miles—forever, if need be.

To this, I wish I could add that they will always be among the ones who are spared and saved. But there is no longer trading any kind of observance for the promise of safety, no illusion that goodness can grant protection, no assurance that everything happens for a reason. This too is one of the losses of this past year, yet there is another kind of comfort to be had from saying things that I actually believe. I have no clear-cut answers to hand them, no theological treatises to offer, but I also don't have to frantically stitch together an unraveling explanation in my hands — faster, faster, in order to keep the threads from coming apart.

"Why did a little boy die?" Josh asks.

"Why?" Layla joins in, and they are looking at me, both of them awaiting an answer. When they were younger, what they needed most was for me to feed them, bathe them, carry them, dress them. Then, what I'd wanted most was a second set of hands. Now what they increasingly need from me is this kind of conversation.

"We don't know, we can't understand it," I begin and continue the best I can. How to be helpers. How to live purposefully. How to be compassionate. These questions belonged to us all. The answers weren't the sole possession of any one religion.

As they both drift off to sleep, I hold them close — these children whom I know so well yet am constantly discovering anew.

"I love you," I say, one of the few sentences I know to be certain and true.

The acts of putting a child to bed — smoothing her hair, caressing his cheek, pulling up the blankets, tucking them in — are small rituals, tiny acts of devotion. Holding them on this night comes closest to locating some part of the goodness I want.

After the divorce, I'd let myself believe that there was only one kind of home and that ours was irreparably broken. But on this night, in this quiet house, home doesn't need those solid unbreachable walls. It feels more like a small nest you could build for yourself and for those whom you love.

Weddings

My sister's wedding is in May, in Israel, and I'm taking the kids out of school for a week to travel there. William is meeting us in Israel two days before the wedding. It's the first time he will be in Israel and the first time he will meet much of my family — the separate parts of my life continuing to merge.

"Are you ready for this?" I ask William.

"Bring it on," he says.

In Israel, a few hours before Shabbat begins, William emerges from a cab in front of the hotel where we are all staying for a weekend of pre-wedding celebration. I rush outside to hug him and give him a kiss under the displeased eyes of a relative, who looks shocked to see me greet a man in this way.

"And who is this?" she asks when we come into the lobby, and on her face I see the suspicious, surveying look I'd once known all too well. Momentarily, I see him through her eyes. He isn't wearing a yarmulke — he's clearly not Orthodox, and unrepentantly so.

At her question, which hangs in the air, I stumble for the right words, all of which feel wrong, here more than anywhere.

"This is William," I say. There is no better answer I could have given, no truer statement of fact.

WILLIAM WEARS A YARMULKE on Friday night for services. I watch him sitting in the men's section with my boys. He is wearing a yarmulke as a sign of respect, but there is no pretense that it stands for something he believes in. He holds his head stiffly, aware of its foreign presence, as though a bird has landed on his head and he is afraid of disturbing its perch. He stands when the other men do, but at the end of Lecha Dodi, the prayer welcoming the Sabbath, he is caught off guard when all the people turn, as required, to the back of the room, bow, then turn back to the front—a dancer unaware of the next move in his chorus line.

"I'm glad it's all in Hebrew. That way I don't understand anything they're saying," he whispers to me at the end of services.

We gather for dinner and the Kiddush is recited. After we do the ceremonial hand-washing and are prohibited from speaking until the blessing over the challah is made, I whisper to him, "Are you okay?"

William looks at me in surprise. "I'm fine," he says, and he *is* fine here, I realize.

For the rest of the night, every time I look up, he is deep in conversation with either my siblings or my parents or one of my other relatives. William is irrepressibly friendly, someone to whom people tell things. A family member I haven't seen in many years asks him about his kids, and he tells them about his two daughters and about his son, who after his long struggle with anxiety has vastly improved. After spending three months in the Utah wilderness, backpacking and living outside in harsh conditions, he is thriving—independent and calm. More than anything, he has learned that he can rely on his own strength.

Even so, the pain is still present in William's voice; as a parent, there is no easy return to an unworried state. He has become someone that other parents call and ask for advice when faced with a similar situation. He doesn't hide how hard it has been. Here, too, to my surprise, this relative whom I'd always thought of as reticent shares a painful situation with her daughter. One person's honesty paves the way for another's. William isn't wondering what others want him to be, isn't trying to match so as not to offend. He's at ease with who he is. I knew this about him before, but here, I'm seeing anew the part of him that I love most.

ON SHABBAT AFTERNOON, there is a game of ultimate Frisbee on the grass behind the hotel. Everyone plays: My children and William, my brother's children, my sister's soon-to-be-husband, and his nephews and nieces. The kids and adults are running back and forth, calling out in a mixture of English and Hebrew. The kids have been shy with one another—gaps of language and a world—but now the reserve loosens.

By this point in the afternoon, William's yarmulke has disappeared. I'm glad he's taken it off, that he's not paying homage to something he doesn't believe. White-fringed tzitzit fly behind my brother's kids as they run. William calls out directions in English, even though the kids understand little. Trying to prevent mass confusion, Noam translates, using the Hebrew he has learned in school. Noam is wearing his yarmulke; Josh is not. Layla is running and weaving through the players, half in the game, half in a game of her own. The nephews wear the knit yarmulkes of the Modern Orthodox and are dressed in shorts and T-shirts. My brother is in his long black coat and dress clothes, standing on the sidelines watching with me. My parents are sitting in chairs looking out at this view of our family. Raised with one vision, we have all nonetheless forged our own paths. If someone were to take a group picture now and hang it next to all the others in my parents' house, there would be no simple game of matching up how we all fit together. Yet, despite this, here we are. Not a family whose members are all the same, but a family in which the love for one another matters more.

The game is ending, and all of the players are red-faced and sweaty and thirsty, and it's impossible to tell which team has won. Or maybe they have forgotten to keep score, because they all seem equally happy as they laugh and trade high-fives.

The wedding is the next day, in a garden overlooking the rocky Judean hills. The air smells like lemon and mint. Flowers bloom from trellises. My sister's white lace dress is decorated with a sea-green ribbon that ties around her waist and cascades down her back.

The wedding is being live-streamed by the videographer so that my grandparents, too frail to make the trip, can watch it from their house in Memphis. My grandmother, who has long awaited this day, bought a dress years before in the hope of Dahlia getting married, and when I imagine her in front of the computer, I hope she's wearing the dress, though only my grandfather will see her in it.

Akiva, his wife, and their kids go down the aisle first. Behind them, I walk with my three kids, who are in Israeli wedding–casual, the boys in navy pants and white button-down shirts, Layla in a pale green dress and hot-pink light-up sneakers.

Dahlia walks down the aisle on the arms of my parents, toward her fiancé. He is wearing the groom's traditional white robe, standing under the white chuppah, waiting for her. The two of them gaze at each other and smile as the wedding benedictions are sung, as she circles him seven times, symbolically building the walls of their home. My brother is the rabbi who marries them, and he stands before them, dressed in his dark suit and hat. The sun is setting behind them, the brown and green landscape now streaked with rays of pink. Still jet-lagged, Layla falls asleep on me as the blessings are recited. Dahlia's veil is lifted, the wine is sipped, and the happiness on her face is evident.

The *ketubah* is read aloud and I'm shaken from my peaceful reverie. To me, it's no longer a mostly incomprehensible document in ancient Aramaic. Even if people pay little attention to the meaning of the words, here it is, in the middle of a wedding ceremony. Amid all the flowers and the bridal tulle, the details of what a groom pays his wife in the event of a divorce. It's a stark reminder that there are so many ways these stories can turn out. It's hard for me to see a wedding in the same way, hard not to think of all the ways hopes can go unfulfilled, innocence can go awry. Even as I'm filled with happiness for my sister, my own wedding comes back to me with unexpected force. On this day, it's hard not to once again be the bride, walking down that aisle.

Even after all these years, I still wish I could go back in time and call to my younger self before her betrothal documents were signed, or catch her eye as she was being reminded about how the bride has a direct line to God; before she sets off down the aisle, a white flower wreath in her hair, her face covered with a pearl-studded veil that makes everything appear blurred and soft. I want to whisper warnings to her — to be the evil fairy who comes uninvited to the festivities, bringing not happy blessings but ugly truths from the future. I want to open her eyes and ask her if she is sure, really sure. Gently remind her that life doesn't always turn out the way it's supposed to, tell her she can wait longer, until she is more sure of who she is. Awaken her curiosity about the other choices that will await her if only she could live with the unknown.

And if she won't listen to these gentle warnings — because of course she won't — then I will hold back nothing. Be relentless and brutal. Show her the artifacts from the future, her red-rimmed eyes and her arms that she squeezes tightly in order to keep herself intact, and the stunned look on her children's faces when she pulls aside the covering on their lives. I will tell her she will have to bear the pain on three young faces that she will love more than anything she could yet imagine.

I will tell her of the anger, held in for too long, that will come spewing forth. Tell her that she will be accused of not trying when she is exhausted from years of trying.

Tell her that she will know that she is doing this to save herself, but even so, there is a price to pay and she must be willing to pay it again and again. That in the end, after dividing everything of the marriage, she will have to bear all the blame.

Tell her this is a story that will divide her life in two, a story she will carry with her always. Tell her this is a story she will want to tell, need to tell, but first she will have to be able to face it herself.

The Sheva Brachot, the seven marriage blessings, are being recited now, but my mind is spinning and I think not of the words praising God who created the groom who rejoices in his bride. Instead, I think of the Sharon Olds poem "I Go Back to May 1937"—hardly good wedding material—about her parents' disastrous marriage.

> *I want to go up to them and say Stop,*
> *don't do it—she's the wrong woman,*
> *he's the wrong man, you are going to do things*
> *you cannot imagine you would ever do*

I still want to go up to her, my bridled, bridal self, and plead with her one last time: Please. You are barely twenty-three, so much younger than you realize. Please. You know so little of the world. You know so little of yourself.

The sound of broken glass returns me to this wedding, to now. My sister, who has waited, who knows herself, is married, and her face is shining, and she and her husband are holding hands and dancing back down the aisle, and the people all around are calling out, "Mazel tov," and I am sitting here, happy to be in this moment, at this time.

But I don't do it. I want to live, concludes Sharon Olds.

I look down at my daughter sleeping in my lap, the softness of her cheek, the rise and fall of her breath, my boys next to me, prodding each other, whispering and smiling, looking mischievous even when dressed in their wedding clothes.

I shake myself from all this backward-looking. It's true, I didn't heed my own voice when I was younger. I waited too long to recognize my doubt. But it's time to acknowledge to myself that the only way to have learned all this was to pass through it.

Do it anyway, I tell that bride. *Walk down that aisle.*

Letting Go

I want to give you a heads-up that I'm getting engaged this week-end, Aaron e-mails me one night at the end of May.

I had known from the kids that he was dating someone, so I'm not surprised. As strange as this all feels, I'm glad for him. I want him to be happy. The complexities, I know, will continue to multiply. Now there will be many families our children are part of, their family trees always multilimbed. It will not be simple, with all the changes still ahead, but a more complicated life carries its own rewards.

With this news replaying in my mind, I drive down the street we used to live on and stop in front of the old house. All this year, I've avoided driving down this street, afraid of the house that had been both cocoon and cage, but now the past is starting to feel less daunting. I can look at the house, at the grass that is neatly mowed and the pink azalea bushes in bloom as they were every spring. The new owners have painted the exterior and taken care of the much-needed repairs on the roof. The house sits innocently — just another blue-shuttered, black-roofed New England home.

The next week, I'm in New York City to give a book talk, and with a few free hours, I walk uptown to the 110th Street apartment where Aaron and I lived when we first got married. A decade has passed since I've been in this neighborhood, but on the corner is the same grocery store where I once shopped. On the blocks nearby are some of the same small restaurants I'd never entered because they weren't kosher. There are newer places too, ones that are cleaner and brighter, distorting the images I'd held on to of these gritty few blocks that were not quite the Upper West Side, not yet Columbia. I walk to what had been our building, set back from the street, with its wide courtyard and green shutters, peeling now as they were then. Gazing upward, I count five flights to what had been our floor. The same wooden, mullioned windows, the same kind of white shades — almost, almost making me feel that if I were to peer in, I could catch a glimpse of that young married girl cooking in her kitchen or lying beside her husband in their new married bed. Like a play that is performed over and over, two figures in a window acting out their happy scene again and again.

So much of the past feels like it has been ravaged in a fire, but is it still possible to rescue any intact memory?

It's easier to think about the years of sadness and loneliness that came after, but this apartment is a stone-and-concrete reminder that here inside these walls, we were once young and innocent and only at the start of our married lives together. It's this fact that has been the hardest to face. There existed a time before the anger and the disappointment and the feeling of entrapment. A time when I wouldn't have believed or wished for this ending.

When I return home to Newton, I finally unpack that old box of photos, read the cards Aaron gave to me over a decade of birthdays and anniversaries. I make myself look at the wedding photos that I'd so long avoided, at the cascading flowers and my bridal whites and the bright smiles on our shining faces. The line between then and now doesn't need to remain as fractured. Yes, I had been young, and yes, we had been in such a hurry, and yes, we hadn't known each other, or ourselves, nearly well enough, and yes, it had ended so terribly and so painfully, but some of these memories can still be salvaged. The end doesn't have to erase the beginning. There is no avoiding the fact that on our faces, in that moment, there is unmistakable happiness.

IN THE MIDDLE OF JUNE, I turn forty-one. In celebration of my birthday — and in belated celebration of my fortieth, which had passed almost unnoticed in the chaos of the divorce — William and I go to the Berkshires for the weekend. We're staying next to a lake, and on Saturday morning, we sit in rickety beach chairs along the shore. The water is so cold that only a few brave adults have waded in. Kids, seemingly impervious to the temperature, swing from a rope tied to a tree branch, soaring into the lake, immune as well to fear.

We decide to brave the water, which is so cold it stings, but even so, I swim out to the middle of the lake, where I float on my back, staring up at the sky domed above me and the trees circling all around — here not to cleanse myself or purify myself but to open myself as much as I can be. Inside my chest, there is a widened, no-longer-knotted feeling, as though more space has been created between my ribs. I didn't know until this year that there is comfort to be derived from being inside not just a community of people, but a body of water and a ring of trees. I didn't know that you could belong to a lake, to a forest, to an expansive vista. Is beauty enough of an alternative? Can you trade the rules of so many books for the green of so many trees?

William swims toward me and I swim toward him and his arms wrap around me. I keep expecting the exhilaration I have when I'm with him to fade, but it has yet to. There is still that urge to pull him closer. This man, whom I love, so different from me and yet with whom I feel entirely intertwined. The life ahead of me is as roadless and unmappable as the water we're swimming in. Nor is there any path back to a pristine, innocent state, even if I still wanted that.

I move in toward him, my arms around his neck, his arms encircling my waist. He brings his face close to mine, my eyes staring forcefully into his. I try to hold on to him without putting all my weight on him, try to keep treading water even as he holds me, in order to keep myself afloat. And this — it always comes down to this — is the answer between us as well. To know that this is who I am, and this is who he is, this is how we are connected, and this is how we will each remain ourselves.

THE SUMMER IS PASSING QUICKLY, too quickly, when Aaron and I stand in the empty parking lot of an office building, lit only by a few street lamps, and talk beside our two cars, which are pulled up next to each other, like reunited members of a herd.

We'd come here to meet with a school counselor, seeking last-minute advice about where Josh should go for this upcoming year. Inside, with the help of the counselor, who talked about the ways she thought public school would be beneficial, we came to the decision that this was what Josh would do

With the meeting over, Aaron and I stand in the dark parking lot, and we talk tentatively about the kids. Until now, e-mail has been the primary way to communicate, but in e-mail, it's easier to be cold and sharp. In person, the mood has become softer, resigned. After our years of fighting with a fierceness that I don't think either of us knew we possessed, the feeling between us is one of being used up. I wish there were some way we could laugh as we once did about the funny things the kids have said, exclaim over how they have grown, and share with each other how proud we are of them. But any departure from this stilted practical conversation might pierce the protective layer that has been set in place.

I still have the wish, futile as it is, to make my story understood, as though it were only a matter of finding the right words in the right combination. I wish there were some way to lay aside the old questions about good and bad and look back and say, *This is who we were and who we became. This is what happened between us and this is who we now are. This is how we were the same and this is how we were different and this is what we each needed and this is how we failed each other.* I know that there is no agreed-upon story between us—it's as though we've constructed entirely different albums, as though we lived inside different marriages and different divorces. We will look back at our shared past in our own ways, learn our own lessons, carry our own stories and our own truths. One more separation that I need to accept.

Before getting into our own cars and driving off to our separate lives, Aaron and I linger for a few minutes more. Tentatively, we talk about how we hope this upcoming school year will be a good one for Josh. This is what we both want more than anything. Even long after everything we once jointly owned has been divided, these three children belong to us both. In this way we remain part of each other as well.

ON ONE OF THE LAST Sundays in August, I drive the kids to the beach. William is spending the day with his own kids, who are home for the summer. I've met his kids and am slowly starting to get to know them. This too will be part of what comes next, more people to whom we will all be connected, more parts of an ever-changing and expanding story.

With the car packed, I pull out of the driveway, still cautious, as though newly piloting a 747. Each time I enter the highway on-ramp, preparing to merge, I feel the specter of fear.

"Do you remember that time," I ask Noam, who is in the front seat next to me, "when I had to pull over because I was too afraid to keep driving?"

He sifts through his memories until he comes up with that night. He was seven, maybe eight — an age when he would have assumed that the mother in the driver's seat was as steady as an autopilot.

"I didn't understand what was going on but I knew something was wrong," he says.

I think of the young mother I was to him, my first child, and the intensity of my urge to shield him from any uncertainty. I think of all the times I pushed him in the stroller up and down the streets of New York City, barely aware that I was only at the beginning of what I would come to know as a mother. I tell him now, as I drive, that I was once so afraid and now I am not. I tell him you can conquer fears, you can make changes when you need to, you can take action, seize control of your life.

"Okay, Mom," he says.

"Really," I say. I've strayed into Mom-offering-valuable-life-lessons mode, but with him on the verge of starting high school, I want to pack in all these moments while I still can.

"Very interesting," he says and gives me a look of exaggerated deep focus, his head nodding in faux deep contemplation. I laugh and he laughs, and Josh and Layla in the back seat want to know what we are laughing at, and even though we can't really explain, they laugh as well.

I change lanes and merge onto Route 3, where the road narrows, becoming less of an interstate and more of a country highway. Soon the Sagamore Bridge gleams ahead. There is the Cape Cod Canal and the boats sailing past and the vastness of the bright sky and the water on both sides that widens and leads to the ocean.

A few miles across the bridge, I get on Route 6A, the scenic highway, even though it will take longer. Along this road is a small art gallery with a nature walk behind it that I once loved.

"We used to do a small hike near here," I tell the kids.

"When?" they ask.

"Every summer, this was the first stop we made on the way to the Cape," I say.

"I remember," Noam says. "There's the really muddy part, and then the high grass and the rickety bridge."

"All of us went there?" Layla asks. She is the one least likely to remember any time before; for her, all of us together will be a story she hears about a seemingly mythical past.

"All of us," I confirm. "Daddy and I came here for the first time when Noam was four and Josh was a baby—I read about it in a book and we decided to stop here, and we loved it. So we came back the following summer, and then every year after that."

"I miss the way it used to be," Josh says.

The rush of guilt and sadness rolls across me and I let it inside me, able to hold this pain, as though my heart has grown an extra chamber. In making more room for my happiness, there is also more space for the sadness—the two don't cancel each other out but exist side by side.

"Tell me what you miss the most," I say.

"We were all together," Josh says.

I take in his words, hold them, mourn them.

"I miss it too," I say and think back to that young family we once were. I held Noam's hand as we walked behind the gallery, Josh snuggled into a baby carrier against me as we passed through the sculpture garden where the ground was covered with iridescent stones, blues and purples and greens. We kept walking as sculptures and statues were scattered among the flowers and grass and trees—as though trees could bloom with metallic flowers and host hammered-silver birds. Farther out, the grass grew taller than the kids, some years even taller than Aaron and me, and we stepped across the slats of a boardwalk, stopped at a covered wood bench, then walked across the rickety hanging bridge.

Each summer, I took pictures of the kids in the same spots. Soon another baby was added to the pictures, Layla in the same carrier I'd once used to hold the boys. In different photos, my hair was shorter or longer, I was heavier or thinner, my face a little older and more worn, Aaron's hair beginning to be flecked with gray. I'd imagined we would come here every year until the kids were grown. I'd planned a decade's worth of these pictures hanging on the walls of our house to mark all the ways we had changed.

Now, as we near the gallery, I consider stopping the car—I could once again walk through with the kids, take pictures as I always have; a return visit to a place that has stayed the same, though we have changed.

The gallery comes up quickly, and I slow but don't stop, preferring to let this one place remain as it exists in my mind. Let the grass grow ever higher, let the gates remain sealed so the inhabitants can fall into a protected hundred-year sleep. I keep driving, to the Orleans rotary where the highways merge and onward to the outer Cape, to Coast Guard Beach. Under the bright sun, we lay out our blanket and sand toys and sandwiches, and the boys and I grab the Boogie Boards and run into the ocean, while Layla plays in the sand.

A huge wave is coming. Noam points, grinning.

"Should we try it?" I ask.

It's far enough away that we can still balk, either by rushing forward to safety or going under to avoid its impact. We do neither. The water is rough and smashes against us, but instead of being toppled, we are lifted up and over the waves.

A New Year

And then there are the final waning weeks of summer, when I want the days to both linger and hurry toward what comes next.

At the end of August, Noam starts high school. He leaves early, taking the bus. As I watch him walk to the corner bus stop, I remember how, when he was a baby, the days used to feel so long, yet every change in him seemed to happen so quickly. In just a few years he will learn to drive. A few years after that, he will leave home, go to college and on to the rest of his life. Without realizing it, I've been preparing for this stage all along.

For now, though, he walks toward the corner, a teenager in jeans and a Red Sox T-shirt, a brightly colored crocheted yarmulke on his head, gray backpack slung over his shoulder, cell phone tucked into his pocket. He looks both ways, then crosses over to the other side.

The following day is the start of kindergarten for Layla. As she gets dressed, I try to brush her hair but she likes to wear it wild, a halo of blond.

At the entryway to the school building, we pass a makeshift band of parents and teachers playing musical instruments. She carries herself into the building with an air of importance. This is the school where her big brothers used to go and now she is one of the big kids as well.

After the parents join the kids for morning circle in the kindergarten classroom, the whole school is summoned to the library. All the parents and teachers and kids are here, and when I look around, I see the class Josh would have been part of had he stayed. I feel a pang at Josh's absence, but more than ever, I'm aware of how each child needs something different. My children won't grow up with the luxury, if that's what it is, of thinking that everyone is the same, that everyone believes as they do. They will make no belated discovery of the fact that there is no one way, no one truth. For better or worse, they will have known from early on that there are multiple ways to live. They will know there is a choice and that it's one they are allowed to make.

With all the kids gathered on the floor, the teachers and parents sitting among them or standing in the back, the principal speaks, new teachers are introduced, a song is taught. It's getting close to the time to say goodbye. Layla's hand had firmly clasped mine as we walked into the building, and she has turned around a few times to make sure I'm still here. Before the kids go off to their classes, and the parents to work, we sing the same blessing sung every year on this day and that always brings tears to my eyes but no year more so than this one: the Shehecheyanu blessing, recited on the occasion of anything new, but really it's a celebration of arrival, of having been able to reach this moment.

The teachers stand up. It's time. Layla looks at me and an expression of fear crosses her face. She takes my arms and wraps them around her. Then a look of resoluteness comes over her. She gives me one last kiss and off she goes.

And then, just after Labor Day, Josh has his first day at the public school that's a few blocks from our house.

"I hope I like it," he says to me as we walk toward the building, where scores of parents and kids are waiting outside. "I hope it feels different."

When each of the kids went off to nursery school or kindergarten, I was surprisingly dry-eyed. But this first day is unlike any other. I'm all too aware of how much Josh's dislike of school has come to define him. Ready to make a fresh start, he's walking into not just a new building but a new version of himself.

And he knows no one. There is no set community, no established group of friends. I feel lonely and lost on his behalf. As we wait for the doors to open, I'm on the verge of bursting into tears, though Josh has warned me not to embarrass him.

"Josh," I hear someone call. A kid hurries up to him — someone he knew briefly from a local sports camp — and gives him a crushing hug, and I'm so relieved I want to hug the kid myself. Josh starts talking to him and to some other kids he is with and then the doors open and he is swept along into the building.

"Today was good," Josh says when I pick him up.

The next day, he wants to walk to school by himself — it's only a few blocks, he argues, and though a parade of kids passes by our house on the way to school, I'm reluctant to let him walk on his own. I draw him a map. I make him tell me each direction he'll turn, and drill him on the rules about strangers and candy and looking both ways.

Eventually I agree, but on the first morning that he walks alone, I tail him in my car, pretending to be invisible as I drive slowly down the street.

"I see you, Mom," he calls, then he hurries off, pretending not to know me. But before he strides past, I see the look of pride on his face.

THE KIDS HAVE HAD just a few days of school when it's time to halt the start of one new year to celebrate another. Rosh Hashanah falls earlier than usual this year, a week after Labor Day, and at first I'd had the same spool of worry about what I would do. Again, as last year, there is the thought of doing nothing — pretending these were simply odd days without the kids. I know I don't want to be inside a synagogue. I know I won't do something obligatory just so I can say that I have marked the day. But the holiday still matters to me — I still want to celebrate this day as the start of something new. I want to be filled with awe, mystery, and majesty — to stand not in prayer but outside in nature.

In bookstores, over the past few weeks I've browsed the travel section. The world, neatly alphabetized, giddily called to me, *Let's go here!* I could go to Ireland, to India, to Morocco, to Mexico. At night, while the kids slept, I Googled the Grand Canyon and Iceland, imagining gaping holes in the earth and blue lagoons inside a white frozen landscape. Both are too far and too expensive, so I searched for closer options. When I read of craggy ocean vistas, of jutting rocks and sprawling mountain views, I decided to go to Acadia National Park, in Maine, a six-hour drive from Boston.

On the day before the holiday, I pack the kids' dress clothes into one bag. In another bag, I pack my hiking boots, which still look new but are slowly starting to be broken in, coated now with dust. Along with them, I pack my jeans, a handful of granola bars, a water bottle, and a map. I talk to Dahlia on the phone as I pack; she is at her in-laws' house, preparing food for the holiday, setting a table, happy to be where she is.

A sweet year, I wish my parents, who are in Memphis, and my brother, who is already on his yearly spiritual pilgrimage to Uman, the birthplace of the rabbi whom he follows.

A sweet year, I wish William as I kiss him goodbye. I'll miss him but I want to take this trip on my own. We are best together when we both have the capacity to be independent.

There is no getting used to being away from the kids for a holiday, but I have become accustomed to being alone. The thought of not being with them doesn't fill me with the same terrible dread; one more painful separation I have learned to endure. I will miss them—I always do—but I know that we will soon return to one another. One day, perhaps, when they are older, one of them, or all of them, will come with me on my new year's excursion, but for now, in what is starting to feel like a ritual all its own, I hug them goodbye, then set off.

JORDAN POND, inside Acadia National Park, is ringed by a path with mountains in the distance. As I'm walking around it in search of a quiet spot, a deer wanders in front of me, seemingly unaware of any human presence. Before I set off on the hike I'd planned, I decide to do *tashlich*—one of the rituals of Rosh Hashanah I intend to keep. By a body of water, we gather to symbolically cast away our sins; we throw in bread as physical embodiments of the sins, which are nullified by the abundant water.

I have no bread to throw in — the popovers dipped in butter and blueberry jam, a Maine specialty that I'd eaten for my Rosh Hashanah lunch, were far too delicious to waste. Instead, I pick up a stone and throw it into the water, wishing to cast off the pieces of myself that still feel hardened and closed up and stale. Wishing to let go of the remaining voices of recrimination in my head.

Into Jordan Pond they go.

It's the kind of day with a glare so bright it's almost blinding, and it feels both warm and cool at the same time, as though I'm standing on the exact dividing line between seasons. Some of the trees are already dusted in gold, a harbinger of what is to come. Until now, fall was merely a backdrop to the holidays. This year, the season steps to the forefront. Fall itself feels like the holiday.

From the guidebook I've been studying, my version of a Rosh Hashanah prayer book, I've selected what sounds like an easy hike. I'm still only aspiring to be a serious hiker, and I like the description of a steep ascent to a vista of sky and sea, and then the Deer Path, which offers a gentle slow-rolling descent. I have the look of someone who has inadvertently wandered too far into the forest; I'm still trying to figure out how to work the hiking app I downloaded on my phone.

I decide to just go — as long as I'm ascending, I'll assume I'm on the right path. The hike starts out as easy as described, just an upward climb among rocks and trees. It's warmer now and I take off my sweatshirt so I'm wearing just my tank top; my shoulders prickle with sensation. The fact that it's Rosh Hashanah once again settles over me, another year gone by. I still feel a longing for holiday tables with family gathered around, the smell of dinner, the sweetness of apples and honey. I can still summon the tunes of the prayers in my head, background music as I make this climb, but mostly what I hear is just the gentle rustle of the wind and the sound of my own footsteps.

I ascend higher, until I reach the top—or at least what appears to be the top, because it's hard to tell exactly where I am on the map. But I'm not going to worry about that, not yet, because I am surrounded by stripes of ocean blue and sandy brown and forest green, and a majestic sky all around. There is no need to cede words like *wonder* and *mystery* and *awe*. No group can lay sole claim to these words; no religion owns this rising, expansive feeling.

If from the top of that mountain I could have seen forward in time as well, past the oceans and all these trees, to the year ahead, I would see a day a year from now, just before another Rosh Hashanah, when I will go back to Crystal Lake. I will carry with me the gold wedding ring I once wore, which bore the inscription *Love Always,* words that turned out not to be true after all. Since the day I removed it from my finger, it has been stored in a small box inside a larger box in my closet. By the shore of the lake, I will bring the ring to my lips, a final goodbye, then toss it into the water. The ring won't go as far as I imagined it would—in my mind, it soared like a small golden sparrow to the middle of the lake before skimming low and dipping beneath. Instead, a few feet from me, it will fall with an almost unnoticeable splash. The water will know what to do with it. The band will sink to the bottom of the lake, where it will remain, the words eventually rubbed out by the water.

And if I could see further forward, into the next year, William and I will get engaged, with a poem he writes and a purple-stoned ring we select together. We will get married in the house where we will all live together, under a chuppah painted by my mother, in a service presided over by my father and William's mother, with promises to each other that I write and with a song that William arranges and sings, and with the Sheva Brachot, the traditional seven blessings, sung by Ariel. We will be surrounded by William's brothers; my brother here from Israel; my sister, who is newly pregnant, and her husband; and all six of our children as we marry each other.

All these are in the future still as I look for the blue streaks of paint that were supposed to mark the path down. But all I see are rocks and scraggly green. I'm out of the range of my iPhone map, no comforting blue circle to find me and illuminate the way.

Finally I see, on a distant rock, a stripe of faded blue. It's not where I expected it to be, but I'm completely turned around now, and seeing no other way to go, I follow it. After I climb down a few rocks, the path grows narrower and steeper, and metal railings are embedded in the stones—hardly the gentle slope promised by the book. The ground is slippery from the recent rain—it's a slippery slope, indeed—and the rocks jut out, offering little clue which way to go. Having betrayed me once, the guidebook offers little help now, and the map I'd picked up at the rangers' station seems unintelligible—I can't retrace my steps because I don't know where I've been.

Who was I to think I knew how to hike, and how did I think I could manage this alone? These voices of old, always able to find me. But there are other ones now that speak alongside them. *Sometimes you need to think only about the step right in front of you. All you can do is trust your own footing and keep going even when you feel lost and afraid.*

I hear footsteps and see a couple coming around a tight bend; in their full hiking gear, they look rugged and confident, the sort of serious hikers I long to be.

"Is this the Deer Path?" I ask, hoping they will tell me that from his point onward, the path will be smooth, my descent easy and assured.

"It's the Cliff Path," one of them says, and they continue their ascent. Up the rocks, around a corner, and they are gone.

The path at least is true to its name. I grab onto the railing and make a tentative first step. I stay close to the wall of stone, grasping the metal bars drilled into the rock, and slowly descend. With each step, my foot feels for solid ground on the wet rocks. There may be a better way to do this, but I decide to go down the steepest of the slippery rocks on my butt, which is a good idea until my jeans catch on a rock and tear. I keep going this way until I feel more steady. Once the rocks become less jagged, and my feet are more secure, I stand and I walk toward the lush green below, and the light streaming through the trees. I've gotten myself up here, and however imperfectly, I can find my way back down.

Acknowledgments

I am thankful to the Hadassah-Brandeis Institute for a grant early on, when I was just beginning to conceive of this memoir.

Joshua Halberstam, Rachel Mesch, Judith Rosenbaum, and Barry Wimpfheimer, gifted scholars and valued friends, read drafts and offered helpful feedback. I am very thankful for the friendship and sage writerly advice of Emily Franklin, Heidi Pitlor, Joanna Rakoff, and Jessica Shattuck. I am immensely grateful to Rachel Kadish, for always being my first reader, for offering smart insights at every stage of the writing process, and for being a cherished friend throughout. And I am lucky to have Sarah Crane as an honorary member of our family; her warm presence makes life run more smoothly and happily.

My family has been an enormous source of support, understanding, and encouragement. Many parents would be nervous to have a novelist in the family, and most would be even more nervous to have a memoirist. I am grateful to my parents for championing my writing and for giving me a love of creativity and remaining steadfast as I have used this in my own way. I am thankful to my brother and his family and to my sister and her family for their anchoring sense of connection and love.

My agent Julie Barer has been an enthusiastic supporter from the very beginning of this book, and I have benefited tremendously from her warmth and her ever-present wisdom and insight. I am also thankful for all that Nicole Cunningham does at The Book Group. Lauren Wein, my editor, has an uncanny ability to see what a book has the potential to be, and with her dazzling intelligence, she has guided and inspired me through every step. And to Pilar Garcia-Brown at Houghton Mifflin Harcourt, for her sure-handed support, and to Tracy Roe, for her truly exceptional copyediting, I am very grateful.

I want to express my gratitude to my husband for his steadying strength, his open-ended love, and his boundless energy, which awakens me and inspires me. Now and always, there is nowhere I'd rather be. To my stepchildren whose presence in my life is a gift, my thanks and appreciation. And to my children, I offer my endless gratitude for every day of their love, good humor, and high spirits. I love them deeply and am so proud of who they are and who they are still becoming.

Reading Group Guide

INTRODUCTION

Several years ago, Tova Mirvis wrote an essay that appeared in the *New York Times* about receiving a get—a Jewish bill of divorce—and recognizing that this religious ceremony marked not just the end of her marriage, but also her belonging to the Orthodox Jewish world in which she was raised. Mirvis received hundreds of emails from readers—men and women, young and old, of all religious backgrounds—who wanted to share their own stories of change and personal transformation. This experience inspired her to write *The Book of Separation*.

In this memoir, Mirvis explores how to leave a world that has shaped her and enter a new way of living—where so much is unmapped. How do you maintain a sense of tradition and remain close with family members who might believe differently than you do? And above all, how do you overcome fear and learn to heed your own voice? These questions that Mirvis addresses in her memoir have prompted discussion and reflection on universal themes that affect so many of her readers, including: motherhood, being a woman, finding home, defining freedom, and more. The following pages contain discussion questions that can spark a conversation among readers, as well as workshop questions that may be used individually or as a group to prompt writing exercises, greater reflection, or deeper analysis about one's own experiences—and how we relate to Mirvis's story and to one other.

ON FEAR

"If you left, you were in danger of losing everyone you loved. If you left, you were in danger of losing yourself." (xii)

"Every day before class, I had to remind myself of what one of my favorite writers, Eudora Welty, had written: 'A sheltered life can be a daring life as well. For all serious daring starts from within.'"(115)

"I feel my clenched resistance begin to give way. It's a little easier to face my fears, a list lying in wait—nightmares of my hands slipping from the roof of a building, of falling off the edge of a cliff, falling from an airplane, falling from a thin wire, falling for no reason at all, just falling. The fear most of all that I would come unmoored from all that was supposed to hold me. What I have most feared is now what I have chosen." (20)

DISCUSSION QUESTION: In overcoming her fear of driving, how does Mirvis express overcoming other fears? What are her other fears?

WORKSHOP QUESTION: Write or talk about a time when you faced a fear. What did that fear come from? Was it a reflection of a familial, social, or other pressure? Can you share the steps you took or what you had to overcome or reconcile to face that fear?

ON LEAVING

"In the years in which I'd lain awake plotting escapes, I'd imagined some dramatic moment of departure. But sometimes leaving happens more quietly, not with any grand proclamations but with a single, still action." (201)

"And this, I understand anew, is why it's so hard to leave. Leaving isn't just about engaging in a set of once-forbidden actions. It's about changing the family story." (76)

"When you're inside, good is a word that automatically belongs to you. When you leave, it's a word you surrender at the gate. Despite the very meaning of my name, being good is something to which I can no longer lay claim." (206–7)

DISCUSSION QUESTION: What does being "good" mean to Mirvis? How has "leaving" made her question or redefine this term and her identity?

"To leave a marriage, to leave a religion, you never go just once. You have to leave again and again." (48)

WORKSHOP QUESTION: Have you experienced this in your own life? Write about or consider the different ways that you have had to leave something or someone.

ON WRITING

"One sentence set free another sentence." (200)

"More than anything, I wanted to write bravely. I wanted to speak openly. I wanted to live freely." (210)

"Anything that did not uphold or affirm—could you think it? Could you say it? Even worse, did you dare write it? Yet being a writer, I was learning, required a willingness to cast aside these restrictions. To write was to enter an underground that was rich and teeming . . . a house with corners and hallways and passageways to explore." (156)

DISCUSSION QUESTION: How does writing help Mirvis find her way?

WORKSHOP QUESTION: In your opinion, what are the goals of writing? How might they sometimes be at odds, if at all, with other frameworks? How might writing help counter—or reconcile—living within a specific set of rules for living?

ON BEING A WOMAN

"Listen to the men recite the prayers, deliver the sermons, make the rules." (11)

"We were always subject to inspection, our bodies divided and measured and mapped." (61)

"The rules had always cloaked me like the long skirts I was supposed to wear, but by getting married, they were poised to enter my body as well." (135)

"If someone were to ask why I covered my hair, I could explain why this ritual felt meaningful to other people, but the truth was that I did it because I wanted to be seen by my community as the type of woman who covered her hair." (157)

DISCUSSION QUESTION: Why did Mirvis initially strive to follow the rules for being an Orthodox woman, including her decision to wear a "fall"? What do you think was the moment, or series of moments, that led to her decision to stop following these rules?

WORKSHOP QUESTION: Consider ways that your gender limits you, is policed, or even frees you. Do you think that it is appropriate for there to be different cultural, religious, or political laws or rules for different genders? Write about a time that your actions, options, or appearance was limited or scrutinized because of your gender. How did that make you feel? Do you agree or disagree with this scrutiny or rule?

ON FINDING HOME

"As I am no longer part of this community, the idea of home feels tenuous, irreparably broken. I stumble over the word home every time I say it, not sure that I can still lay claim to its comforts." (72)

"After the divorce, I'd let myself believe that there was only one kind of home and that ours was irreparably broken. But on this night, in this quiet house, home doesn't need those solid unbreachable walls. It feels more like a small nest you could build for yourself and for those whom you love." (273)

"I didn't know until this year that there is comfort to be derived from being inside not just a community of people, but a body of water and a ring of trees. I didn't know that you could belong to a lake, to a forest, to an expansive vista. Is beauty enough of an alternative? Can you trade the rules of so many books for the green of so many trees?" (285)

DISCUSSION QUESTION: How did Mirvis define home within the Orthodox community? How did that definition change once she left?

WORKSHOP QUESTION: How do you define home? Have you ever had to forge your own home after leaving a home into which you were born or were already accepted? What were the challenges? What were the rewards?

ON BEING A MOTHER

"In motherhood, all of you is demanded, but sometimes that means giving your children the parts of you that are uncertain and unresolved." (84)

"My daughter slept and she woke and she continued to nurse. 'Be happy,' I whispered in her small soft ear. 'Be free.'" (185)

"'Oh, Josh,' I say, and as I look into his eyes, I feel my heart breaking open. Even at his young age, he knows the price to be paid for not following the rules." (154)

"This, more than anything, was the iron bar across the exit door—love was what tied you and kept you inside. Love was

what you risked losing if you wanted to choose for yourself."
(154)

DISCUSSION QUESTION: What are some of the ways that Mirvis redefined her role as a mother when she decided to leave the Orthodox community? How did this change her relationship with her children, if at all?

WORKSHOP QUESTION: How have you reconciled freedom versus structure with your child (or parent)? In what ways are these two ideas intertwined? In what ways are they at odds?

FREEDOM

"I keep going, each word a tiny key unlocking one more tiny door. I had once thought that others could unlock these doors for you, but over this year, I've come to realize that no one can offer freedom to you. It's yours to choose and to claim." (255)

"To be free, I'm learning, is to allows others to be free as well." (248)

"In this moment, it feels clear to me: I still want to participate in this tradition with my children. Surely freeing yourself means being able to choose what to let go of as well as what to keep. By leaving, I don't have to leave it all." (244)

"I wanted freedom, and here it is—not the freedom of escape, not the freedom of fantasy, but a freedom that is confusing and daunting and complicated. In this freedom, there are no preordained questions, no easy answers, no ready definitions. No as-

surances of truth, no endless castigations about badness, but also no ready promises of goodness." (207)

DISCUSSION QUESTION: How did Mirvis's definition of freedom change as she continued her journey with the Orthodox community? As a partner and a mother? What were some of the moments that helped her redefine freedom?

WORKSHOP QUESTION: What is your definition of freedom? Have you changed that definition at any point in your life? How do you see your definition of freedom evolving as you age or your roles change? Do you define freedom differently within different situations or relationships?

If you are interested in having Tova Mirvis join your book discussion via Skype, please visit TovaMirvis.com for more information.

A Conversation with Tova Mirvis

The Book of Separation originated with an essay you published in the New York Times called "Divorcing My Husband, and My Faith." What was that essay about and what was the response to it?

I wrote an essay about my experience of having an Orthodox Jewish divorce ceremony, the ancient, highly scripted ritual used to end a marriage in the religious world in which I lived. In the essay I wrote about how, as I followed the minute details of this ceremony, I came to understand that I was leaving not just a marriage but a religious world. This ceremony, for me, marked the end of my willingness to stay inside a faith in which I didn't sufficiently believe.

The essay was published in the *New York Times*, and it was widely shared and became one of the most emailed essays of the day—except I wasn't aware of that at the time. I didn't know when exactly the piece was going to run, and I happened to be in a remote part of Costa Rica, in a rain forest with very little email access. But it actually worked out very well, because if I've learned one thing as a writer, it's that when you put your most private story in the *New York Times,* a remote rain forest with no internet access is not the worst place to be.

But once I was home, I saw that my inbox was flooded with emails—from family and friends, of course, but mostly from strangers. I had emails from people who read the essay, men and women, old and young, from all religious backgrounds, who wanted to share their stories with me. Stories of leaving a marriage or leaving a religion. Or stories about undergoing some sort of painful transformation. It was the most moving experience I've had as a writer. When I was writing the piece, I was very nervous about putting this essay to the world, but in the response to the piece, I came to realize anew how much people respond to that kind of vulnerability. Being honest about your story and being willing to share it allows other people to be honest and share their own stories.

And that essay was the beginning of what would become The Book of Separation? *Can you talk a little bit about what the book explores?*

That essay, and the response to it, persuaded me to write this memoir.

One of the things that struck me, as I was going through the process of getting a religious divorce, was the fact that the biblical term for the Jewish divorce document is *sefer kritut.* This translates as a book of rending, or tearing, or a book of separation. In that religious ceremony, everything was scripted according to very specific laws. The document had to follow an exact legal formulation. In ritual, there might be a script to follow, but in life, of course, there's no such agreed-upon script. No one kind of marriage, no one sort of divorce, no one experience of faith. The stories we each live every day are always so much more complicated. I decided that I wanted to write my own book of separation — my own version of this ancient document.

The Book of Separation follows the first year of leaving my marriage and this religious world, and it explores what it means to leave a way of life that is scripted and mapped, and instead to enter into a world where there are far fewer expectations and rules. The book explores how you shed a world that has shaped you and asks whether you can you leave parts of it while holding on to some of it, in my case, a closeness with family and a sense of tradition. It's a book about letting go and starting over, a book about learning to live with uncertainty and to heed your own voice. It's also a book about parenting (I have three children) when there is this rupture between then and now, and when, as a result, there are no easy answers.

Even though the memoir explores separating from both your husband and your faith, you don't need to have been once married or a religious person to appreciate the larger story. What do you hope people take away from reading it?

I think that at its core, this is a memoir about change and over-coming fear and being willing to face the parts of ourselves that are scary. What happens when we feel the painful need to upend the fixed parts of our lives? What happens when we look at our lives and feel that the way we live doesn't match what we really believe? All change comes with loss. It's very hard to leave what is secure and known. Even when we are unhappy, sometimes it's preferable to stay where we are, rather than take a chance at what is unknown. Making a big change can feel like taking a leap off a skyscraper, but sometimes, sometimes, we are ready — ready to change course, ready to let our lives look different than we imagined they would.

A phrase you use when talking about the book is "late doubt." Can you discuss that idea? And can this book be seen as a sort of midlife coming of age?

Late doubt is a phrase I've thought about a lot. I was raised with the idea that you were supposed to know who you were at a very young age. I grew up in a religious community where I tried to be the quintessential good girl. I stayed inside, and I married someone at a young age, from a similar religious world, and I began to raise my kids in this world as well. I sometimes chafed at the rules, bothered by what I saw as the limitations of my world, but I didn't act on any of these feelings. I knew that to do so could upend the foundations on which my life was built. I hoped that these doubts would disappear, or at least sit quietly, and I could somehow make it through unscathed.

But one of the things I've learned is that doubt doesn't just disappear. No one gets to make it through unscathed. Sooner or later we have to face the unresolved questions, and for me, as I got older, I felt a renewed sense of religious doubt, one that was too strong to ignore. Could you make yourself believe in something? I asked myself this over and over. I knew you could make yourself act as though you believed — but was this enough? This late-arriving doubt forced me to look at the painful questions I had, both about my marriage and my religious world, and eventually enabled me to make changes in order to live more honestly and authentically.

And in this way, this is a book about a midlife coming of age. We don't all come of age in our early twenties, and we don't always come of age just once. Maybe we are always in the process of coming of age, again and again, as we encounter new experiences and undergo new challenges and allow ourselves to grow in new ways.

What was it like for you to put this personal story to the world? Can you describe some of the reactions to it?

Before the book came out, I was very nervous about sharing something so personal. But once the book was published, I was immensely moved by the flood of reaction.

Soon after the publication — and after an excerpt of the book ran as a "Modern Love" essay in the *New York Times* — I started to get emails, hundreds of them, from so many people, of so many different backgrounds. I received emails from people who had been through a divorce and understood the pain of making that kind of change. People who felt trapped inside their marriages but were unsure about what to do. People who'd left other religious communities — many fellow former Orthodox Jews, of course, but also those raised inside devout Christian, Catholic, and Muslim communities. People who remained committed to religion but understood what it was to doubt. People who were alienated from family members due to religious differences. People who'd become more religious than their families and knew what it meant to want to live a life in which you really believed. I heard from people who had overcome long-held fears, people who had to let go of a particular stage in their lives for a variety of reasons, including illness and the death of loved ones. Maybe we are all leave-takers of one kind or another, separating from stages in our lives, from homes, from our own notion of who we are supposed to be.

In the midst of any of these life changes, it's so easy to feel that you are the only one, to feel so incredibly alone. But in all these emails, I felt people wanting to connect — to say, "your story touched me, and here, in return, is my story." It made me realize that when you write something personal and put it to the world, you open up a kind of conversation.

There was one community for which my story seems to have had special resonance: those who'd left, or were in the process of leaving, the Mormon world. In the many emails I received, I felt that though the particulars varied, there was a deep sense of shared experience. These people writing to me described their own experience of trying to navigate what it means to raise your children in a new way. They too felt that sometimes-searing loss of faith and the surround of community. Each time someone from the post-Mormon world wrote to me and said that I was telling their story, it reminded me of the power of memoir — of personal narrative — to speak to a universal experience.

When you leave a fixed world you set out down an un-mapped path, you have to walk alone. But sometimes you discover that there are a great many others walking their own individual paths alongside you.